Public Administration and Policy

The CONTEMPORARY ESSAYS Series

GENERAL EDITOR: LEONARD W. LEVY

Public Administration and Policy

Selected Essays

Edited by

Peter Woll

HARPER TORCHBOOKS ▼ The Academy Library

Harper & Row, Publishers, New York

This book is dedicated to
Ethel A. Crowther
and to the memory of
Samuel Crowther

PUBLIC ADMINISTRATION AND POLICY

Printed in the United States of America.

First Edition: HARPER TORCHBOOKS, 1966
Harper & Row, Publishers, Incorporated
49 East 33rd Street, New York, N.Y. 10016.

Library of Congress Catalog Card Number: 66-21602.

Designed by Darlene Starr Carbone

Contents

Preface

This book brings together a number of significant articles in the area of public administration and policy development. A broad approach is taken to illustrate the vital role now played by administrative agencies in the governmental process. The nature of agencies, the functions they perform, and the problems they create within our system of constitutional democracy are discussed in detail.

The book is designed to stimulate the interest of both students and general readers concerned with recent trends in government and public administration. It will immediately become clear that administration and politics are connected in a way that makes the study of one without the other meaningless. The administrative process must be analyzed within the broad context of the political system, and the fact that the administrative branch is often the dominant force in policy-making requires that its relationship to Congress, the Presidency, and the courts be clarified in any attempt to understand the character of these traditional branches of our government.

In making this compilation I am indebted to Leonard W. Levy who originally suggested the idea for the book. Susan Diamondstone provided invaluable assistance in tracking down the articles and in the general preparation of the manuscript.

PETER WOLL

Introduction

Peter Woll

The administrative branch today stands at the very center of our governmental process; it is the keystone of the structure. And administrative agencies exercise legislative and judicial as well as executive functions—a fact that is often overlooked. In the selections that follow, classics in the field, we will see the growth of public administration as a discipline, with particular emphasis upon the political role of administration and the way in which the bureaucracy is involved in policy-making. Many proposals are contained in the selections dealing with methods of bringing bureaucracy under control.

How should we view American bureaucracy? Ultimately, the power of government comes to rest in the administrative branch. Agencies are given the responsibility of making concrete decisions carrying out vague policy initiated in Congress or by the President. The agencies can offer expert advice, closely attuned to the most interested pressure groups, and they often not only determine the policies that the legislature and executive recommends in the first place, but also decisively affect the policy-making process. Usually it is felt that the bureaucracy is politically "neutral," completely under the domination of the President, Congress, or the courts. We will see that this is not entirely the case, and that the President and Congress have only sporadic control over the administrative process.

The bureaucracy is a semi-autonomous branch of the government, often dominating Congress, exercising strong influence on the President, and only infrequently subject to review by the courts. If our constitutional democracy is to be fully analyzed, we must focus attention upon the administrative branch. What is the nature of public administration? How are administration and politics intertwined? How are administrative constituencies determined? What is the relationship between agencies and their constituencies? What role should the President assume in relation to the administrative branch? How far should Congress go in controlling agencies which in fact tend to dominate the legislative process? Should judicial review be expanded? What are the conditions of judicial review? How do administrative agencies perform judicial functions, and how do these activities affect the ability of courts to oversee their actions? These questions confront us with what is called the problem of administrative responsibility: that is, how can we control the activities of the administrative branch? In order to approach an understanding of this difficult problem, it is necessary to appreciate the nature of the administrative process and how it interacts with other branches of the government and with the general public. It is also important to understand the nature of our constitutional system, and the political context within which agencies function.

CONSTITUTIONAL DEMOCRACY AND BUREAUCRATIC POWER

We operate within the framework of a constitutional democracy. This means, first, that the government is to be limited by the separation of powers and Bill of Rights. Another component of the system, federalism, is designed in theory to provide states with a certain amount of authority when it is not implied at the national level. Our separation of powers, the system of checks and balances, and the federal system, help to explain some of the differences between administrative organization here and in other countries. But the Constitution does not explicitly provide for the administrative branch, which has become a new fourth branch of government. This raises the question of how to control the bureaucracy when there are no clear constitutional limits upon it. The second aspect of our system, democracy, is of course implied in the Constitution itself, but has expanded greatly since it was adopted. We are confronted, very broadly speaking, first with the problem of constitutional limitation, and secondly with the problem of democratic participation in the activities of the bureaucracy. The bureaucracy must be accommodated within the framework of our system of constitutional democracy. This is the crux of the problem of administrative responsibility.

Even though the Constitution does not explicitly provide for the bureaucracy, it has had a profound impact upon the structure, functions, and general place that the bureaucracy occupies in government. The administrative process was incorporated into the constitutional system under the heading of "The Executive Branch." But the concept of "administration" at the time of the adoption of the Constitution was a very simple one, involving the "mere execution" of "executive details," to use the phrases of Hamilton in *The Federalist*. The idea, at that time, was simply that the President as Chief Executive would be able to control the executive branch in carrying out the mandates of Congress. In *Federalist* 72, after defining administration in this very narrow way, Hamilton stated:

> . . . The persons, therefore, to whose immediate management the different administrative matters are committed ought to be considered as Assistants or Deputies of the Chief Magistrate, and on this account, they ought to derive their offices from his appointment, at least from his nomination, and ought to be subject to his superintendence.

It was clear that Hamilton felt the President would be responsible for administrative action as long as he was in office. This fact later turned up in what can be called the "presidential supremacy" school of thought, which held and still holds that the President is *constitutionally* responsible for the administrative branch, and that Congress should delegate to him all necessary authority for this purpose. Nevertheless, whatever the framers of the Constitution might have planned if they could have foreseen the nature of bureaucratic development, the fact is that the system they constructed in many ways supported bureaucratic organization and functions independent of the President. The role they assigned to Congress in relation to administration assured this result, as did the general position of Congress in the governmental system as a check or balance to the power of the President. Congress has a great deal of authority over the administrative process.

If we compare the powers of Congress and the President over the bureaucracy it becomes clear that they both have important constitutional responsibility. Congress retains primary control over the organization of the bureaucracy. It alone creates and destroys agencies, and determines whether they are to be located within the executive branch or outside it. This has enabled Congress to create a large number of *independent* agencies beyond presidential control. Congress has the authority to control appropriations and may thus exercise a great deal of power over the administrative arm, although increasingly the Bureau of the Budget and the President have the initial, and more often than not the final say over the budget. Congress also has the authority to define the jurisdiction of agencies. Finally, the Constitution gives to the legislature the power to interfere in presidential appointments, which must be "by and with the advice and consent of the Senate."

Congress may extend the sharing of the appointive power when it sets up new agencies. It may delegate to the President pervasive authority to control the bureaucracy. But one of the most important elements of the separation of powers is the electoral system, which gives to Congress a constituency which is different from and even conflicting with that of the President. This means that Congress often decides to set up agencies beyond presidential purview. Only rarely will it grant the President any kind of final authority to structure the bureaucracy. During World War II, on the basis of the War Powers Act, the President had the authority to reorganize the administrative branch. Today he has the same authority, provided that Congress does not veto presidential proposals within a certain time limit. In refusing to give the President permanent reorganization authority, Congress is jealously guarding one of its important prerogatives.

Turning to the constitutional authority of the President over the bureaucracy, it is somewhat puzzling to see that it gives him a relatively small role. He appoints certain officials by and with the advice and consent of the Senate. He has directive power over agencies that are placed within his jurisdiction by Congress. His control over patronage, once so important, has diminished sharply under the merit system. The President is Commander-in-Chief of all military forces, which puts him in a controlling position over the Defense Department and Agencies involved in military matters. In the area of international relations, the President is by constitutional authority the "Chief Diplomat," to use Rossiter's phrase. This means that he appoints Ambassadors (by and with the advice and consent of the Senate), and generally directs national activities in the international arena—a crucially important executive function. But regardless of the apparent intentions of some of the framers of the Constitution as expressed by Hamilton in *The Federalist*, and in spite of the predominance of the Presidency in military and foreign affairs, the fact remains that we seek in vain for explicit constitutional authorization for the President to be "Chief Administrator."

This is not to say that the President does not have an important responsibility to act as Chief of the bureaucracy, merely that there is no constitutional mandate for this. As our system evolved, the President was given more and more responsibility until he became, in practice, Chief Administrator. At the same time the constitutional system has often impeded progress in this direction. The President's Committee on Administrative Management in 1937, and later the Hoover Commissions of 1949 and 1955, called upon Congress to initiate a series of reforms increasing presidential authority over the administrative branch. It was felt that this was necessary to make democracy work. The President is the only official elected nationally, and if the administration is to be held democratically accountable, he alone can stand as its representative. But meaningful control from the White House requires that the President have a comprehensive program which encompasses the activities of the bureaucracy. He must be informed as to what they are doing, and be able to control them. He must understand the complex responsibilities of the bureaucracy. Moreover, he must be able to call on sufficient political support to balance the support which the agencies draw from private clientele groups and congressional committees. This has frequently proven a difficult and often impossible task for the President. He may have the *authority* to control the bureaucracy in many areas, but not enough *power*.

On the basis of the Constitution, Congress feels it quite proper that when it delegates legislative authority to administrative agencies it can relatively often place these groups outside the control of the President. For example, in the case of the Interstate Commerce Commission, the subject of an important case study in this book, Congress has delegated final authority to that agency to control railroad mergers and other aspects of transportation activity, without giving the President the right to veto. The President may feel that a particular merger is undesirable because it is in violation of the antitrust laws, but the Interstate Commerce Commission is likely to feel differently. In such a situation, the President can do nothing because he does not have the *legal authority* to take any action. If he could muster enough political support to exercise influence over the ICC, he would be able to control it, but the absence of legal authority is an important factor in such cases and diminishes presidential power. Moreover, the ICC draws strong support from the railroad industry, which has been able to counterbalance the political support possessed by the President and other groups that have wished to control it. Analogous situations exist with respect to other regulatory agencies.

Besides the problem of congressional and presidential control over the bureaucracy, there is the question of judicial review of administrative decisions. The rule of law is a central element in our Constitution. The rule of law means that decisions judicial in nature should be handled by common law courts, because of their expertise in rendering due process of law. When administrative agencies engage in adjudication their decisions should be subject to judicial review—at least, they should if one supports the idea of the supremacy of law. Judicial decisions are supposed to be rendered on an independent and impartial basis, through the use of tested procedures, in order to arrive at the accurate determination of the truth. Administrative adjudication should not be subject to presidential or congressional control, which would mean political determination of decisions that should be rendered in an objective manner. The idea of the rule of law, derived from the common law and adopted within the framework of our constitutional system, in theory limits legislative and executive control over the bureaucracy.

The nature of our constitutional system poses very serious difficulties to the development of a system of administrative responsibility. The Constitution postulates that the functions of government must be separated into different branches with differing constituencies and separate authority. The idea is that the departments should oppose each other, thereby preventing the arbitrary exercise of political power. Any combination of functions was considered to lead inevitably to arbitrary government. This is a debatable point, but the result of the Constitution is quite clear. The administrative process, on the other hand, often combines various functions of government in the same hands. Attempts are made, of course, to separate those who exercise judicial functions from those in the prosecuting arms of the agencies. But the fact remains that there is a far greater combination of functions in the administrative process than can be accommodated by strict adherence to the Constitution.

It has often been proposed, as a means of alleviating what may be considered the bad effects of combined powers in administrative agencies, to draw a line of control from the original branches of the government to those parts of the bureaucracy exercising similar functions. Congress would control the legislative activities of the agencies, the President the executive aspects, and the courts the judicial functions. This would maintain the symmetry of the constitutional system. But this solution is not feasible, because other parts of the Constitution, giving different authority to these three branches make symmetrical control of this kind almost impossible. The three branches of the government are not willing to give up whatever powers they may have over administrative agencies. For example, Congress is not willing to give the President complete control over all executive functions, nor to give the courts the authority to review all the decisions of the agencies. At present, judicial review takes place only if Congress authorizes it, except in those rare instances where constitutional issues are involved.

Another aspect of the problem of control is reflected in the apparent paradox that the three branches do not always use to the fullest extent their authority to regulate the bureaucracy, even though they wish to retain their power to do so. The courts, for example, have exercised considerable self-restraint in their review of administrative decisions. They are not willing to use all their power over the bureaucracy. Similarly, both Congress and the President will often limit their dealings with the administrative branch for political and practical reasons.

In the final analysis, we are left with a bureaucratic system that has been fragmented by the Constitution, and in which administrative discretion is inevitable. The bureaucracy reflects the general fragmentation of our political system. It is often the battleground for the three branches of government, and for outside pressure groups which seek to control it for their own purposes.

THE RISE OF THE ADMINISTRATIVE PROCESS

What has caused the development of this large administrative branch which exercises all the functions of government, usually within the same agency? The reasons for the rise of the bureaucracy can be largely explained by observing how the transfer of legislative, executive, and judicial functions has occurred from the primary branches of the government.

Administrative agencies exercise legislative power because Congress and the President are unable and unwilling to cope with all the legislative problems of the nation. The President is "Chief Legislator." Congress is supposed to exercise the primary legislative function. But clearly, given the scope of modern government, it would be impossible for the President and

Congress to deal on a continuous basis with the myriad legislative concerns that arise. The President's "program" is necessarily incomplete. It deals with major legislative problems which happen to be of interest to him and of concern to the nation at a particular time. Much of the President's program is formulated by the bureaucracy. In any event, it ultimately has to be carried out by administrative agencies, provided Congress approves.

For the most part Congress is concerned with formulating policy in very broad terms. It has neither the technical information nor the time to cope with the intricate phases of modern legislation. Moreover, it is often unwilling to deal with difficult political questions, for this would necessitate taking sides and alienating various segments of the public. It frequently passes on to the bureaucracy the burden of reconciling group conflict. The bureaucracy receives the unresolved disputes that come both to Congress and to the President, making it one of the most important political arms of the government. The concept of the bureaucracy as neutral is actually contrary to the facts.

Turning to the judicial arena, the development of administrative law has taken place because of the need for a more flexible mechanism for resolving cases and controversies arising under new welfare and regulatory statutes. The idea that the functions of government can be divided into legislative, executive, and judicial categories, and segregated into three separate branches of the government, is outdated because of the growth of a complex and interdependent economy requiring government regulation. Effective regulatory power often requires a combination of legislative and judicial functions.

Examples of the Development of Administrative Agencies. At the beginning of the republic, our bureaucracy was very small. It was quite capable of domination by the President, and at that time the President was the Chief Administrator in fact as well as in theory. No one then could conceive of the growth of a complex bureaucracy such as we know today, and it was only proper to feel that the activities of the executive branch would be, for the most part, politically neutral under the control of the President and Congress. The fact that the President was supposed to be politically neutral gave the concept of a neutral bureaucracy real meaning.

The original bureaucracy consisted of the War, Navy, State, and Treasury Departments, along with the office of Attorney General (the Department of Justice was created in 1870). These departments were extraordinarily small, and although distance and the difficulty of communications may have created some barriers to presidential domination over an agency such as the State Department, most agencies were easily subject to scrutiny by both Congress and the White House. This was the only time in American history when it was accurate to picture the administrative branch as a hierarchical structure with the President at the apex.

The development of administrative agencies after the Civil War resulted from public pressure which in turn reflected changing economic, social, and political conditions. For the most part agencies were created to deal with specific problems. The growth of the major departments reflected the expansion of government generally. The *laissez faire* ideal of a government remote from the community began to prove inadequate at the end of the nineteenth century. At this time, expanded powers were given to the Justice Department under the Sherman Act of 1890. This was necessary, it was felt, to deal with the rising restraints of trade and the growth of monopolies. In the regulatory area, the Interstate Commerce Commission was created in 1887 as the first national regulatory agency to supervise the railroad industry. The general expansion of the government was reflected in the establishment of the Justice Department in 1870, the Post Office Department in 1882, and the Department of Agriculture in 1889, succeeding the Commissioner of Agriculture, an office established in 1862. Present day bureaucracy has its roots in the latter part of the nineteenth century. But even then the administrative branch was fairly small and relatively powerless.

In examining the characteristics of nineteenth century bureaucracy, it can be seen that although the ideal of *laissez faire* had begun to tarnish, nevertheless it was still powerful and was reflected in the domination of big business interests within the governmental process. Although the frontier had receded significantly, it was still an important factor in absorbing excess energy and alleviating at least some of the grievances caused by economic interdependence. National communications were not highly developed. The integrative force of a strong Presidency was just beginning to be felt. The concept of the welfare state, which led to the vast expansion of the bureaucracy during the New Deal period, was unknown. Both theoretical and practical considerations militated against the creation at that time of a significant and pervasive administrative process. There was, it is true, a great deal of agitation and demand for government action to curb economic abuses. This was quite evident, for example, in the strong agitation of agricultural interests leading to the creation of the ICC. However, these protests were largely ineffective.

The real growth of the administrative process came in the twentieth century, when added powers were given to agencies which were already established, and new agencies were developed to expand government influence.

Expansion of the Bureaucracy in the Twentieth Century. The twentieth century saw the growth of a welfare philosophy of government, an enlargement of the problems created by the interdependence of economic groups, and the development of the country into a national community where the impact of activity in one area was felt in many others. There was increased political pressure for more government action which in turn required an expanded administrative process. Neither Congress, the Presidency, nor the judiciary could cope with the tremendous increase in the workload of government. Nor could they meet all the needs for innovation in the governmental process. Where a new type of adjudication was required to handle an increasing number of complex cases, the common law framework as well as the Constitution prevented the judiciary from embarking upon necessary programs and new procedures. Congress continued to work in modern times much as it had in the past, dealing with problems through a rather cumbersome hearing process.

It would be very difficult for Congress radically to change

the legislative process because of constitutional as well as political limitations. These create obstacles to unity and continuity in the legislature. The courts too are constrained by the system. To take an example: suppose the judiciary decided to change the "case and controversy" rule, which requires that they adjudicate only cases properly brought before them involving concrete controversies. This would clearly violate Article 3 of the Constitution, and would be very difficult to bring about without a constitutional Amendment. These are the kinds of factors that led increasingly to the growth of bureaucracy. New forms of government were needed, and the administrative branch, which was not hampered by constitutional restrictions to the same degree as the original three branches, was able to fill this need.

Turning to some examples of agencies created in the twentieth century: the Federal Reserve Board, established in 1913 to stand at the head of a Federal Reserve system, was necessitated by changes in the banking industry which had resulted in a need for some kind of national control and standards. The Federal Trade Commission, created in 1914, was designed to expand the control of the national government over restraints of trade and deceptive business practices. The FTC reflects the need for a separate administrative agency with authority distinct from that of the courts and the Justice Department. This need indicated in part the failure of the Sherman Act of 1890 as it had been administered by the Justice Department through an unsympathetic judiciary. By 1920, the Federal Power Commission had been created, and in 1927 initial steps were taken to regulate the communications industry with the establishment of a Federal Radio Commission, which in 1934 was transformed into the Federal Communications Commission.

The proliferation of agencies during the New Deal can be seen in the Securities and Exchange Commission of 1933, the National Labor Relations Board of 1935, the Civil Aeronautics Board and Civil Aeronautics Administration (now the Federal Aviation Agency) created in 1937 and reorganized in 1958. New regulatory bureaus were created in the Department of

Agriculture and other executive departments. Many New Deal agencies were created on the basis of presidential support rather than on the demands of private interests. This contrasted with the Interstate Commerce Commission which was created primarily because of strong agrarian demands for government control. The New Deal period was a time when President Roosevelt acted as a focal point for the expansion of the bureaucracy, and it was his ingenuity and power that often provided the balance of political support necessary for this purpose.

Since the New Deal period, there has been a notable expansion of bureaucratic power in the Defense Department, which has been put on a permanent basis since World War II and has strong political support from the armaments industry. Also an agency such as NASA reflects changing technology and subsequent innovations in governmental policy. NASA has now become one of our most important agencies, employing a large number of people and receiving huge appropriations.

CHARACTERISTICS OF ADMINISTRATIVE AGENCIES

Administrative agencies are generally characterized by their size, the complexity of the decisions that they must make, specialization, and the combination of several governmental functions. Another characteristic of primary importance is the fact that no agency can exist without strong political support. All agencies have constituencies to which they are responsible. Their constituencies include congressional committees with which they negotiate appropriations and policy changes; the White House; the courts, which will review certain of their decisions provided the conditions of judicial review are met; and private groups. Administrative agencies operate within a highly charged political environment and this fact immediately distinguishes government bureaucracy from private business. The administrative process in government cannot be considered similar to that in business, except in a very limited range of activities. And insofar as their activities are not political, they are not particularly significant for the study of government.

THE PROBLEM OF ADMINISTRATIVE RESPONSIBILITY

How do the agencies perform the tasks that have been assigned to them? Are they acting responsibly within the framework of our constitutional democracy? These questions involve an analysis of administrative procedure and accountability. The bureaucracy must be viewed as a political decision-making arena, and the appropriateness of particular decisions must be analyzed in terms of the goals that have been set for society and for government. Are agencies making the best decisions possible? Are they fair when they render adjudicative decisions? Are their activities sufficiently coordinated to assure a certain minimum level of efficiency? Does the President have the kind of controls that he needs over the bureaucracy? Should Congress become more or less involved in administrative activities? Is it feasible to expand judicial review, given the nature and characteristics of the administrative process? These and other questions will be examined in the following essays. Complete answers to them cannot be given, but the information gathered here equips the reader to make a sound approach towards a solution.

I. Politics and Administration

EDITORIAL NOTE. The following two articles present a striking contrast. The first, by Woodrow Wilson, calls for a systematic study of administration in the United States. It is notable because of its separation of administration and politics, a dichotomy understandable in light of the times in which it was written. The article preceded the tremendous growth of bureaucracy, and the recognition that administration and politics are inevitably connected. It reflects the constant American dream of an objective administration, a bureaucracy which is somehow removed from the political process, but nevertheless subject to public scrutiny. This selection, written in 1887, was the first serious attempt to deal with the subject of American public administration.

The second selection, in contrast, illustrates the fact that the American governmental system inevitably places administrators in the field of politics. They must be able to achieve a favorable measure of political support in order to implement their programs. They are politicians in the true sense, in that they are constantly striving for the necessary power to carry out public policy. Insofar as "principles of administration," which Wilson hoped would be developed, are capable of statement, they are as much concerned with "politics" as with "administration." The two cannot be separated.

1. THE STUDY OF ADMINISTRATION

Woodrow Wilson

I suppose that no practical science is ever studied where there is no need to know it. The very fact, therefore, that the eminently practical science of administration is finding its way into college courses in this country would prove that this country needs to know more about administration, were such proof of the fact required to make out a case. It need not be said, however, that we do not look into college programmes for proof of this fact. It is a thing almost taken for granted among us, that the present movement called civil service reform must, after the accomplishment of its first purpose, expand into efforts to improve, not the *personnel* only, but also the organization and methods of our government offices: because it is plain that their organization and methods need improvement only less than their *personnel.* It is the object of administrative study to discover, first, what government can properly and successfully do, and, secondly, how it can do these proper things with the utmost possible efficiency and at the least possible cost either of money or of energy. On both these points there is obviously much need of light among us; and only careful study can supply that light.

Before entering on that study, however, it is needful:

I. To take some account of what others have done in the same line; that is to say, of the history of the study.

II. To ascertain just what is its subject-matter.

III. To determine just what are the best methods by which to develop it, and the most clarifying political conceptions to carry with us into it.

Unless we know and settle these things, we shall set out without chart or compass.

I.

The science of administration is the latest fruit of that study of the science of politics which was begun some twenty-two hundred years ago. It is a birth of our own century, almost of our own generation.

Why was it so late in coming? Why did it wait till this too busy century of ours to demand attention for itself? Administration is the most obvious part of government; it is government in action; it is the executive, the operative, the most visible side of government, and is of course as old as government itself. It is government in action, and one might very naturally expect to find that government in action had arrested the attention and provoked the scrutiny of writers of politics very early in the history of systematic thought.

But such was not the case. No one wrote systematically of administration as a branch of the science of government until the present century had passed its first youth and had begun to put forth its characteristic flower of systematic knowledge. Up to our own day all the political writers whom we now read had thought, argued, dogmatized only about the *constitution* of government; about the nature of the state, the essence and seat of sovereignty, popular power and kingly prerogative; about the greatest meanings lying at the heart of government, and the high ends set before the purpose of government by man's nature and man's aims. The central field of controversy was that great field of theory in which monarchy rode tilt against democracy, in which oligarchy would have built for itself strongholds of privilege, and in which tyranny sought opportunity to make good its claim to receive submission from all competitors. Amidst this high warfare of principles, administration could command no pause for its own consideration. The question was always: Who shall make law, and what shall that law be? The other question, how law should be administered with enlightenment, with equity, with speed, and without friction, was put aside as "practical detail" which clerks could arrange after doctors had agreed upon principles.

That political philosophy took this direction was of course no accident, no chance preference of perverse whim of political philosophers. The philosophy of any time is, as Hegel says, "nothing but the spirit of that time expressed in abstract thought"; and political philosophy, like philosophy of every other kind, has only held up the mirror to contemporary affairs. The trouble in early times was almost altogether about the constitution of government; and consequently that was what engrossed men's thoughts. There was little or no trouble about administration—at least little that was heeded by administrators. The functions of government were simple because life itself was simple. Government went about imperatively and compelled men, without thought of consulting their wishes. There was no complex system of public revenues and public debts to puzzle financiers; there were, consequently, no financiers to be puzzled. No one who possessed power was long at a loss how to use it. The great and only question was: Who shall possess it? Populations were of manageable numbers; property was of simple sorts. There were plenty of farms, but no stocks and bonds: more cattle than vested interests.

I have said that all this was true of "early times"; but it was substantially true also of comparatively late times. One does not have to look back of the last century for the beginnings of the present complexities of trade and perplexities of commercial speculation, nor for the portentous birth of national debts. Good Queen Bess, doubtless, thought that the monopolies of the sixteenth century were hard enough to handle without burning her hands; but they are not remembered in the presence of the giant monopolies of the nineteenth century. When Blackstone lamented that corporations had no bodies to be kicked and no souls to be damned, he was anticipating the proper time for such regrets by full a century. The perennial discords between master and workmen which now so often disturb industrial society began before the Black Death and the Statute of Laborers; but never before our own day did they assume such ominous proportions as they wear now. In brief, if difficulties of governmental action are to be seen gathering in other centuries, they are to be seen culminating in our own.

This is the reason why administrative tasks have nowadays to be so studiously and systematically adjusted to carefully tested standards of policy, the reason why we are having now what we never had before, a science of administration. The weightier debates of constitutional principle are even yet by no means concluded; but they are no longer of more immediate practical moment than questions of administration. It is getting to be harder to *run* a constitution than to frame one.

Here is Mr. Bagehot's graphic, whimsical way of depicting the difference between the old and the new in administration:

> In early times, when a despot wishes to govern a distant province, he sends down a satrap on a grand horse, and other people on little horses; and very little is heard of the satrap again unless he send back some of the little people to tell what he has been doing. No great labour of superintendence is possible. Common rumour and casual report are the sources of intelligence. If it seems certain that the province is in a bad state, satrap No. 1 is recalled, and satrap No. 2 sent out in his stead. In civilized countries the process is different. You erect a bureau in the province you want to govern; you make it write letters and copy letters; it sends home eight reports *per diem* to the head bureau in St. Petersburg. Nobody does a sum in the province without some one doing the same sum in the capital, to "check" him, and see that he does it correctly. The consequence of this is, to throw on the heads of departments an amount of reading and labour which can only be accomplished by the greatest natural aptitude, the most efficient training, the most firm and regular industry.[1]

There is scarcely a single duty of government which was once simple which is not now complex; government once had but a few masters; it now has scores of masters. Majorities formerly only underwent government; they now conduct government. Where government once might follow the whims of a court, it must now follow the views of a nation.

And those views are steadily widening to new conceptions of state duty; so that, at the same time that the functions of government are every day becoming more complex and difficult, they are also vastly mutliplying in number. Administration is everywhere putting its hands to new undertakings. The utility, cheapness, and success of the government's postal service, for instance, point towards the early establishment of governmental control of the telegraph system. Or, even if our government is not to follow the lead of the governments of

[1] Essay on William Pitt.

Europe in buying or building both telegraph and railroad lines, no one can doubt that in some way it must make itself master of masterful corporations. The creation of national commissioners of railroads, in addition to the older state commissions, involves a very important and delicate extension of administrative functions. Whatever hold of authority state or federal governments are to take upon corporations, there must follow cares and responsibilities which will require not a little wisdom, knowledge, and experience. Such things must be studied in order to be well done. And these, as I have said, are only a few of the doors which are being opened to offices of government. The idea of the state and the consequent ideal of its duty are undergoing noteworthy change; and "the idea of the state is the conscience of administration." Seeing every day new things which the state ought to do, the next thing is to see clearly how it ought to do them.

This is why there should be a science of administration which shall seek to straighten the paths of government, to make its business less unbusinesslike, to strengthen and purify its organization, and to crown its duties with dutifulness. This is one reason why there is such a science.

But where has this science grown up? Surely not on this side of the sea. Not much impartial scientific method is to be discerned in our administrative practices. The poisonous atmosphere of city government, the crooked secrets of state administration, the confusion, sinecurism, and corruption ever and again discovered in the bureaus at Washington forbid us to believe that any clear conceptions of what constitutes good administration are as yet very widely current in the United States. No; American writers have hitherto taken no very important part in the advancement of this science. It has found its doctors in Europe. It is not of our making; it is a foreign science, speaking very little of the language of English or American principle. It employs only foreign tongues; it utters none but what are to our minds alien ideas. Its aims, its examples, its conditions, are almost exclusively grounded in the histories of foreign races, in the precedents of foreign systems, in the lessons of foreign revolutions. It has been developed by French and German professors, and is consequently in all parts adapted to the needs of a compact state, and made to fit highly centralized forms of government; whereas, to answer our purposes, it must be adapted, not to a simple and compact, but to a complex and multiform state, and made to fit highly decentralized forms of government. If we would employ it, we must Americanize it, and that not formally, in language merely, but radically, in thought, principle, and aim as well. It must learn our constitutions by heart; must get the bureaucratic fever out of its veins; must inhale much free American air.

If an explanation be sought why a science manifestly so susceptible of being made useful to all governments alike should have received attention first in Europe, where government has long been a monopoly, rather than in England or the United States, where government has long been a common franchise, the reason will doubtless be found to be twofold: first, that in Europe, just because government was independent of popular assent, there was more governing to be done; and, second, that the desire to keep government a monopoly made the monopolists interested in discovering the least irritating means of governing. They were, besides, few enough to adopt means promptly.

It will be instructive to look into this matter a little more closely. In speaking of European governments I do not, of course, include England. She has not refused to change with the times. She has simply tempered the severity of the transition from a polity of aristocratic privilege to a system of democratic power by slow measures of constitutional reform which, without preventing revolution, has confined it to paths of peace. But the countries of the continent for a long time desperately struggled against all change, and would have diverted revolution by softening the asperities of absolute government. They sought so to perfect their machinery as to destroy all wearing friction, so to sweeten their methods with consideration for the interests of the governed as to placate all hindering hatred, and so assiduously and opportunely to offer their aid to all classes of undertakings as to render themselves indispensable to the industrious. They did at last give the people constitutions and the franchise; but even after that they obtained leave to continue despotic by becoming paternal. They made themselves too efficient to be dispensed with, too smoothly operative to be noticed, too enlightened to be inconsiderately questioned, too benevolent to be suspected, too powerful to be coped with. All this has required study; and they have closely studied it.

On this side of the sea we, the while, had known no great difficulties of government. With a new country, in which there was room and remunerative employment for everybody, with liberal principles of government and unlimited skill in practical politics, we were long exempted from the need of being anxiously careful about plans and methods of administration. We have naturally been slow to see the use or significance of those many volumes of learned research and painstaking examination into the ways and means of conducting government which the presses of Europe have been sending to our libraries. Like a lusty child, government with us has expanded in nature and grown great in stature, but has also become awkward in movement. The vigor and increase of its life has been altogether out of proportion to its skill in living. It has gained strength, but it has not acquired deportment. Great, therefore, as has been our advantage over the countries of Europe in point of ease and health of constitutional development, now that the time for more careful administrative adjustments and larger administrative knowledge has come to us, we are at a signal disadvantage as compared with the transatlantic nations; and this for reasons which I shall try to make clear.

Judging by the constitutional histories of the chief nations of the modern world, there may be said to be three periods of growth through which government has passed in all the most highly developed of existing systems, and through which it promises to pass in all the rest. The first of these periods is that of absolute rulers, and of an administrative system adapted to absolute rule; the second is that in which constitutions are framed to do away with absolute rulers and substitute popular control, and in which administration is neglected for these higher concerns; and the third is that in which the sovereign people undertake to develop administration under this new constitution which has brought them into power.

Those governments are now in the lead in administrative practice which had rulers still absolute but also enlightened when those modern days of political illumination came in which it was made evident to all but the blind that governors are properly only the servants of the governed. In such governments administration has been organized to subserve the general weal with the simplicity and effectiveness vouchsafed only to the undertakings of a single will.

Such was the case in Prussia, for instance, where administration has been most studied and most nearly perfected. Frederic the Great, stern and masterful as was his rule, still sincerely professed to regard himself as only the chief servant of the state, to consider his great office a public trust; and it was he who, building upon the foundations laid by his father, began to organize the public service of Prussia as in very earnest a service of the public. His no less absolute successor, Frederic William III, under the inspiration of Stein, again, in his turn, advanced the work still further, planning many of the broader structural features which give firmness and form to Prussian administration today. Almost the whole of the admirable system has been developed by kingly initiative.

Of similar origin was the practice, if not the plan, of modern French administration, with its symmetrical divisions of territory and its orderly gradations of office. The days of the Revolution—of the Constituent Assembly—were days of constitution-*writing*, but they can hardly be called days of constitution-*making*. The Revolution heralded a period of constitutional development,—the entrance of France upon the second of those periods which I have enumerated,—but it did not itself inaugurate such a period. It interrupted and unsettled absolutism, but did not destroy it. Napoleon succeeded the monarchs of France, to exercise a power as unrestricted as they had ever possessed.

The recasting of French administration by Napoleon is, therefore, my second example of the perfecting of civil machinery by the single will of an absolute ruler before the dawn of a constitutional era. No corporate, popular will could ever have effected arrangements such as those which Napoleon commanded. Arrangements so simple at the expense of local prejudice, so logical in their indifference to popular choice, might be decreed by a Constituent Assembly, but could be established only by the unlimited authority of a despot. The system of the year VIII was ruthlessly thorough and heartlessly perfect. It was, besides, in large part, a return to the despotism that had been overthrown.

Among those nations, on the other hand, which entered upon a season of constitution-making and popular reform before administration had received the impress of liberal principle, administrative improvement has been tardy and half-done. Once a nation has embarked in the business of manufacturing constitutions, it finds it exceedingly difficult to close out that business and open for the public a bureau of skilled, economical administration. There seems to be no end to the tinkering of constitutions. Your ordinary constitution will last you hardly ten years without repairs or additions; and the time for administrative detail comes late.

Here, of course, our examples are England and our own country. In the days of the Angevin kings, before constitutional life had taken root in the Great Charter, legal and administrative reforms began to proceed with sense and vigor under the impulse of Henry II's shrewd, busy, pushing, indomitable spirit and purpose; and kingly initiative seemed destined in England, as elsewhere, to shape governmental growth at its will. But impulsive, errant Richard and weak, despicable John were not the men to carry out such schemes as their father's. Administrative development gave place in their reigns to constitutional struggles; and Parliament became king before any English monarch had had the practical genius or the enlightened conscience to devise just and lasting forms for the civil service of the state.

The English race, consequently, has long and successfully

studied the art of curbing executive power to the constant neglect of the art of perfecting executive methods. It has exercised itself much more in controlling than in energizing government. It has been more concerned to render government just and moderate than to make it facile, well-ordered, and effective. English and American political history has been a history, not of administrative development, but of legislative oversight,—not of progress in governmental organization, but of advance in law-making and political criticism. Consequently, we have reached a time when administrative study and creation are imperatively necessary to the well-being of our governments saddled with the habits of a long period of constitution-making. That period has practically closed, so far as the establishment of essential principles is concerned, but we cannot shake off its atmosphere. We go on criticizing when we ought to be creating. We have reached the third of the periods I have mentioned—the period, namely, when the people have to develop administration in accordance with the constitutions they won for themselves in a previous period of struggle with absolute power; but we are not prepared for the tasks of the new period.

Such an explanation seems to afford the only escape from blank astonishment at the fact that, in spite of our vast advantages in point of political liberty, and above all in point of practical political skill and sagacity, so many nations are ahead of us in administrative organization and administrative skill. Why, for instance, have we but just begun purifying a civil service which was rotten full fifty years ago? To say that slavery diverted us is but to repeat what I have said—that flaws in our constitution delayed us.

Of course all reasonable preference would declare for this English and American course of politics rather than for that of any European country. We should not like to have had Prussia's history for the sake of having Prussia's administrative skill; and Prussia's particular system of administration would quite suffocate us. It is better to be untrained and free than to be servile and systematic. Still there is no denying that it would be better yet to be both free in spirit and proficient in practice. It is this even more reasonable preference which impels us to discover what there may be to hinder or delay us in naturalizing this much-to-be-desired science of administration.

What, then, is there to prevent?

Well, principally, popular sovereignty. It is harder for democracy to organize administration than for monarchy. The very completeness of our most cherished political successes in the past embarrasses us. We have enthroned public opinion; and it is forbidden us to hope during its reign for any quick schooling of the sovereign in executive expertness or in the conditions of perfect functional balance in government. The very fact that we have realized popular rule in its fullness has made the task of *organizing* that rule just so much the more difficult. In order to make any advance at all we must instruct and persuade a multitudinous monarch called public opinion—a much less feasible undertaking than to influence a single monarch called a king. An individual sovereign will adopt a simple plan and carry it out directly: he will have but one opinion, and he will embody that one opinion in one command. But this other sovereign, the people, will have a score of differing opinions. They can agree upon nothing simple: advance must be made through compromise, by a compounding of differences, by a trimming of plans and a suppression of too straightforward principles. There will be a succession of resolves running through a course of years, a dropping fire of commands running through a whole gamut of modifications.

In government, as in virtue, the hardest of hard things is to make progress. Formerly the reason for this was that the single person who was sovereign was generally either selfish, ignorant, timid, or a fool—albeit there was now and again one who was wise. Nowadays the reason is that the many, the people, who are sovereign have no single ear which one can approach, and are selfish, ignorant, timid, stubborn, or foolish with the selfishness, the ignorances, the stubbornnesses, the timidities, or the follies of several thousand persons—albeit there are hundreds who are wise. Once the advantage of the reformer was that the sovereign's mind had a definite locality, that it was contained in one man's head, and that consequently it could be gotten at; though it was his disadvantage that that mind learned only reluctantly or only in small quantities, or was under the influence of some one who let it learn only the wrong things. Now, on the contrary, the reformer is bewildered by the fact that the sovereign's mind has no definite locality, but is contained in a voting majority of several million heads; and embarrassed by the fact that the mind of this sovereign also is under the influence of favorites, who are none the less favorites in a good old-fashioned sense of the word because they are not persons but preconceived opinions; *i.e.*, prejudices which are not to be reasoned with because they are not the children of reason.

Wherever regard for public opinion is a first principle of government, practical reform must be slow and all reform must be full of compromises. For wherever public opinion exists it must rule. This is now an axiom half the world over, and will presently come to be believed even in Russia. Whoever would effect a change in a modern constitutional government must first educate his fellow-citizens to want *some* change. That done, he must persuade them to want the particular change he wants. He must first make public opinion willing to listen and then see to it that it listen to the right things. He must stir it up to search for an opinion, and then manage to put the right opinion in its way.

The first step is not less difficult than the second. With opinions, possession is more than nine points of the law. It is next to impossible to dislodge them. Institutions which one generation regards as only a makeshift approximation to the realization of a principle, the next generation honors as the nearest possible approximation to that principle, and the next worships as the principle itself. It takes scarcely three generations for the apotheosis. The grandson accepts his grandfather's hesitating experiment as an integral part of the fixed constitution of nature.

Even if we had clear insight into all the political past, and could form out of perfectly instructed heads a few steady, infallible, placidly wise maxims of government into which all sound political doctrine would be ultimately resolvable, *would the country act on them?* That is the question. The bulk of mankind is rigidly unphilosophical, and nowadays the bulk of mankind votes. A truth must become not only plain but also commonplace before it will be seen by the people who go to their work very early in the morning; and not to act upon it must involve great and pinching inconveniences before these same people will make up their minds to act upon it.

And where is this unphilosophical bulk of mankind more multifarious in its composition than in the United States? To know the public mind of this country, one must know the mind, not of Americans of the older stocks only, but also of Irishmen, of Germans, of Negroes. In order to get a footing for new doctrine, one must influence minds cast in every mould of race, minds inheriting every bias of environment, warped by the histories of a score of different nations, warmed or chilled, closed or expanded by almost every climate of the globe.

So much, then, for the history of the study of administration, and the peculiarly difficult conditions under which, entering upon it when we do, we must undertake it. What, now, is the subject-matter of this study, and what are its characteristic objects?

II.

The field of administration is a field of business. It is removed from the hurry and strife of politics; it at most points stands apart even from the debatable ground of constitutional study. It is a part of political life only as the methods of the counting-house are a part of the life of society; only as machinery is part of the manufactured product. But it is, at the same time, raised very far above the dull level of mere technical detail by the fact that through its greater principles it is directly connected with the lasting maxims of political wisdom, the permanent truths of political progress.

The object of administrative study is to rescue executive methods from the confusion and costliness of empirical experiment and set them upon foundations laid deep in stable principle.

It is for this reason that we must regard civil-service reform in its present stages as but a prelude to a fuller administrative reform. We are now rectifying methods of appointment; we must go on to adjust executive functions more fitly and to prescribe better methods of executive organization and action. Civil service reform is thus but a moral preparation for what is to follow. It is clearing the moral atmosphere of official life by establishing the sanctity of public office as a public trust, and, by making the service unpartisan, it is opening the way for making it businesslike. By sweetening its motives it is rendering it capable of improving its methods of work.

Let me expand a little what I have said of the province of administration. Most important to be observed is the truth already so much and so fortunately insisted upon by our civil-service reformers; namely, that administration lies outside the proper sphere of *politics*. Administrative questions are not political questions. Although politics sets the tasks for administration, it should not be suffered to manipulate its offices.

This is distinction of high authority; eminent German writers insist upon it as a matter of course. Bluntschli,[2] for instance, bids us separate administration alike from politics and from law. Politics, he says, is state activity "in things great and universal," while "administration, on the other hand," is "the activity of the state in individual and small things. Politics is thus the special province of the statesman, administration of the technical official." "Policy does nothing without the aid of administration"; but administration is not therefore politics. But we do not require German authority for this position; this discrimination between administration and politics is now, happily, too obvious to need further discussion.

There is another distinction which must be worked into all

[2] Politik, S. 467.

our conclusions, which, though but another side of that between administration and politics, is not quite so easy to keep sight of: I mean the distinction between *constitutional* and administrative questions, between those governmental adjustments which are essential to constitutional principle and those which are merely instrumental to the possibly changing purposes of a wisely adapting convenience.

One cannot easily make clear to every one just where administration resides in the various departments of any practicable government without entering upon particulars so numerous as to confuse and distinctions so minute as to distract. No lines of demarcation, setting apart administrative from non-administrative functions, can be run between this and that department of government without being run up hill and down dale, over dizzy heights of distinction and through dense jungles of statutory enactment, hither and thither around "ifs" and "buts," "whens" and "howevers," until they become altogether lost to the common eye not accustomed to this sort of surveying, and consequently not acquainted with the use of the theodolite of logical discernment. A great deal of administration goes about *incognito* to most of the world, being confounded now with political "management," and again with constitutional principle.

Perhaps this ease of confusion may explain such utterances as that of Niebuhr's: "Liberty," he says, "depends incomparably more upon administration than upon constitution." At first sight this appears to be largely true. Apparently facility in the actual exercise of liberty does depend more upon administrative arrangements than upon constitutional guarantees; although constitutional guarantees alone secure the existence of liberty. But—upon second thought—is even so much as this true? Liberty no more consists in easy functional movement than intelligence consists in the ease and vigor with which the limbs of a strong man move. The principles that rule within the man, or the constitution, are the vital springs of liberty or servitude. Because dependence and subjection are without chains, are lightened by every easy-working device of considerate, paternal government, they are not thereby transformed into liberty. Liberty cannot live apart from constitutional principle; and no administration, however perfect and liberal its methods, can give men more than a poor counterfeit of liberty if it rest upon illiberal principles of government.

A clear view of the difference between the province of constitutional law and the province of administrative function ought to leave no room for misconception; and it is possible to name some roughly definite criteria upon which such a view can be built. Public administration is detailed and systematic execution of public law. Every particular application of general law is an act of administration. The assessment and raising of taxes, for instance, the hanging of a criminal, the transportation and delivery of the mails, the equipment and recruiting of the army and navy, *etc.*, are all obviously acts of administration; but the general laws which direct these things to be done are as obviously outside of and above administration. The broad plans of governmental action are not administrative; the detailed execution of such plans is administrative. Constitutions, therefore, properly concern themselves only with those instrumentalities of government which are to control general law. Our federal constitution observes this principle in saying nothing of even the greatest of the purely executive offices, and speaking only of that President of the Union who was to share the legislative and policy-making functions of government, only of those judges of highest jurisdiction who were to interpret and guard its principles, and not of those who were merely to give utterance to them.

This is not quite the distinction between Will and answering Deed, because the administrator should have and does have a will of his own in the choice of means for accomplishing his work. He is not and ought not to be a mere passive instrument. The distinction is between general plans and special means.

There is, indeed, one point at which administrative studies trench on constitutional ground—or at least upon what seems constitutional ground. The study of administration, philosophically viewed, is closely connected with the study of the proper distribution of constitutional authority. To be efficient it must discover the simplest arrangements by which responsibility can be unmistakably fixed upon officials; the best way of dividing authority without hampering it, and responsibility without obscuring it. And this question of the distribution of authority, when taken into the sphere of the higher, the originating functions of government, is obviously a central constitutional question. If administrative study can discover the best principles upon which to base such distribution, it will have done constitutional study an invaluable service. Montesquieu did not, I am convinced, say the last word on this head.

To discover the best principle for the distribution of authority is of greater importance, possibly, under a democratic system, where officials serve many masters, than under others where they serve but a few. All sovereigns are suspicious of their servants, and the sovereign people is no exception to the rule; but how is its suspicion to be allayed by *knowledge?* If that suspicion could but be clarified into wise vigilance, it would be altogether salutary; if that vigilance could be aided by the unmistakable placing of responsibility, it would be altogether beneficent. Suspicion in itself is never healthful either in the private or in the public mind. *Trust is strength* in all relations of life; and, as it is the office of the constitutional reformer to create conditions of trustfulness, so it is the office of the administrative organizer to fit administration with conditions of clear-cut responsibility which shall insure trustworthiness.

And let me say that large powers and unhampered discretion seem to me the indispensable conditions of responsibility. Public attention must be easily directed, in each case of good or bad administration, to just the man deserving of praise or blame. There is no danger in power, if only it be not irresponsible. If it be divided, dealt out in shares to many, it is obscured; and if it be obscured, it is made irresponsible. But if it be centred in heads of the service and in heads of branches of the service, it is easily watched and brought to book. If to keep his office a man must achieve open and honest success, and if at the same time he feels himself intrusted with large freedom of discretion, the greater his power the less likely is he to abuse it, the more is he nerved and sobered and elevated by it. The less his power, the more safely obscure and unnoticed does he feel his position to be, and the more readily does he relapse into remissness.

Just here we manifestly emerge upon the field of that still larger question,—the proper relations between public opinion and administration.

To whom is official trustworthiness to be disclosed, and by whom is it to be rewarded? Is the official to look to the public for his meed of praise and his push of promotion, or only to his superior in office? Are the people to be called in to settle administrative discipline as they are called in to settle constitutional principles? These questions evidently find their root in what is undoubtedly the fundamental problem of this whole study. That problem is: What part shall public opinion take in the conduct of administration?

The right answer seems to be that public opinion shall play the part of authoritative critic.

But the *method* by which its authority shall be made to tell? Our peculiar American difficulty in organizing administration is not the danger of losing liberty, but the danger of not being able or willing to separate its essentials from its accidents. Our success is made doubtful by that besetting error of ours, the error of trying to do too much by vote. Self-government does not consist in having a hand in everything, any more than housekeeping consists necessarily in cooking dinner with one's own hands. The cook must be trusted with a large discretion as to the management of the fires and the ovens.

In those countries in which public opinion has yet to be instructed in its privileges, yet to be accustomed to having its own way, this question as to the province of public opinion is much more readily soluble than in this country, where public opinion is wide awake and quite intent upon having its own way anyhow. It is pathetic to see a whole book written by a German professor of political science for the purpose of saying to his countrymen, "Please try to have an opinion about national affairs"; but a public which is so modest may at least be expected to be very docile and acquiescent in learning what things it has *not* a right to think and speak about imperatively. It may be sluggish, but it will not be meddlesome. It will submit to be instructed before it tries to instruct. Its political education will come before its political activity. In trying to instruct our own public opinion, we are dealing with a pupil apt to think itself quite sufficiently instructed beforehand.

The problem is to make public opinion efficient without suffering it to be meddlesome. Directly exercised, in the oversight of the daily details and in the choice of the daily means of government, public criticism is of course a clumsy nuisance, a rustic handling delicate machinery. But as superintending the greater forces of formative policy alike in politics and administration, public criticism is altogether safe and beneficent, altogether indispensable. Let administrative study find the best means for giving public criticism this control and for shutting it out from all other interference.

But is the whole duty of administrative study done when it has taught the people what sort of administration to desire and demand, and how to get what they demand? Ought it not to go on to drill candidates for the public service?

There is an admirable movement towards universal political education now afoot in this country. The time will soon come when no college of respectability can afford to do without a well-filled chair of political science. But the education thus imparted will go but a certain length. It will multiply the number of intelligent critics of government, but it will create no competent body of administrators. It will prepare the way for the development of a sure-footed understanding of the general principles of government, but it will not necessarily foster skill in conducting government. It is an education which will equip legislators, perhaps, but not executive officials. If we are to improve public poinion, which is the motive power of government, we must prepare better officials as the *apparatus* of government. If we are to put in new boilers and to mend the fires which drive our governmental machinery, we must not leave the old wheels and joints and valves and bands to creak and buzz and clatter on as best they may at bidding of the new force. We must put in new running parts wherever there is the least lack of strength or adjustment. It will be necessary to organize democracy by sending up to the competitive examinations for the civil service men definitely prepared for standing liberal tests as to technical knowledge. A technically schooled civil service will presently have become indispensable.

I know that a corps of civil servants prepared by a special schooling and drilled, after appointment, into a perfected organization, with appropriate hierarchy and characteristic discipline, seems to a great many very thoughtful persons to contain elements which might combine to make an offensive official class—a distinct, semi-corporate body with sympathies divorced from those of a progressive, free-spirited people, and with hearts narrowed to the meanness of a bigoted officialism. Certainly such a class would be altogether hateful and harmful in the United States. Any measures calculated to produce it would for us be measures of reaction and of folly.

But to fear the creation of a domineering, illiberal officialism as a result of the studies I am here proposing is to miss altogether the principle upon which I wish most to insist. That principle is, that administration in the United States must be at all points sensitive to public opinion. A body of thoroughly trained officials serving during good behavior we must have in any case: that is a plain business necessity. But the apprehension that such a body will be anything un-American clears away the moment it is asked, What is to constitute good behavior? For that question obviously carries its own answer on its face. Steady, hearty allegiance to the policy of the government they serve will constitute good behavior. That *policy* will have no taint of officialism about it. It will not be the creation of permanent officials, but of statesmen whose responsibility to public opinion will be direct and inevitable. Bureaucracy can exist only where the whole service of the state is removed from the common political life of the people, its chiefs as well as its rank and file. Its motives, its objects, its policy, its standards, must be bureaucratic. It would be difficult to point out any examples of impudent exclusiveness and arbitrariness on the part of officials doing service under a chief of department who really served the people, as all our chiefs of departments must be made to do. It would be easy, on the other hand, to adduce other instances like that of the influence of Stein in Prussia, where the leadership of one statesman imbued with true public spirit transformed arrogant and perfunctory bureaus into public-spirited instruments of just government.

The ideal for us is a civil service cultured and self-sufficient enough to act with sense and vigor, and yet so intimately connected with the popular thought, by means of elections and constant public counsel, as to find arbitrariness or class spirit quite out of the question.

III.

Having thus viewed in some sort the subject-matter and the objects of this study of administration, what are we to conclude as to the methods best suited to it—the points of view most advantageous for it?

Government is so near us, so much a thing of our daily familiar handling, that we can with difficulty see the need of any philosophical study of it, or the exact point of such study, should it be undertaken. We have been on our feet too long to study now the art of walking. We are a practical people, made so apt, so adept in self-government by centuries of experimental drill that we are scarcely any longer capable of perceiving the awkwardness of the particular system we may be using, just because it is so easy for us to use any system. We do not study the art of governing: we govern. But mere unschooled genius for affairs will not save us from sad blunders in administration. Though democrats by long inheritance and repeated choice, we are still rather crude democrats. Old as democracy is, its organization on a basis of modern ideas and conditions is still an unaccomplished work. The democratic state has yet to be equipped for carrying those enormous burdens of administration which the needs of this industrial and trading age are so fast accumulating. Without comparative studies in government we cannot rid ourselves of the misconception that administration stands upon an essentially different basis in a democratic state from that on which it stands in a non-democratic state.

After such study we could grant democracy the sufficient honor of ultimately determining by debate all essential questions affecting the public weal, of basing all structures of policy upon the major will; but we would have found but one rule of good administration for all governments alike. So far as administrative functions are concerned, all governments have a strong structural likeness; more than that, if they are to be uniformly useful and efficient, they *must* have a strong structural likeness. A free man has the same bodily organs, the same executive parts, as the slave, however different may be his motives, his services, his energies. Monarchies and democracies, radically different as they are in other respects, have in reality much the same business to look to.

It is abundantly safe nowadays to insist upon this actual likeness of all governments, because these are days when abuses of power are easily exposed and arrested, in countries like our own, by a bold, alert, inquisitive, detective public thought and a sturdy popular self-dependence such as never existed before. We are slow to appreciate this; but it is easy to appreciate it. Try to imagine personal government in the United States. It is like trying to imagine a national worship of Zeus. Our imaginations are too modern for the feat.

But, besides being safe, it is necessary to see that for all governments alike the legitimate ends of administration are the same, in order not to be frightened at the idea of looking into foreign systems of administration for instruction and suggestion; in order to get rid of the apprehension that we might perchance blindly borrow something incompatible with our principles. That man is blindly astray who denounces attempts to transplant foreign systems into this country. It is impossible: they simply would not grow here. But why should we not use such parts of foreign contrivances as we want, if they be in any way serviceable? We are in no danger of using them in a foreign way. We borrowed rice, but we do not eat it with chopsticks. We borrowed our whole political language from England, but we leave the words "king" and "lords" out of it. What did we ever originate, except the action of the federal government upon individuals and some of the functions of the federal supreme court?

We can borrow the science of administration with safety and profit if only we read all fundamental differences of condition into its essential tenets. We have only to filter it through our constitutions, only to put it over a slow fire of criticism and distil away its foreign gases.

I know that there is a sneaking fear in some conscientiously patriotic minds that studies of European systems might signalize some foreign methods as better than some American methods; and the fear is easily to be understood. But it would scarcely be avowed in just any company.

It is the more necessary to insist upon thus putting away all prejudices against looking anywhere in the world but at home for suggestions in this study, because nowhere else in the whole field of politics, it would seem, can we make use of the historical, comparative method more safely than in this province of administration. Perhaps the more novel the forms we study the better. We shall the sooner learn the peculiarities of our own methods. We can never learn either our own weaknesses or our own virtues by comparing ourselves with ourselves. We are too used to the appearance and procedure of our own system to see its true significance. Perhaps even the English system is too much like our own to be used to the most profit in illustration. It is best on the whole to get entirely away from our own atmosphere and to be most careful in examining such systems as those of France and Germany. Seeing our own institutions through such *media,* we see ourselves as foreigners might see us were they to look at us without preconceptions. Of ourselves, so long as we know only ourselves, we know nothing.

Let it be noted that it is the distinction, already drawn, between administration and politics which makes the comparative method so safe in the field of administration. When we study the administrative systems of France and Germany, knowing that we are not in search of *political* principles, we need not care a peppercorn for the constitutional or political reasons which Frenchmen or Germans give for their practices when explaining them to us. If I see a murderous fellow sharpening a knife cleverly, I can borrow his way of sharpening the knife without borrowing his probable intention to commit murder with it; and so, if I see a monarchist dyed-in-the-wool managing a public bureau well, I can learn his business methods without changing one of my republican spots. He may serve his king; I will continue to serve the people; but I should like to serve my sovereign as well as he serves his. By keeping this distinction in view—that is, by studying administration as a means of putting our own politics into convenient practice, as a means of making what is democratically politic towards all administratively possible towards each—we are on perfectly safe ground, and can learn without error what foreign systems have to teach us. We thus devise an adjusting weight for our comparative method of study. We can thus scrutinize the anatomy of foreign governments without fear of getting any of their diseases into our veins; dissect alien systems without apprehension of blood-poisoning.

Our own politics must be the touchstone for all theories. The principles on which to base a science of administration for America must be principles which have democratic policy very much at heart. And, to suit American habit, all general theories must, as theories, keep modestly in the background, not in open argument only, but even in our own minds—lest opinions satisfactory only to the standards of the library should be dogmatically used, as if they must be quite as satisfactory to the standards of practical politics as well. Doctrinaire devices must be postponed to tested practices. Arrangements not only sanctioned by conclusive experience elsewhere but also congenial to American habit must be preferred without hesitation to theoretical perfection. In a word, steady, practical statesmanship must come first, closet doctrine second. The cosmopolitan what-to-do must always be commanded by the American how-to-do-it.

Our duty is, to supply the best possible life to a *federal* organization, to systems within systems; to make town, city, county, state, and federal governments live with a like strength and an equally assured healthfulness, keeping each unquestionably its own master and yet making all interdependent and co-operative, combining independence with mutual helpfulness. The task is great and important enough to attract the best minds.

This interlacing of local self-government with federal self-government is quite a modern conception. It is not like the arrangements of imperial federation in Germany. There local government is not yet, fully, local *self*-government. The bureaucrat is everywhere busy. His efficiency springs out of *esprit de corps,* out of care to make ingratiating obeisance to the authority of a superior, or, at best, out of the soil of a sensitive conscience. He serves, not the public, but an irresponsible minister. The question for us is, how shall our series of governments within governments be so administered that it shall always be to the interest of the public officer to serve, not his superior alone but the community also, with the best efforts of his talents and the soberest service of his conscience? How shall such service be made to his commonest interest by contributing abundantly to his sustenance, to his dearest interest by furthering his ambition, and to his highest interest by advancing his honor and establishing his character? And how shall this be done alike for the local part and for the national whole?

If we solve this problem we shall again pilot the world. There is a tendency—is there not?—a tendency as yet dim, but already steadily impulsive and clearly destined to prevail, towards, first the confederation of parts of empires like the British, and finally of great states themselves. Instead of centralization of power, there is to be wide union with tolerated divisions of prerogative. This is a tendency towards the American type—of governments joined with governments for the pursuit of common purposes, in honorary equality and honorable subordination. Like principles of civil liberty are everywhere fostering like methods of government; and if comparative studies of the ways and means of government should enable us to offer suggestions which will practicably combine openness and vigor in the administration of such governments with ready docility to all serious, well-sustained public criticism, they will have approved themselves worthy to be ranked among the highest and most fruitful of the great departments of poiltical study. That they will issue in such suggestions I confidently hope.

2. POWER AND ADMINISTRATION

Norton Long

There is no more forlorn spectacle in the administrative world than an agency and a program possessed of statutory life, armed with executive orders, sustained in the courts, yet stricken with paralysis and deprived of power. An object of contempt to its enemies and of despair to its friends.

The lifeblood of administration is power. Its attainment, maintenance, increase, dissipation, and loss are subjects the practitioner and student can ill afford to neglect. Loss of realism and failure are almost certain consequences. This is not to deny that important parts of public administration are so deeply entrenched in the habits of the community, so firmly supported by the public, or so clearly necessary as to be able to take their power base for granted and concentrate on the purely professional side of their problems. But even these islands of the blessed are not immune from the plague of politics, as witness the fate of the hapless Bureau of Labor Statistics and the perennial menace of the blind 5 per cent across-the-board budget cut. Perhaps Carlyle's aphorism holds here. "The healthy know not of their health but only the sick." To stay healthy one needs to recognize that health is a fruit, not a birthright. Power is only one of the considerations that must be weighed in administration, but of all it is the most overlooked in theory and the most dangerous to overlook in practice.

The power resources of an administrator or an agency are not disclosed by a legal search of titles and court decisions or by examining appropriations or budgetary allotments. Legal authority and a treasury balance are necessary but politically insufficient bases of administration. Administrative rationality requires a critical evaluation of the whole range of complex and shifting forces on whose support, acquiescence, or temporary impotence the power to act depends.

Analysis of the sources from which power is derived and the limitations they impose is as much a dictate of prudent administration as sound budgetary procedure. The bankruptcy that comes from an unbalanced power budget has consequences far more disastrous than the necessity of seeking a deficiency appropriation. The budgeting of power is a basic subject matter of a realistic science of administration.

It may be urged that for all but the top hierarchy of the administrative structure the question of power is irrelevant. Legislative authority and administrative orders suffice. Power adequate to the function to be performed flows down the chain of command. Neither statute nor executive order, however, confers more than legal authority to act. Whether Congress or President can impart the substance of power as well as the form depends upon the line-up of forces in the particular case. A price control law wrung from a reluctant Congress by an amorphous and unstable combination of consumer and labor groups is formally the same as a law enacting a support price program for agriculture backed by the disciplined organizations of farmers and their congressmen. The differences for the scope and effectiveness of administration are obvious. The Presidency, like Congress, responds to and translates the pressures that play upon it. The real mandate contained in an Executive order varies with the political strength of the group demand embodied in it, and in the context of other group demands.

Both Congress and President do focus the general political energies of the community and are so considerably more than mere means for transmitting organized pressures. Yet power is not concentrated by the structure of government or politics into the hands of a leadership with a capacity to budget it among a diverse set of administrative activities. A picture of the Presidency as a reservoir of authority from which the lower echelons of administration draw life and vigor is an idealized distortion of reality.

A similar criticism applies to any like claim for an agency head in his agency. Only in varying degrees can the powers of subordinate officials be explained as resulting from the chain of command. Rarely is such an explanation a satisfactory account of the sources of power.

To deny that power is derived exclusively from superiors in the hierarchy is to assert that subordinates stand in a feudal relation in which to a degree they fend for themselves and acquire support peculiarly their own. A structure of interests friendly or hostile, vague and general or compact and well-defined, encloses each significant center of administrative discretion. This structure is an important determinant of the scope of possible action. As a source of power and authority it is a competitor of the formal hierarchy.

Not only does political power flow in from the sides of an organization, as it were; it also flows up the organization to the center from the constituent parts. When the staff of the Office of War Mobilization and Reconversion advised a hard-pressed agency to go out and get itself some popular support so that the President could afford to support it, their action reflected the realities of power rather than political cynicism.

It is clear that the American system of politics does not generate enough power at any focal point of leadership to provide the conditions for an even partially successful divorce of politics from administration. Subordinates cannot depend on the formal chain of command to deliver enough political power to permit them to do their jobs. Accordingly they must supplement the resources available through the hierarchy with those they can muster on their own, or accept the consequences in frustration—a course itself not without danger. Administrative rationality demands that objectives be determined and sights set in conformity with a realistic appraisal of power position and potential.

The theory of administration has neglected the problem of the sources and adequacy of power, in all probability because of a distaste for the disorderliness of American political life and a belief that this disorderliness is transitory. An idealized picture of the British parliamentary system as a Platonic form to be realized or approximated has exerted a baneful fascination in the field. The majority party with a mandate at the polls and a firmly seated leadership in the Cabinet seems to solve adequately the problem of the supply of power necessary to permit administration to concentrate on the fulfillment of accepted objectives. It is a commonplace that the American party system provides neither a mandate for a platform nor a mandate for a leadership.

Accordingly, the election over, its political meaning must be explored by the diverse leaders in the executive and legislative branches. Since the parties have failed to discuss issues, mobilize majorities in their terms, and create a working political consensus on measures to be carried out, the task is left for others—most prominently the agencies concerned. Legislation passed and powers granted are frequently politically premature. Thus the Council of Economic Advisers was given legislative birth before political acceptance of its functions existed. The agencies to which tasks are assigned must devote themselves to the creation of an adequate consensus to permit administration. The mandate that the parties do not supply must be attained through public relations and the mobilization of group support. Pendleton Herring and others have shown just how vital this support is for agency action.

The theory that agencies should confine themselves to communicating policy suggestions to executive and legislature, and refrain from appealing to their clientele and the public, neglects the failure of the parties to provide either a clear-cut decision as to what they should do or an adequately mobilized political support for a course of action. The bureaucracy under the American political system has a large share of responsibility for the public promotion of policy and even more in organizing the political basis for its survival and growth. It is generally recognized that the agencies have a special competence in the technical aspects of their fields which of necessity gives them a rightful policy initiative. In addition, they have or develop a shrewd understanding of the politically feasible in the group structure within which they work. Above all, in the eyes of their supporters and their enemies they represent the institutionalized embodiment of policy, an enduring organization actually or potentially capable of mobilizing power behind policy. The survival interests and creative drives of administrative organizations combine with clientele pressures to compel such mobilization. The party system provides no enduring institutional representation for group interest at all comparable to that of the bureaus of the Department of Agriculture. Even the subject matter committees of Congress function in the shadow of agency permanency.

The bureaucracy is recognized by all interested groups as a major channel of representation to such an extent that Congress rightly feels the competition of a rival. The weakness in party structure both permits and makes necessary the present dimensions of the political activities of the administrative branch—permits because it fails to protect administration from pressures and fails to provide adequate direction and support, makes necessary because it fails to develop a consensus on a leadership and a program that makes possible administration on the basis of accepted decisional premises.

Agencies and bureaus more or less perforce are in the business of building, maintaining, and increasing their political support. They lead and in large part are led by the diverse groups whose influence sustains them. Frequently they lead and are themselves led in conflicting directions. This is not due to a dull-witted incapacity to see the contradictions in their behavior but is an almost inevitable result of the contradictory nature of their support.

Herbert Simon has shown that administrative rationality depends on the establishment of uniform value premises in the decisional centers of organization. Unfortunately, the value premises of those forming vital elements of political support are often far from uniform. These elements are in Barnard's and Simon's sense "customers" of the organization and therefore parts of the organization whose wishes are clothed with a very real authority. A major and most time-consuming aspect of administration consists of the wide range of activities designed to secure enough "customer" acceptance to survive and, if fortunate, develop a consensus adequate to program formulation and execution.

To varying degrees, dependent on the breadth of acceptance of their programs, officials at every level of significant discretion must make their estimates of the situation, take stock of their resources, and plan accordingly. A keen appreciation of the real components of their organization is the beginning of wisdom. These components will be found to stretch far beyond the government payroll. Within the government they will encompass Congress, congressmen, committees, courts, other agencies, presidential advisers, and the President. The Aristotelian analysis of constitutions is equally applicable and equally necessary to an understanding of administrative organization.

The broad alliance of conflicting groups that makes up presidential majorities scarcely coheres about any definite pattern of objectives, nor has it by the alchemy of the party system had its collective power concentrated in an accepted leadership with a personal mandate. The conciliation and maintenance of this support is a necessary condition of the attainment and retention of office involving, as Madison so well saw, "the spirit of party and faction in the necessary and ordinary operations of government." The President must in large part be, if not all things to all men, at least many things to many men. As a consequence, the contradictions in his power base invade administration. The often criticized apparent cross-purposes of the Roosevelt regime cannot be put down to inept administration until the political facts are weighed. Were these apparently self-defeating measures reasonably related to the general maintenance of the composite majority of the Administration? The first objective—ultimate patriotism apart—of the administrator is the attainment and retention of the power on which his tenure of office depends. This is the necessary pre-condition for the accomplishment of all other objectives.

The same ambiguities that arouse the scorn of the naive in the electoral campaigns of the parties are equally inevitable in administration and for the same reasons. Victory at the polls does not yield either a clear-cut grant of power or a unified majority support for a coherent program. The task of the Presidency lies in feeling out the alternatives of policy which are consistent with the retention and increase of the group support on which the Administration rests. The lack of a budgetary theory (so frequently deplored) is not due to any incapacity to apply rational analysis to the comparative contribution of the various activities of government to a determinate hierarchy of purposes. It more probably stems from a fastidious distaste for the frank recognition of the budget as a politically expedient allocation of resources. Appraisal in terms of their political contribution to the Administration provides almost a sole common denominator between the Forest Service and the Bureau of Engraving.

Integration of the administrative structure through an overall purpose in terms of which tasks and priorities can be established is an emergency phenomenon. Its realization, only partial at best, has been limited to war and the extremity of depression. Even in wartime the Farm Bureau Federation, the American Federation of Labor, the Congress of Industrial Organizations, the National Association of Manufacturers, the Chamber of Commerce, and a host of lesser interests resisted coordination of themselves and the agencies concerned with their interests. A Presidency temporarily empowered by intense mass popular support acting in behalf of a generally accepted and simplified purpose can, with great difficulty, bribe, cajole, and coerce a real measure of joint action. The long-drawn-out battle for conversion and the debacle of orderly reconversion underline the difficulty of attaining, and the transitory nature of, popularly based emergency power. Only in crises are the powers of the Executive nearly adequate to impose a common plan of action on the executive branch, let alone the economy.

In ordinary times the manifold pressures of our pluralistic society work themselves out in accordance with the balance of forces prevailing in Congress and the agencies. Only to a limited degree is the process subject to responsible direction or review by President or party leadership.

The program of the President cannot be a Gosplan for the government precisely because the nature of his institutional and group support gives him insufficient power. The personal unity of the Presidency cannot perform the function of Hobbes' sovereign since his office lacks the authority of Hobbes' contract. Single-headedness in the executive gives no assurance of singleness of purpose. It only insures that the significant pressures in a society will be brought to bear on one office. Monarchy solves the problem of giving one plan to a multitude only when the plentitude if its authority approaches dictatorship. Impatient social theorists in all ages have turned to the philosopher king as a substitute for consensus. Whatever else he may become, it is difficult to conceive of the American president ruling as a philosopher king, even with the advice of the Executive Office. The monarchical solution to the administrative problems posed by the lack of a disciplined party system capable of giving firm leadership and a program to the legislature is a modern variant of the dreams of the eighteenth century savants and well nigh equally divorced from a realistic appraisal of social realities.

Much of administrative thought, when it does not assume the value of coordination for coordination's sake, operates on the assumption that there must be something akin to Rousseau's *volonté générale* in administration to which the errant *volunté de tous* of the bureaus can and should be made to conform. This will-o'-the-wisp was made the object of an illuminating search by Pendleton Herring in his *Public Administration and the Public Interest.* The answer for Rousseau was enlightened dictatorship or counting the votes. The administrative equivalent to the latter is the resultant of the relevant pressures, as Herring shows. The first alternative seems to require at least the potency of the British Labour party, and elsewhere has needed the disciplined organization of a fascist, nazi, or communist party to provide the power and consensus necessary to coordinate the manifold activities of government to a common plan.

Dictatorship, as Sigmund Neumann has observed, is a substitute for institutions which is required to fill the vacuum when traditional institutions break down. Force supplies the compulsion and guide to action in place of the normal routines of unconscious habit. Administrative organizations, however much they may appear the creations of art, are institutions produced in history and woven in the web of social relationships that gives them life and being. They present the same refractory material to the hand of the political artist as the rest of society of which they form a part.

Just as the economists have attempted to escape the complexities of institutional reality by taking refuge in the frictionless realm of theory, so some students of administration, following their lead, have seen in the application of the doctrine of opportunity costs a clue to a science of administration. Valuable as this may be in a restricted way, Marx has more light to throw on the study of institutions. It is in the dynamics and interrelations of institutions that we have most hope of describing and therefore learning to control administrative behavior.

The difficulty of coordinating government agencies lies not only in the fact that bureaucratic organizations are institutions having survival interests which may conflict with their rational adaptation to over-all purpose, but even more in their having roots in society. Coordination of the varied activities of a modern government almost of necessity involves a substantial degree of coordination of the economy. Coordination of government agencies involves far more than changing the behavior and offices of officials in Washington and the field. It involves the publics that are implicated in their normal functioning. To coordinate fiscal policy, agricultural policy, labor policy, foreign policy, and military policy, to name a few major areas, moves beyond the range of government charts and the habitat of the bureaucrats to the market place and to where the people live and work. This suggests that the reason why government reorganization is so difficult is that far more than government in the formal sense is involved in reorganization. Our could overlook this in the limited government of the nineteenth century but the multi-billion dollar government of the mid-twentieth permits no facile dichotomy between government and economy. Economy and efficiency are the two objectives a laissez faire society can prescribe in peacetime as over-all government objectives. Their inadequacy either as motivation or standards has long been obvious. A planned economy clearly requires a planned government. But, if one can afford an unplanned economy, apart from gross extravagance, there seems no compelling and therefore, perhaps, no sufficiently powerful reason for a planned government.

Basic to the problems of administrative rationality is that of organizational identification and point of view. To whom is one loyal—unit, section, branch, division, bureau, department, administration, government, country, people, world history, or what? Administrative analysis frequently assumes that organizational identification should occur in such a way as to merge primary organization loyalty in a larger synthesis. The good of the part is to give way to the reasoned good of the whole. This is most frequently illustrated in the rationalizations used to counter self-centered demands of primary groups for funds and personnel. Actually the competition between governmental power centers, rather than the rationalizations, is the effective instrument of coordination.

Where there is a clear common product on whose successful production the sub-groups depend for the attainment of their own satisfaction, it is possible to demonstrate to almost all participants the desirability of cooperation. The shoe factory produces shoes, or else, for all concerned. But the government as a whole and many of its component parts have no such identifiable common production on which all depend. Like the proverbial Heinz, there are fifty-seven or more varieties unified, if at all, by a common political profit and loss account.

Administration is faced by somewhat the same dilemma as economics. There are propositions about the behavior patterns conducive to full employment—welfare economics. On the other hand, there are propositions about the economics of the individual firm—the counsel of the business schools. It is possible to show with considerable persuasiveness that sound considerations for the individual firm may lead to a depression if generally adopted, a result desired by none of the participants. However, no single firm can afford by itself to adopt the course of collective wisdom; in the absence of a common power capable of enforcing decisions premised on the supremacy of the collective interest, *sauve qui peut* is common sense.

The position of administrative organizations is not unlike the position of particular firms. Just as the decisions of the firms could be coordinated by the imposition of a planned economy so could those of the component parts of the government. But just as it is possible to operate a formally unplanned economy by the loose coordination of the market, in the same fashion it is possible to operate a government by the loose coordination of the play of political forces through its institutions.

The unseen hand of Adam Smith may be little in evidence in either case. One need not believe in a doctrine of social or administrative harmony to believe that formal centralized planning—while perhaps desirable and in some cases necessary—is not a must. The complicated logistics of supplying the city of New York runs smoothly down the grooves of millions of well adapted habits projected from a distant past. It seems naive on the one hand to believe in the possibility of a vast, intricate, and delicate economy operating with a minimum of formal over-all direction, and on the other to doubt that a relatively simple mechanism such as the government can be controlled largely by the same play of forces.

Doubtless the real reasons for seeking coordination in the government are the same that prompt a desire for economic planning. In fact, apart from waging war with its demand for rapid change, economic planning would seem to be the only objective sufficiently compelling and extensive to require a drastic change in our system of political laissez faire. Harold Smith, testifying before the Senate Banking and Currency Committee on the Employment Act of 1946, showed how extensive a range of hitherto unrelated activities could be brought to bear on a common purpose—the maintenance of maximum employment and purchasing power. In the flush of the war experience and with prophecies of reconversion unemployment, a reluctant Congress passed a pious declaration of policy. Senator Flanders has recorded the meager showing to date.

Nevertheless, war and depression apart, the Employment Act

of 1946 for the first time provides an inclusive common purpose in terms of which administrative activities can be evaluated and integrated. While still deficient in depth and content, it provides at least a partial basis for the rational budgeting of government activities. The older concept of economy and efficiency as autonomous standards still lingers in Congress, but elsewhere their validity as ends in themselves is treated with skepticism.

If the advent of Keynesian economics and the erosion of laissez faire have created the intellectual conditions requisite for the formulation of over-all government policy, they do not by any means guarantee the political conditions necessary for its implementation. We can see quite clearly that the development of an integrated administration requires an integrating purpose. The ideals of Locke, Smith, Spencer, and their American disciples deny the need for such a purpose save for economy and efficiency's sake. Marx, Keynes, and their followers by denying the validity of the self-regulating economy have endowed the state with an over-arching responsibility in terms of which broad coordination of activities is not only intellectually possible but theoretically, at least, necessary. Intellectual perception of the need for this coordination, however, has run well ahead of the public's perception of it and of the development of a political channeling of power adequate to its administrative implementation.

Most students of administration are planners of some sort. Most congressmen would fly the label like the plague. Most bureaucrats, whatever their private faith, live under two jealous gods, their particular clientele and the loyalty check. Such a condition might, if it exists as described, cast doubt on whether even the intellectual conditions for rational administrative coordination exist. Be that as it may, the transition from a government organized in clientele departments and bureaus, each responding to the massive feudal power of organized business, organized agriculture, and organized labor, to a government integrated about a paramount national purpose will require a political power at least as great as that which tamed the earlier feudalism. It takes a sharp eye or a tinted glass to see such an organized power on the American scene. Without it, administrative organization for over-all coordination has the academic air of South American constitution making. One is reminded of the remark attributed to the Austrian economist Mises; on being told that the facts did not agree with his theory, he replied "*desto schlechter für die Tatsache.*"

It is highly appropriate to consider how administrators should behave to meet the test of efficiency in a planned polity; but in the absence of such a polity and while, if we like, struggling to get it, a realistic science of administration will teach administrative behavior appropriate to the existing political system.

A close examination of the presidential system may well bring one to conclude that administrative rationality in it is a different matter from that applicable to the British ideal. The American Presidency is an office that has significant monarchical characteristics despite its limited term and elective nature. The literature on court and palace has many an insight applicable to the White House. Access to the President, reigning favorites, even the court jester, are topics that show the continuity of institutions. The maxims of LaRochefoucauld and the memoirs of the Duc de Saint Simon have a refreshing realism for the operator on the Potomac.

The problem of rival factions in the President's family is as old as the famous struggle between Jefferson and Hamilton, as fresh and modern as the latest cabal against . . . [a cabinet officer]. Experience seems to show that this personal and factional struggle for the President's favor is a vital part of the process of representation. The vanity, personal ambition, or patriotism of the contestants soon clothes itself in the generalities of principle and the clique aligns itself with groups beyond the capital. Subordinate rivalry is tolerated if not encouraged by so many able executives that it can scarcely be attributed to administrative ineptitude. The wrangling tests opinion, uncovers information that would otherwise never rise to the top, and provides effective opportunity for decision rather than mere ratification of prearranged plans. Like most judges, the Executive needs to hear argument for his own instruction. The alternatives presented by subordinates in large part determine the freedom and the creative opportunity of their superiors. The danger of becoming a Merovingian is a powerful incentive to the maintenance of fluidity in the structure of power.

The fixed character of presidential tenure makes it necessary that subordinates be politically expendable. The President's men must be willing to accept the blame for failures not their own. Machiavelli's teaching on how princes must keep the faith bears re-reading. Collective responsibility is incompatible with a fixed term of office. As it tests the currents of public opinion, the situation on the Hill, and the varying strength of the organized pressures, the White House alters and adapts the complexion of the Administration. Loyalties to programs or to groups and personal pride and interest frequently conflict with whole-souled devotion to the Presidency. In fact, since such devotion is not made mandatory by custom, institutions, or the facts of power, the problem is perpetually perplexing to those who must choose.

The balance of power between executive and legislature is constantly subject to the shifts of public and group support. The latent tendency of the American Congress is to follow the age-old parliamentary precedents and to try to reduce the President to the role of constitutional monarch. Against this threat and to secure his own initiative, the President's resources are primarily demagogic, with the weaknesses and strengths that dependence on mass popular appeal implies. The unanswered question of American government—"who is boss?"—constantly plagues administration. The disruption of unity of command is not just the problem of Taylor's functional foreman, but goes to the stability and uniformity of basic decisional premises essential to consequent administration.

It is interesting to speculate on the consequences for administration of the full development of congressional or presidential government. A leadership in Congress that could control the timetable of the House and Senate would scarcely content itself short of reducing the President's Cabinet to what in all probability it was first intended to be, a modified version of the present Swiss executive. Such leadership could scarcely arise without centrally organized, disciplined, national parties far different from our present shambling alliances of state and local machines.

A Presidency backed by a disciplined party controlling a majority in Congress would probably assimilate itself to a premiership by association of legislative leadership in the formulation of policy and administration. In either line of development the crucial matter is party organization. For the spirit of the party system determines the character of the government.

That the American party system will develop toward the British ideal is by no means a foregone conclusion. The present oscillation between a strong demagogic Presidency and a defensively powerful congressional oligarchy may well prove a continuing pattern of American politics, as it was of Roman. In the absence of a party system providing an institutionalized centripetal force in our affairs, it is natural to look to the Presidency as Goldsmith's weary traveler looked to the throne.

The Presidency of the United States, however, is no such throne as the pre-World War I *Kaiserreich* that provided the moral and political basis for the Prussian bureaucracy. Lacking neutrality and mystique, it does not even perform the function of the British monarchy in providing a psychological foundation for the permanent civil service. A leaderless and irresponsible Congress frequently makes it appear the strong point of the republic. The Bonapartist experience in France, the Weimar Republic, and South American examples nearer home, despite important social differences, are relevant to any thoughtful consideration of building a solution to legislative anarchy on the unity of the executive.

The present course of American party development gives little ground for optimism that a responsible two party system capable of uniting Congress and Executive in a coherent program will emerge. The increasingly critical importance of the federal budget for the national economy and the inevitable impact of world power status on the conduct of foreign affairs make inescapable the problem of stable leadership in the American system. Unfortunately they by no means insure a happy or indeed any solution.

Attempts to solve administrative problems in isolation from the structure of power and purpose in the polity are bound to prove illusory. The reorganization of Congress to create responsibility in advance of the development of party responsibility was an act of piety to principle, of educational value; but as a practical matter it raised a structure without foundation. In the same way, reorganization of the executive branch to centralize administrative power in the Presidency while political power remains dispersed and divided may effect improvement, but in a large sense it must fail. The basic prerequisite to the administration of the textbooks is a responsible two party system. The means to its attainment are a number one problem for students of administration. What Schattschneider calls the struggle for party government may sometime yield us the responsible parliamentary two party system needed to underpin our present administrative theory. Until that happy time, exploration of the needs and necessities of our present system is a high priority task of responsible scholarship.

II. Agencies and Their Constituencies

EDITORIAL NOTE. The two case studies in this Chapter vividly portray the political nature of bureaucracy. The first is a classic, dealing with the Interstate Commerce Commission, and illustrating the way in which regulatory agencies tend to become the captives of the groups that they regulate. Students of government should ask themselves what alternatives are available to administrators confronted with the dilemma of having to achieve political support in order to survive. The second selection bears out the thesis of the first, and demonstrates how pressure groups will attempt to influence the agencies which regulate them by trying to control presidential appointments.

3. THE MARASMUS OF THE ICC: THE COMMISSION, THE RAILROADS, AND THE PUBLIC INTEREST

Samuel P. Huntington

Among the myriad federal agencies concerned with transportation, the Interstate Commerce Commission has long been preeminent. It is the oldest transportation regulatory commission, and with the exception of the Corps of Engineers it is the oldest federal agency of any type with major transportation responsibilities. It is the only federal agency immediately concerned with more than one type of carrier: its activities directly affect four of the five major forms of commercial transportation. It is one of the few significant transportation bodies which have not been absorbed by the Department of Commerce, and it is the only important transportation agency completely independent of the executive branch. It is the sole administrative agency to which Congress has delegated the responsibility for enforcing the National Transportation Policy.[1] During its sixty-five years of existence the Commission developed an enviable reputation for honesty, impartiality, and expertness. Its age, prestige, and scope combined to make it the premier federal agency in the transportation field.

Despite this impressive past, however, there are many indications that the ICC is now losing its position of leadership. New developments threaten to bring about the end of the agency or to reduce it to a secondary position. The level of its appropriations and the number of its employees have been either stationary or declining. Its decisions are more frequently reversed in the courts than previously. Its leadership and staff have manifestly deteriorated in quality. The general praise which it once received has been replaced by sharp criticism. And, most importantly, it is now challenged by the rise of a new agency, the Office of the Undersecretary of Commerce for Transportation, which appears to be assuming federal transportation leadership. It is the purpose of this Article to analyze the causes of the decline of the ICC and the probable and desirable future position of this agency.

Successful adaptation to changing environmental circumstances is the secret of health and longevity for administrative

[1] "It is hereby declared to be the national transportation policy of the Congress to provide for fair and impartial regulation of all modes of transportation subject to the provisions of this Act, so administered as to recognize and preserve the inherent advantages of each; to promote safe, adequate, economical, and efficient service and foster sound economic conditions in transportation and among the several carriers; to encourage the establishment and maintenance of reasonable charges for transportation services, without unjust discriminations, undue preferences or advantages, or unfair or destructive competitive practices; to cooperate with the several States and the duly authorized officials thereof; and to encourage fair wages and equitable working conditions:—all to the end of developing, coordinating, and preserving a national transportation system by water, highway, and rail, as well as other means, adequate to meet the needs of the commerce, of the United States, of the Postal Service, and of the national defense. All the provisions of this Act shall be administered and enforced with a view to carrying out the above declaration of policy." Preamble to the Interstate Commerce Act, 54 STAT. 899 (1940).

as well as biological organisms. Every government agency must reflect to some degree the "felt needs" of its time. In the realm of government, felt needs are expressd through political demands and political pressures. These demands and pressures may come from the president, other administrative agencies and officials, congressmen, political interest groups, and the general public. If an agency is to be viable it must adapt itself to the pressures from these sources so as to maintain a net preponderance of political support over political opposition. It must have sufficient support to maintain and, if necessary, expand its statutory authority, to protect it against attempts to abolish it or subordinate it to other agencies, and to secure for it necessary appropriations. Consequently, to remain viable over a period of time, an agency must adjust its sources of support so as to correspond with changes in the strength of their political pressures. If the agency fails to make this adjustment, its political support decreases relative to its political opposition, and it may be said to suffer from administrative marasmus. The decline of the ICC may be attributed to its susceptibility to this malady.

I. HISTORICAL BACKGROUND

The history of the ICC in terms of its political support divides naturally into two fairly distinct periods. The Commission was created in 1887 after the Supreme Court invalidated state attempts to regulate the railroads' abuse of their monopoly power. The driving force behind these early state regulatory laws and commissions were the farmers, who had suffered severely from exorbitant rates and discriminatory practices. This group plus equally dissatisfied commercial shippers were the political force responsible for the Act to Regulate Commerce. In addition, general public indignation and disgust at railroad financial and business practices provided a favorable climate of opinion for the creation of the Commission. President Cleveland endorsed the legislation and enhanced the Commission's reputation by appointing Judge Cooley and other prominent figures as its first members.

From 1887 down to the First World War the support of the

Commission came primarily from the groups responsible for its creation. Opposition came principally from the railroads and the courts. In its first two decades the Commission was severely hampered by the combined action of these two groups. Subsequently farmer and shipper interests with the vigorous support of President Roosevelt secured the passage of the Hepburn Act of 1906. This enlarged the Commission, extended its jurisdiction, gave it the power to prescribe future maximum rates, and prohibited railroads from owning the products they transported. The decade which followed the passage of this Act was the peak of the Commission's power and prestige while still dependent upon consumer, public and presidential support.

The end of the First World War marked a definite change in the nature of the transportation problem and in the attitudes of the various interests towards railroad regulation. The vigorous actions of the ICC in the period immediately prior to the war had eliminated the worst discriminatory practices and had convinced the railroads that the path of wisdom was to accept regulation and to learn to live with the Commission. This domestication of the carriers consequently reduced the interest and political activity of shipper groups. And increased urbanization reduced the power of farm groups which had been such a significant source of support to the Commission. Finally, "normalcy" had supplanted progressivism and Harding and Coolidge were significantly different from T. Roosevelt and Wilson. Consequently there was little likelihood that restrictive regulation would find much support from either the public or the White House.

All these factors dictated not only the shift in public policy which was made in the Transportation Act of 1920 but also a shift by the Commission in the sources to which it looked for support.[2] Continued reliance upon the old sources of support

[2] The Transportation Act of 1920 required the Commission to fix rates so that the railroad industry as a whole would earn a "fair return upon the aggregate value" of its invested capital. Other provisions (1) extended the power of the Commission over the issuance of railroad securities, new construction and abandonments, car service, and minimum rates, (2) permitted poolings subject to Commission approval, (3) directed the Commission to

would have resulted in decreasing viability. Therefore the Commission turned more and more to the railroad industry itself, particularly the railroad management group. This development was aided by the expansion of the Commission's activities and the resulting increased dependence of the Commission upon the cooperation of regulated groups for the successful administration of its program.[3] The support which the Commission received from the railroads sustained it down to World War II and enabled it both to expand its authority over other carrier groups and to defend itself against attempts to subject it to executive control.

The present marasmus of the ICC is due to continued dependence upon railroad support. The transportation industry is not only large, it is also dynamic. Technological changes and economic development are basically altering the nation's transportation pattern. The tremendous expansion of air and motor transport, the resulting increase in competition, the economic development of the South and West, the rise of private carriage, and the increased significance of defense considerations all make today's transportation system fundamentally different from that of twenty-five years ago. These technological and economic developments have given rise to new political demands and pressures, and have drastically altered the old balance of political forces in the transportation arena. A quarter of a century ago commercial transportation was railroad transportation. Today, railroads are a declining, although still major, segment of the transportation industry. Their economic decline has been matched by a decrease in political influence. The ICC, however, remains primarily a "railroad" agency. It has not responded to the demands of the new forces in transportation. It has not duplicated the successful adjustment of its sources of political support that it carried out after World

---

draw up a plan for the consolidation of the railroads into a limited number of systems, and (4) provided for the recapture of excess railroad profits and their use for the benefit of the weaker roads.

[3] See HERRING, PUBLIC ADMINISTRATION AND THE PUBLIC INTEREST 183–93 (1936).

War I. Consequently, it is losing its leadership to those agencies which are more responsive to the needs and demands of the times.

II. RAILROAD SUPPORT OF THE ICC

Railroad Praise of the ICC

The attitude of the railroads towards the Commission since 1935 can only be described as one of satisfaction, approbation, and confidence. At times the railroads have been almost effusive in their praise of the Commission. The ICC, one sub-committee of the Association of American Railroads has declared, "is eminently qualified by nearly sixty years of experience to handle transportation matters with a maximum of satisfaction to management, labor and the public." Another representative of the same association has similarly stated that "[w]hat is needed for the solution of the tremendously important problems of transport regulation is the impartiality, deliberation, expertness, and continuity of policy that have marked the history of the Interstate Commerce Commission." Railroad officials and lawyers have commended the Commission as a "conspicuous success," a "constructive force," and as a "veteran and generally respected tribunal." The American Short Line Railroad Association has commented upon the "fair, intelligent treatment" its members have been accorded by the Commission, and the Pennsylvania Railroad has been lavish in its praise of the latter's policies. The ICC is probably the only regulatory body in the federal government which can boast that a book has been written about it by counsel for a regulated interest in order to demonstrate "how well" the Commission has "performed its duty."[4]

The railroads and the Commission have both praised their harmonious relations. "The railroad industry," it has been said, "in wide contrast to other industry, has learned to live under government regulation." The editors of *Railway Age* have similarly spoken highly of the "collaboration" which exists between

[4] Walter, Introduction to DRAYTON, TRANSPORTATION UNDER TWO MASTERS, xii (1946).

the Commission and its regulated enterprises and have remarked that this "stands out in strong contrast to the animosity and distrust which now separates many regulatory bodies from the areas of industry which they supervise." The Commission itself has noted with pride the lack of criticism which its administration of the Interstate Commerce Act has received from the carriers and has pointed out that while some interests have urged the abandonment of regulation the "railroads have never joined in that suggestion."

Railroad Defense of Commission Independence

The railroads have vigorously defended the independence of the ICC from control by other governmental units and have opposed all attempts to subordinate it to other agencies or to transfer from the Commission any of its functions. This support for the Commission has taken three principal forms.

Opposition to ICC reorganization. The railroads have successfully opposed all reorganization proposals to subordinate the ICC or transfer any of its functions to the executive branch. In 1937 the President's Committee on Administrative Management recommended that the ICC along with all other regulatory commissions be divided into administrative and judicial sections and be placed in an executive department. The administrative section would be a regular bureau within the department; the judicial section would be in the department for "housekeeping" purposes only. These proposals raised a storm of protest from the ICC-railroad block and legislation to effect them was defeated in Congress. Over a decade later similar opposition was expressed by the railroads to legislation designed to create a Department of Transportation which would absorb the "executive" functions of the ICC. The Hoover Commission recommendations that the equipment inspection, safety, and car service functions of the Commission be transferred to the Department of Commerce were likewise opposed by the rail carriers. In general, the railroads have repeatedly emphasized the desirability of maintaining the independence of the Commission against all forms of executive encroachment.

The significance of railroad support for the Commission in this connection was perhaps best demonstrated by the fate of the presidential reorganization plan designed to centralize administrative authority within the Commission in a chairman appointed by the president. This plan was one of six, all submitted by the president at the same time, and devised to effectuate similar reforms in five other commissions as well as the ICC. Resolutions of disapproval of four of these plans were introduced in the Senate and referred to the Committee on Expenditures in Executive Departments.[5] This committee reported three of the resolutions unfavorably; the fourth, that disapproving of the ICC reorganization, was reported favorably. The explanation of this obviously inconsistent action (since all four plans were virtually identical) can, in the words of the minority report, "easily be found by reading the roster of the regulated interests (and their lawyers) which appeared in opposition." The hearings on the plans had been largely monopolized by railroad and associated witnesses appearing to defend the "independence" of the ICC. In the debate on the floor of the Senate the railroads were given primary credit for the committee's peculiar action, and in the end the ICC resolution was approved by a substantial majority. Railroad support saved the ICC from a reorganized fate to which five other commissions succumbed.

Opposition to the creation of new agencies which might rival the ICC. Within the last decade the railroads have generally opposed the establishment of new agencies which might in any way infringe upon or limit the powers of the ICC. In 1938 the railroad Committee of Six did recommend the creation of a new transportation authority which would take over the Commission's powers in regard to finance, entry, and abandonment, and the establishment of a special court to handle railroad reorganizations. Both recommendations, however, were opposed by numerous rail carriers and officials. Typical of the usual railroad attitude was the rejection in 1946 by one Association of

[5] ICC: Reorganization Plan No. 7 of 1950.

American Railroads group of the proposal for a new transportation planning body because apparently this "would provide another agency duplicating the work of the Interstate Commerce Commission, and further complicate a situation now made difficult by the intervening of various government departments." Representatives of the AAR also opposed the creation of the new office of Undersecretary of Commerce for Transportation on the grounds that the ICC was the leading federal agency concerned with transportation and that this new official could only duplicate its functions and challenge its authority. Similarly, railroad opposition to the creation of a Department of Transportation has in large part been based upon the fear that even if this body did not initially absorb the ICC it would eventually encroach upon the Commission's functions. Railroads have frequently urged the creation of a single regulatory commission for all forms of transportation; the implicit or explicit assumption in all such proposals, however, is that this Commission would be an enlarged and reorganized ICC.

Opposition to the interference of existing agencies with the Commission. Attempts by existing agencies to influence or dictate ICC policy through intervention in proceedings before the Commission, informal pressure upon commissioners, or by other means, have been severely attacked by the railroads. The argument is that the ICC has the responsibility to act in the public interest, and other agencies, if they interfere, must be doing so on behalf of some parochial interest. Appearances of the Secretary of Agriculture before the Commission have frequently been objected to, and the intervention of price control agencies in the general rate cases has likewise been attacked. The heaviest criticism along this line has been directed at the Department of Justice for its frequent interventions before the ICC and attempts to influence Commission policy in cases raising antitrust issues. On a much broader level, the railroads and associated groups have been staunch defenders of the independence of the Commission from presidential and congressional interference.

Railroad Support for the Expansion of ICC Power

In addition to defending the ICC against intrusions upon its powers by other agencies the raliroads have fairly consistently in recent decades advocated the expansion of the Commission's authority. There are four principal points in the railroad program as it has developed.

Transfer to the ICC of all existing regulatory functions affecting the railroads. In the words of the Pennsylvania Railroad:

> All regulation of the railroads should be in the Interstate Commerce Commission and not part under that Commission and part under the Securities and Exchange Commission or other Commissions. In other words, the Interstate Commerce Commission should be the only governmental agency regulating the railroads.

Since 1941 the principal activity of the railroads in this area has been the drive to get the enforcement of the antitrust laws as applied to common carriers transferred from the Department of Justice to the ICC. The railroads argued that they were subject to two conflicting types of regulation and that the Antitrust Division was unfamiliar with and unsympathetic to their problems. In the end, the carriers were successful and the Reed-Bulwinkle Act of 1948 gave the ICC power to exempt rate conferences and bureaus from the antitrust laws.

Expansion of ICC regulatory authority over unregulated railroad-competitive groups. During the 1930's the railroads consistently urged the extension of ICC authority over unregulated carriers, particularly motor and inland water carriers. Their efforts in regard to the former achieved success in the Motor Carrier Act of 1935, which was the culmination of a determined legislative push by the railroads and the ICC. The latter itself had recognized in 1932 that:

> . . . there is substantially no demand for public regulation of the charges of motor trucks to protect shippers against exorbitant or discriminatory charges. The demand

has been chiefly from the railroads, and for the prescription of minimum rather than maximum charges.

Yet the Commission in that year endorsed the regulation of motor carriers, and in succeeding years regularly gave its support to measures designed to achieve that end. The recommendations of ICC Commissioner Eastman in his capacity as Federal Coordinator of Transportation gave additional impetus to the drive for regulation. The strongest political support, however, came from the railroads themselves, and representatives of the Association of Railroad Executives actively participated in the drafting of motor carrier legislation. The great bulk of the motor carriers initially opposed regulation. The approval of the American Trucking Association was achieved only in the later stages after they had received assurances that enforcement of the new legislation would be placed in a separate ICC bureau completely divorced from the existing railroad-regulating bureaus. Motor carrier regulation was also strongly opposed by all the principal farm organizations and most of the industrial shipper groups.

A comparable pattern prevailed in the struggle over the regulation of inland water carriers. The ICC, the Federal Coordinator, and the railroads strongly supported regulation. The farm organizations, the shippers, and the bulk of the water carriers themselves were equally strongly opposed. The strength of this latter combination was sufficient to delay the enactment of regulatory legislation until 1940 when the Transportation Act of that year gave the ICC control over these carriers.

Since the achievement of these two major objectives of basic ICC control over water and motor carriers, the railroads have attempted to fill in the gaps left in the regulatory jurisdiction of the Commission. They have urged that the exemptions given motor carriers of agricultural commodities and water carriers of bulk commodities be removed, and that private carriage and contract carriers likewise be subjected to the authority of the ICC. The AAR has also urged in recent years that the Commission be given power to charge tolls for the use of the inland waterways.

Transfer of regulatory controls over railroad-competitive groups from other agencies to the ICC. Where the railroads have been unsuccessful in preventing the assignment to other agencies of regulatory functions over competing carriers they have waged prolonged campaigns for the transfer of these functions to the ICC. In the debates over the Transportation Act of 1940 the AAR urged that ICC authority be extended over all forms of transportation subject to federal regulation. In particular, the Association wished to transfer authority over coastwise and intercoastal shipping from the Maritime Commission to the ICC and to have the ICC assume the functions of the Civil Aeronautics Authority. Legislation introduced at the instigation of the railroads contained these provisions. The railroads were successful in achieving only the first of their objectives. Rail groups have subsequently regularly attacked the independent position of the Civil Aeronautics Board, and urged either its abolition and the transfer of its functions to the ICC or, in more general terms, the centralization of all regulatory activities affecting transportation in one agency.

Concentration of all federal transportation activities in the ICC. The culmination of these various railroad policies towards the expansion of ICC authority was reached in 1950 when the AAR advanced the position that all government activities—regulatory and promotional—affecting all forms of transportation should be placed in the ICC. The representative of the railroads testifying before the Senate Interstate and Foreign Commerce Committee was quite explicit in stating that such agencies as the Bureau of Public Roads should be under the Commission. He left some doubt, however, as to the extent to which this recommendation also included such transportation service agencies as the Coast Guard, Weather Bureau, and Coast and Geodetic Survey. In addition, the AAR advocated that the authority of the ICC be extended so that all projects for improving the inland waterways proposed by the Chief of Engineers, United States Army, be submitted to the ICC for approval before their transmission to Congress. Insofar as the scope of its authority is concerned, no stronger support could be asked by the ICC than that which the Association of American Railroads has given to the Commission.

Railroad support in all its forms has been the basis of the Interstate Commerce Commission's viability. Other interests have at times supported individual actions of the Commission or defended the Commission against specific attempts to curb its authority. But such action on the part of these interests has always been sporadic and balanced by severe criticism of the Commission and opposition to it in other lines of policy. The railroads are alone among the interests surrounding the Commission in their constant and comprehensive support of that body. By their continuous praise of the Commission, by their defense of its independence and by their efforts to protect and to extend its authority the railroads have made the Commission the beneficiary of what has been their not inconsiderable political power. But in the rough world of competitive politics nothing comes for free. Political support must be purchased, and the price which the ICC has paid for its railroad support may be traced through almost all important phases of its policy and behavior.

III. ICC AID TO THE RAILROADS

An exhaustive analysis of the ramifications of the ICC-railroad affiliation throughout Commission policy is obviously beyond the scope of this Article. Instead it is here proposed to indicate briefly the consequences of this affiliation in four major areas of Commission activity: (1) the level of rates and fares; (2) monopoly and antitrust; (3) rail-motor competition; (4) rail-water competition.

The Level of Rates and Fares

The ease with which the railroads in recent years have obtained advances in rates and fares from the ICC has been the subject of considerable unfavorable comment. The significance of this Commission acquiescence to railroad demands can only be appreciated by a comparison of ICC policy in this field before and after it became dependent upon railroad support.

The Commission received the power to prescribe future maximum rates in the Hepburn Act of 1906. The first general request for rate advances came from the carriers in 1911 after the Mann-Elkins Act had broadened the Commission's powers in this area. These requests were denied, with the Commission laying down rigorous criteria for the justification of rate advances. During the next few years, in a series of general rate cases, the Commission either denied the railroad requests for increases or granted only a minor fraction of their demands. As a consequence of this policy, freight rates remained stable and in general harmony with wholesale prices from 1908 through 1915. In 1916, however, wholesale prices started to skyrocket, and the railroads renewed their demands for rate advances. But the ICC remained adamant throughout 1917, and it was not until March 1918 that the railroads were able to secure any substantial relief. ICC policy during this period directly reflects its shipper and farmer sources of political support.

In 1920, as its support from non-railroad sources was beginning to weaken, the Commission approved a major increase in railroad rates. After prices plummeted in 1921, freight rates were considerably out of line, and the Commission in 1922 ordered a ten per cent decrease. Despite the pressure of agricultural interests, however, the Commission did not restore the prewar relationship between prices and rates. Instead, the Commission from 1924 through 1929 stabilized freight rates at about 165% of the 1913 level, whereas prices had fallen back to about 140% of that level. It was during this period that the Commission lost its farmer and shipper support and developed close railroad affiliations. The changing attitudes of the former toward the Commission are reflected in the Hoch-Smith resolution of 1925, and the year 1926 marks the last time that the Commission denied in toto a railroad request for a general rate advance.

By the advent of the thirties the ICC was exercising a benevolent paternalism in regard to the rate level. Whereas in 1932 the wholesale price index had fallen off over 30% from its 1929 level, the Commission by granting "emergency" increases had actually slightly increased the level of freight rates. Throughout the depression the Commission maintained the rate level by approval of additional "emergency" increases and surcharges, by the rejection in 1933 of a shipper petition for rate reduction, and by the approval in 1938 of a general ten per cent rise. The result was that freight rates never dropped more than eleven per cent from their 1929 level. When wholesale prices increased in the early forties, freight rates went up also: the price index for 1945 was 151.6 and the freight rate index 173.8. Thus from 1924 through 1945 the Commission was able to maintain the rate level well above the price level. The significant gap between wholesale prices and freight rates during this period is graphic measure of the price of railroad support.

The removal of price controls in 1946 sent wholesale prices shooting upward. In three years the wholesale index had risen to 236.4. The ICC made valiant efforts to keep up with these skyrocketing prices. In June 1946 the Commission approved the first of a series of ten general rate increases embodied in four major proceedings. By September 1951 the cumulative percentage increases granted by the Commission amounted to an increase of 67.6% in basic freight rates over the June 1946 level. The actual increase in the rate level from 1946 to 1950 was 35.6% The drastic rise in wholesale prices has made it impossible for the Commission to maintain the 1945 cushion between prices and rates. The Commission has, however, been successful in preserving the 1913 relationship: in 1949 the rate index was 231.2, the price index 222.1; in 1950 the rate index was 229.5 and the price index 231.4. Considering the normal tendency of regulated and administered prices to lag far behind violent fluctuations in the general price level, the action of the Commission in moving rates up along with prices is eloquent testimony to its sensitivity to railroad interests. The speed of the ICC in increasing freight rates during this period contrasts with its tardiness during the World War I inflation and has evoked praise from the railroads and envy from other carrier groups regulated by less considerate commissions.

The responsiveness of the ICC to rail freight rate demands

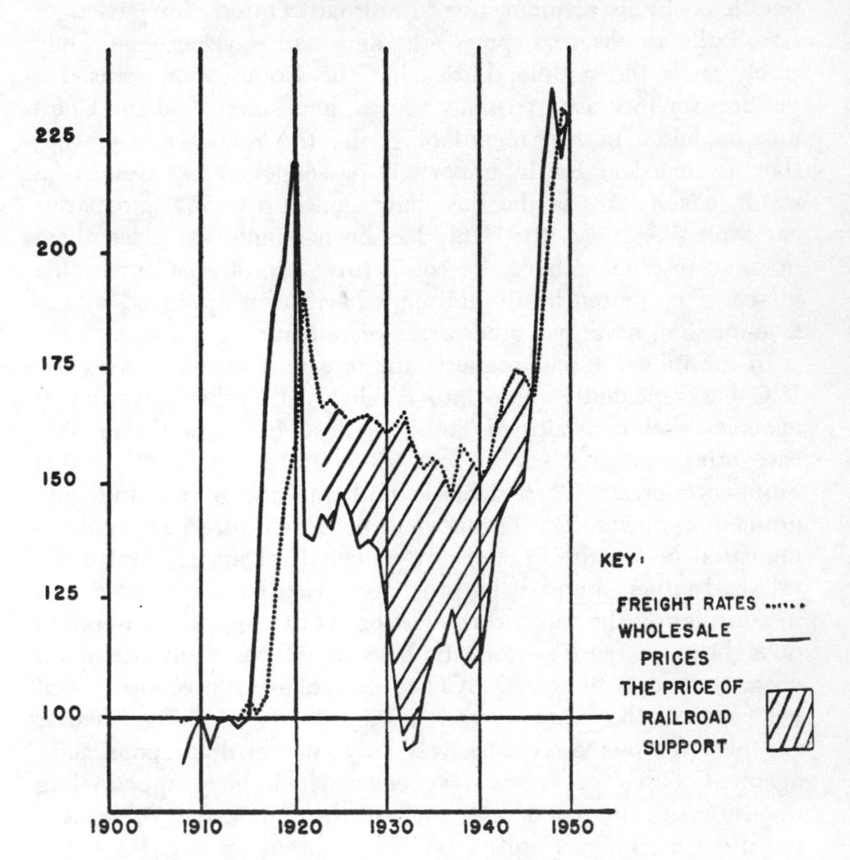

SOURCE: For indexes from 1908 through 1947 the source is Transcript of Record, p. 3, Exhibit No. 54, testimony of C. E. Childe, *Ex Parte* No. 168, Increased Freight Rates, 1948, 272 I.C.C. 695 (1948), 276 I.C.C. 9 (1949). For indexes from 1948 through 1950 the source is letter of C. E. Childe to the author, Jan. 23, 1952. Mr. Childe compiled the freight rate level index from data in the annual issues of ICC, STATISTICS OF RAILWAYS IN THE UNITED STATES. The figures for the years from 1908 through 1949 are all steam railways. The figures for 1950 are based upon data for Class I steam railways only. The wholesale price index is calculated from the index published by the Bureau of Labor Statistics.

since it became dependent upon railroad support has been paralleled by its acquiescence to railroad requests for passenger fare, Pullman charge, express rate, and mail pay increases. Only rarely since the middle thirties has the Commission refused a petition for increased passenger fares, and since 1940 the Commission has a perfect record of giving the roads exactly what they have asked for in important passenger fare cases. As a result, coach fares in the East have gone up 68.75% and parlor car fares 50% since 1940. This has been enough to place them in some instances above the competitive air fares. Comparable increases requested by the railroads have been approved by the Commission in various other areas of rail pricing.

In granting railroad requests for rate and fare increases the ICC has repeatedly come into conflict with other government agencies and non-railroad groups. These fall into three main categories.

Shipper interests. These include both private groups and government agencies. The Department of Agriculture has regularly appeared before the Commission in behalf of agricultural interests and either opposed the procedure used by the Commission in considering the railroad request or, as in most cases, opposed outright an increase in rates. In 1948 the Department attempted without success to get the ICC to investigate the economy and efficiency of the railroads with a view to determining whether the plea for increased rates was only the result of poor management. Other government agencies which have appeared in opposition to increased rates include the Tennessee Valley Authority, Consumers Counsel for the Bituminous Coal Commissions, Office of Solid Fuels Coordinator, General Services Administration, Department of Commerce, and the Department of the Interior. In a 1951 rate case the Attorney General appeared on behalf of the United States in opposition to the interim increase.

Price stabilization interests. During and immediately after the Second World War the OPA and the Economic Stabilization Agency frequently came into conflict with the ICC. Under the provisions of the price control acts the authority of these agencies did not extend to prices otherwise subject to federal regulation. The OPA was successful in 1943 in getting the ICC to suspend its previously granted six per cent freight rate increase but not in securing the removal of the ten per cent increase in passenger fares granted at the same time. Subsequently the OPA tried unsuccessfully to get the Commission to cancel the suspended rates, and in 1946 unsuccessfully opposed further rate increases. Throughout most of the war there was a running battle between the OPA and the ICC over the extent to which the ICC in enforcing the Interstate Commerce Act was bound by the policies of the price control acts. A series of Commission decisions and court cases on this question was finally resolved in favor of the ICC. During the present period of price controls the Office of Price Stabilization has resumed the battle with the Commission. It unsuccessfully opposed the 1951 freight rate increases and has also appeared in opposition to a commuter fare rise.

State and local interests. The ICC has generally been much more favorable to rate and fare increases than have state and local regulatory bodies. Consequently the Commission has frequently come into conflict with such agencies over the extent to which Commission-approved increases for interstate traffic should be extended to intrastate traffic. Under the law the Commission can prescribe rates upon the latter when it finds that the existing rates cause undue, unjust or unreasonable disadvantage to or discrimination against interstate commerce. State regulatory bodies have jealously defended their jurisdictions against the Commission's efforts to intrude thereon for the benefit of the railroads.

Monopoly and Antitrust

The Commission received its principal powers with respect to combinations and competition in the Transportation Act of 1920. Consequently it was only rarely that it acted in this area while dependent upon shipper and public support. In the few instances in which it did consider problems of monopoly prior to 1920 it was vigorously critical of the railroads. Its interpretations of the Transportation Act of 1920, on the other hand, have always been colored by its dependence upon railroad support. The Commission has advanced the individual and collective interests of the railroads by facilitating the reduction of competition among them and by aiding their development of cooperative devices designed to increase group solidarity.

In carrying out this necessary consequence of its railroad affiliation, the Commission has repeatedly come into conflict with the Antitrust Division and other groups interested in the maintenance of competition. The Commission early adopted the views of the railroads that collective price-fixing through rate bureaus and conferences was not only necessary and legal but also highly desirable. This position conflicts with judicial interpretations of the Sherman Act holding (1) that the act is applicable to carriers regulated by the Commission, and (2) that cooperative price-fixing by competing companies is per se a violation of the antitrust laws. It is, hence, significant that of eleven major antitrust proceedings instituted between 1935 and 1948 by the Department of Justice against carriers subject to ICC regulation, only one, which was against a motor carrier rate bureau, was based upon information referred to the Department by the ICC. In another suit, also against a motor carrier, there was "close cooperation" between the Division and the Commission in the investigation preceding the indictment. In regard to the railroads, however, the Commission has not turned over to the Department evidence of antitrust violations uncovered in the performance of its duties. At least some members of the Commission, for instance, were aware in 1939 of the activities of the railroads and motor carriers in Central Freight Association Territory which became the basis of a grand jury investigation, subsequently terminated without indictment because of the war. Of considerably greater significance was Commission awareness, if not sponsorship, of the Western Commissioner Agreement in 1932 among the major railroads operating west of the Mississippi. This established elaborate machinery for the settlement of rate disputes among the participant carriers. Members of the ICC were aware of the existence of the agreement during the eleven years it was in force. No attempt was made, however, to discover its provisions in detail or to require it to be filed with the Commission in accordance with Sec. 6(5) of the Interstate Commerce Act. The Justice Department consequently did not learn of it until 1943. It requested a copy from the railroads on April 9th of that year. It got a copy on April 14th. The same day the agreement was filed with the ICC. Nine days later the participating railroads canceled it. This agreement subsequently became the basis of the Department's Lincoln suit against the Association of American Railroads, the Western Association of Railway Executives, and forty-seven individual carriers.

Going beyond non-cooperation, the Commission has in some instances positively affected the conclusion of antitrust suits by the Government. Since it began to become dependent upon railroad support the Commission has in effect reversed successful antitrust suits by approving under Section 5 of the Interstate Commerce Act, and thereby exempting from the antitrust laws, practices which had previously been found to be in vioaltion of those laws. Similarly, in the recent *Pullman* case the Commission approved the sale of the Pullman operating company to the railroads over the objections of the Antitrust Division. Also, the approval by the Commission of the Western Traffic Association Agreement after the passage of the Reed-Bulwinkle Bill has obstructed the Justice Department's suit against the western railroads.

During the Second World War the ICC and its affiliated agency, the Office of Defense Transportation, endeavored to protect railroad rate bureaus from antitrust prosecution. The Small Business Concerns Act of 1942 authorized the chairman of the War Production Board, after consultation with the Attorney General, to certify to the latter that specified acts of private concerns were approved by him and were "requisite to the prosecution of the war." Such acts would then be immune from attack under the antitrust laws. During 1942 and 1943 the ICC and the ODT engaged in an administrative battle with the Antitrust Division to get the chairman of the WPB to exempt rate bureaus from antitrust prosecutions. The specific issue between the two agencies was whether certain restrictions regulating the practices of the bureaus and proposed by the Division should be written into the WPB certificate. In a much broader sense, the issue was one of competition versus regulated monopoly in railroad rate-making. In the end, the two transportation agencies were successful and the certificate was issued with the inclusion of only one minor provision recommended by the Division. After the termination of hostilities, the expiration date of the certificate was first fixed for October 1, 1945. However, at the request of ICC Commissioner Johnson, director of the ODT, the life of the certificate was extended another year. Despite renewed requests for further extension a year later, the Civilian Production Administrator permitted it to go out of effect on Oct. 1, 1946.

In addition to this administrative battle, the ICC lobbied before Congress for legislation to exempt permanently the rate bureaus from the danger of prosecution. Such a bill was introduced by Senator Wheeler in 1943 at the request of the ICC. The Justice Department immediately proposed that the same restrictions be written into this measure that it had unsuccessfully urged be included in the WPB certificate. This resulted in a conflict between the two agencies and, since with the issuance of the certificate the issue became temporarily dormant, the legislation was not pushed at that time. Subsequently in the 79th and 80th Congresses the ICC and the railroads renewed their efforts. . . . The Commission in its annual report issued at the beginning of 1945 urged the amendment of the Interstate Commerce Act to authorize itself to regulate carrier associations and to exempt them from the antitrust laws. Shortly thereafter Representative Bulwinkle introduced a bill designed to accomplish this purpose. The bill was endorsed by the Commission with suggestions for minor changes, and ICC representatives testified in its favor at the hearings. The need for this legislation likewise became more urgent from the Commission's viewpoint when the WPB exemptions certificate expired in 1946. In the second session of the 79th Congress and in the 80th Congress the Commission renewed its endorsement of legislation along the lines of the Bulwinkle Bill, and in 1948 it approved the conference report of the bill in the form in which it was finally enacted over the President's veto.

Under Sections 5 and 5a of the Interstate Commerce Act, the ICC may approve poolings of carriers, consolidations, mergers, acquisitions of control, and agreements relating to rate and charges, and thereby exempt carriers participating in such actions from the antitrust laws. The policy of the ICC in enforcing these sections has generally coincided with the views of the railroads. It is rare that applications to purchase, merge, or lease railroad lines or to acquire ownership of such lines or to enter into operating agreements with such lines are turned down by the Commission. Applications to permit interlocking directorates are also almost invariably approved. In one significant case concerning the consolidation of eight motor carriers in which it was alleged that there was a railroad interest, the Commission rejected the arguments of the Antitrust Division, the Department of Agriculture and other groups that the Commission ought not approve transactions which would result in an unreasonable restraint of competition within the meaning of the antitrust laws. The Supreme Court, on appeal, sustained the Commission, in a divided decision. In applying the provisions of the Reed-Bulwinkle Bill the ICC has also followed a lenient policy and interpreted broadly the scope of the permissible exemption from the antitrust laws.

Rail-Motor Competition

The affiliation of the ICC with the railroads has resulted in an ambiguous relationship between the Commission and the principal railroad-competitive group, the motor carriers. On the one hand, there is a close affiliation between the motor carrier industry and the ICC's Bureau of Motor Carriers, with the two cooperating in the enforcement of the Motor Carrier Act of 1935. The Bureau has consequently been praised by the motor carriers and criticized by the railroads. On the other hand, the relationship between the motor carrier industry and the Commission apart from the BMC has been cool and frequently antagonistic. The reason for this is Commission partiality towards the railroads in conflicts of interest between the two carrier groups. The price of railroad affiliation has been motor carrier alienation.

Because a large portion of railroad traffic is non-competitive and must move by rail, the Commission has been able to aid the railroads by permitting selective rate-cutting during periods of intense rail-motor competition such as that from 1935 through 1941. For three years from 1937 to 1940 the Commission required motor carriers to bear the burden of proof in making competitive rate cuts while at the same time not requiring the railroads to do so. This policy was continued after Congress in 1938 amended the Motor Carrier Act to make its provisions concerning burden of proof identical with those applicable to the railroads. During this same period the Commission put further barriers in the way of motor carrier competition by prescribing comprehensive minimum rate levels for motor carriers in the northeast and middle west. Although initially requested by the motor carriers, the subsequent effect of these orders was, as Commissioner Eastman pointed out in one dissent, to substitute a much more difficult procedure for motor carriers wishing to lower rates than for railroads. The Commission rejected, however, motor carrier petitions to remedy the situation. Throughout this period the Commission in a number of cases encouraged the railroads to exercise their managerial discretion by meeting motor carrier competition through various devices. The injurious effects of proposed railroad competitive rates upon motor carriers were not sufficient cause to invalidate the rates. Railroads were usually permitted to meet motor carrier competition by rate reductions, and to regain by this means traffic which had been lost of the truckers. Relief from the provisions of Section 4 of the Act prohibiting the charging of a higher rate for a short haul than for a longer one was frequently granted the railroads in this connection. Rate reductions on competitive traffic not accompanied by reductions upon similar noncompetitive traffic were held not to be prejudicial or discriminatory. On the other hand, attempts by the motor carriers to meet railroad competition or to undercut railroads were usually disapproved by the Commission.

ICC action in regard to the most heavily competitive commodities was almost invariably favorable to railroads. The most competitive traffic between the two types of carriers was that which had normally up to that time moved at railroad less-than-carload (LCL) ratings. It was openly admitted that railroad rates on this traffic did not cover costs. Despite this, the railroads vigorously attempted to keep this traffic from falling to the motor carriers, and in carrying out their program to this end they received the cooperation of the Commission. In 1936 the Commission permitted the railroads to introduce free pick-up and delivery services and in the following four years gave them further assistance. The climax of the railroad drive was reached in 1940 when the southern roads filed reduced ratings on some 3,500 commodities and the Commission permitted these changes to go into effect over the most vigorous motor carrier opposition without even suspending them for investigation. In the regulation of other highly competitive traffic, such as automobiles, petroleum, and meats ICC actions and policies likewise tended to favor the railroads. Typical of ICC decisions at this time was one important case dealing with naval stores in which the Commission refused to set minimums beyond which the railroads might not go in meeting motor carrier competition.

The railroads during this period were frequently permitted to quote competitive rates of a type denied to the motor carriers. The Commission required the truckers to base their rates upon the fully allocated cost (constant and variable costs) theory of rate-making while the railroads were permitted to establish rates upon an added cost basis (variable costs only). The railroads were permitted to introduce volume minimum rates (rates applicable only to a minimum volume larger than a carload or truckload); the same privilege was denied to motor carriers. Similarly, for six years motor carriers were not allowed to utilize all freight rates (rates applicable to carloads of mixed commodities regardless of the latter's classification ratings) while at the same time railroads were permitted to do so. Also, freight forwarders and motor carriers were not allowed to charge joint rates (single rates quoted by two or more participating carriers) nor were motor carriers allowed to charge proportional rates (lower rates on through traffic) on freight forwarder traffic.

The incidence of ICC policy during these years can be measured by the criticism from the motor carriers. During the war the situation eased somewhat as there was plenty of traffic for everyone. After the war when the motor carriers again began to cut into railroad business the latter, encouraged by the Commission, commenced a series of competitive rate reductions. Again they received the favor and indulgence of the ICC, and again the motor carriers felt called upon to protest the "tendency upon the part of the ICC to treat 'public interest' and 'railroad interest' as synonymous terms. . . ."

While competitive rate-making has been the single most important field of Commission behavior favoring railroads in their struggle with the motor carriers, other actions and policies of the Commission also deserve mention. In the discussion prior to the passage of the Motor Carrier Act the industry only consented to regulation by the "railroad-minded" ICC on the condition that a separate motor carrier bureau and division be established. These two bodies became the representatives of the industry within the Commission and as such anathemas to the railroads, who consistently urged the Commission to organize itself on a "functional" rather than an "industry" basis. In line with these desires the Commission has gradually emasculated the motor carrier units. The division has been stripped of its responsibilities in regard to rates, securities, consolidations, mergers, purchases, accounts, and penalties; the bureau has lost its Section of Traffic, its Section of Accounts, and its functions in connection with motor carrier securities. In other fields of activity, the Commission has narrowly interpreted the "grandfather clause" (statutory authorization of operating rights to carriers for bona fide operations on a given date) so as to deny certificates and permits to many operating truck lines. When it has approved such rights it has frequently severely restricted them as to the territory or classes of shippers which might be served or the commodities which might be transported. For almost a decade the Commission interpreted the acquisition, certificate, and affiliation clauses of the Interstate Commerce Act in such a manner as to facilitate railroad penetration into the motor carrier industry and to raise genuine fears in the motor carriers as to the extent to which the Commission really wished to preserve the independent trucker. Only recently the Commission announced a policy which would seem to indicate that motor carriers are to be barred from operating upon a transcontinental scale.

The cumulative result of these ICC policies has been the alienation of the motor carriers from the Commission. Motor carrier criticism of the ICC has been consistent and vigorous. At the end of the war, the truckers seriously considered initiating a drive to free themselves from ICC control. After much discussion and the consideration of alternative plans, the industry now supports the break-up of the ICC into separate regulatory commissions for each type of transportation with an appellate commission to have jurisdiction over controversies involving two or more classes of carriers, the transfer of the executive functions of the ICC to an executive agency, and the further development of a general control over transportation by the Undersecretary of Commerce.

Rail-Water Competition

Its affiliation with the railroads has dominated Commission action concerning water carriers and rail-water competition since the middle twenties when the Commission became dependent upon railroad support. Previous to this time the Commission had, with the exception of its administration of the Panama Canal Act, adequately balanced the interests of the two types of carriers. Beginning in this period, however, the railroads instituted a concerted competitive drive against the water carriers. In this they had the virtually complete cooperation of the ICC. The twenty per cent differential which had been established by the Director General of the railroads during World War I for water rail-competitive rates was reduced to ten or fifteen per cent in a number of cases. The persistent refusal of the railroads to enter into joint rates and through routes with the water carriers was acquiesced in by the Commission despite congressional pressure to the contrary. Where joint rates were established, the participating water carrier was made to bear the full burden of the differential, and the Commission on occasion even permitted the railroad division of the joint rate to be considerably higher than the local rate to the point of interchange, thus virtually penalizing the water carrier for entering into such a relationship. Reversing a previous policy adopted when it was dependent upon farmer and shipper support, the Commission began to permit railroads to charge discriminatory rates on traffic which had a prior or subsequent haul by water. Liberal use was made of the provisions of the Fourth Section of the Interstate Commerce Act allowing the ICC to permit railroads to charge a higher rate for a shorter haul than for a longer one, and the Commission frequently granted "flexible" relief permitting the railroads to meet automatically any competitive reductions by the water carriers. In many cases, the Commission cooperated with the railroads to evade the statutory requirement that railroads not be allowed to raise depressed rates solely because of the elimination of water competition. In approving general rate increases during this period the Commission frequently acquiesced to railroad requests for the exemption from such increases of heavily water-competitive traffic. The Commission also showed a marked tendency to permit the railroads to lower rates on highly competitive items, at times such reductions going below the fully compensatory level. In a series of cases concerning the important citrus fruit movement from Florida the Commission engaged in an administrative duel with the Maritime Commission: each agency successively reducing the rates of the carriers subject to its regulation. In the one significant instance during this period in which the ICC was called upon to express its views on federal development of the inland waterways, the Commission delivered a report on a proposed Lake Erie-Ohio River canal which was hostile to waterways interests and favorable to the railroads.

As a result of these policies the water carriers, during the thirties, struggled against the extension over them of the power of the "railroad-minded" ICC. Unlike the motor carriers, they never acquiesced to Commission regulation. In 1940, however, the railroads and the Commission triumphed and the water carrier industry was brought under a comprehensive system of control. This did not ameliorate the antagonism between the water carriers and the Commission, and, again unlike the motor carriers, the water carrier industry never developed affiliations with any significant segment of the ICC. The Commission does not have a separate water carrier division, and, whereas the Bureau of Motor Carriers is the Commission's largest bureau, the Bureau of Water Carriers and Freight Forwarders is one of its smallest. In 1950 this bureau had only twenty-one employees, and in addition to its water carrier duties it also supervised the regulation of freight forwarders and rate bureaus. The water carriers have consequently frequently complained that their interests are neglected, but these complaints have not produced any remedies. The Commission has remained closely affiliated with the railroads.

In applying the provisions of the Transportation Act of 1940 to the inland waterways operators the ICC has continued most of the policies which alienated the barge lines in the 1930's. The Commission is still reluctant to require railroads to enter into through routes and joint rates with the water lines. In considering complaints initiated in the middle 1930's as to the rail-barge differential under the all-rail rate, the Commission, in the words of the Hoover Commission study, prolonged the proceeding "beyond all reasonable length," and did not reach a decision until July 1948. This long delay helped the railroads and was burdensome to the water lines. The final decision of the Commission rejected requests of water carrier interests for a substantial differential under the rail rate. It held that cost-of-service considerations did not justify differentials at all, but also held that congressional policy embodied in Sec. 307(d) of the Interstate Commerce Act required it to maintain some differential beneficial to the water carriers. The ICC has also endeavored to permit railroads to maintain rates discriminating against traffic receiving a water haul. In one notable controversy concerning the shipment of ex-barge grain from Chicago to the east, the Commission's approval of the higher rates charged on such grain was eventually invalidated by the Supreme Court. Despite this action, the Commission has allowed the railroads to maintain similar discriminatory rates on a large volume of traffic, this necessitating further legal action on the part of the water carriers. The continued liberality of the Commission in granting Fourth Section relief, particularly for rates established on an "out-of-pocket" cost basis, has likewise evoked severe criticism from waterway interests. The Commission's interpretation of the certificate provisions of the 1940 Act has also hamstrung the water carriers in a number of ways. These various policies reflecting the Commission's railroad affiliation have caused the inland waterways operators to maintain their critical and even hostile attitude toward the Commission.

While the barge lines have suffered from the Commission's railroad partiality, they have at least been able to stay in business. Such has not been the case with the coastwise and intercoastal carriers. The combination of the war, railroad competition, and the unsympathetic attitude of the ICC has drastically weakened the domestic ocean shipping industry. Service was suspended during the war, the traffic went to the rails, and with ICC concurrence it has stayed there. For a year and a half, from the end of the war until July 1947, the War Shipping Administration and the Maritime Commission operated a common and contract carrier service in the intercoastal and coastwise trades. The difficulties encountered in this operation made it clear that the resumption of private service would be dependent upon a readjustment of railroad water-competitive rates. Consequently in March 1946 the two maritime agencies asked the Commission to initiate an investigation of these rates.

Nine months later the ICC began to comply with this request and instituted the first of five major investigations into water-rail competitive rates. The net result of these investigations has been virtually inconsequential. The water carriers have repeatedly been denied substantial relief which would permit them to resume operations on anything remotely resembling their prewar scale. Practically the only rate increases which have been ordered have been minor ones readily acquiesced to by the railroads. At the same time the Commission allowed the railroads to introduce lower increases on water-competitive traffic in their general rate advance cases, and also to put into effect in the last few years new lower rates on highly competitive individual items. The result of these policies has been vigorous criticism of the Commission by the alienated water carriers, and various suggestions from them for the reorganization of water carrier regulation.

IV. RAILROAD AFFILIATION AND COMMISSION VIABILITY

The pattern of affiliation of the Commission with the railroads described in the preceding pages is the basic reason for the decreasing viability of the Commission. The decline has four significant aspects:

(1) The alienation of non railroad interest groups. This process has been described in regard to the water carriers and motor carriers. The fourth major type of transportation, the air carriers, also recognize the Commission's railroad affiliations and have blocked the extension of Commission power into their field. Among shippers the Commission can only command qualified support from the large industrial shippers of the National Industrial Traffic League, which has always been closely associated with the railroads. Other shippers, and agricultural groups in particular, are generally hostile towards the Commission.

(2) The alienation of other government agencies. With some agencies, such as the Department of Agriculture and the Maritime Commission, estrangement has developed because these bodies are closely affiliated with interest groups alienated from

the Commission. In a larger number of instances, however, it has been because the Commission's espousal of the relatively narrow interests of the railroads has conflicted with the responsibility felt by these other agencies to some broader interest and their dependence upon some broader basis of political support. This is particularly true of such agencies as the Departments of Commerce, Interior, and Defense, the Antitrust Division, and the price stabilization agencies.

(3) Subversion of congressional intent. In interpreting the Interstate Commerce Act in the interests of the railroads it is quite obvious that the Commission is applying the law in a manner not intended by the Congress. In 1940 Congress declared the national transportation policy to include "fair and impartial regulation of all modes of transportation." Congress also wrote into the acts of 1935 and 1940 various provisions designed to insure that this policy would be carried out. The failure of the Commission to do this has resulted in increased criticism of the Commission in Congress.

(4) Passivity and loss of leadership. The general purpose of the railroads during the past quarter century has been first the preservation, and then subsequently, after it had been lost, the restoration of their transportation monopoly. Because of its affiliation with the railroads the Commission has, like them, become a defender of the status quo. To this end it has maintained an outdated, formalistic type of procedure. It has been slow to introduce the most simple and accepted new techniques of modern management. It has failed to develop effective devices for representing the public interest. It has neglected administrative planning, and has failed to develop a coherent transportation policy aside from that of giving the railroads what they want. As a result, it has been slow to recognize and deal with obvious evils, such as the freight classification problem or the question of state limitations on truck sizes and weights. It has also been unable to adjust its thinking and actions to the new demands of an era in which defense considerations are paramount. These failures of the Commission have inevitably led to the formation within the executive branch

of a responsible office which can take the lead in national transportation policy and planning.

Given this situation in regard to the ICC, what, then, is desirable public policy? The independence of a regulatory commission is based upon the premise that this independence will aid it in being objective and impartial. When such a commission loses its objectivity and impartiality by becoming dependent upon the support of a single narrow interest group, obviously the rationale for maintaining its independence has ceased to exist, and it becomes necessary to subordinate this agency to some other agency possessing a broader outlook and a broader basis of political support. It is undoubtedly desirable to have an agency within the federal government affiliated with the railroads and able to represent their interests. It is undoubtedly undesirable to have such an agency independent of all administrative supervision, masquerading as an impartial tribunal, and controlling competing carrier groups. Fortunately the recent reorganization of the Maritime Commission suggests a pattern for application to the ICC.

The Interstate Commerce Commission should be abolished as an independent agency. Its executive functions should be transferred, as the Hoover Commission recommended, to the Secretary of Commerce. The motor and water carriers should be emancipated by dividing the regulatory functions of the ICC among three separate commissions dealing respectively with rail, water, and highway transportation. These three commissions should all be placed within the Department of Commerce in a position similar to that of the Maritime Board and subject to the same general policy guidance of the Secretary.

The Supreme Court of the United States once remarked that: "The outlook of the Commission and its powers must be greater than the interest of the railroads or of that which may affect those interests. It must be as comprehensive as the interest of the whole country." This is not only a norm of public policy; it is also a requisite for administrative viability. The railroads may still, at least in the immediate future, furnish the Commission with powerful political support. But the prolonged failure of the Commission to adhere to the Court's standard must eventually make the Commission unviable and lead to its replacement by other instrumentalities better able to act in the public interest

4. THE SENATORIAL REJECTION OF LELAND OLDS: A CASE STUDY

Joseph P. Harris

One of the most important powers of the United States Senate—but one largely neglected in studies of Congress—is that of passing upon presidential appointments. At its regular session in 1950, the Senate granted its "advice and consent" to 25,590 nominations and rejected 4; in addition, 6 nominations were withdrawn by the President and 99 were not acted upon. The great bulk of these cases, some 23,056 of them, involved the promotions of military and naval officers, and were routinely approved. Another 1,197 nominations were of postmasters, now appointed after a civil service examination, whose approval by the Senate is *pro forma*. The remaining 1,446 nominations submitted by the President were for "other civilian" offices.[1] It is with regard to this last group that the function of senatorial confirmation takes on importance. Even this number is much too great for the Senate as a body to consider, and during each session of Congress there are ordinarily less than a dozen contested confirmation cases which require consideration by the Senate itself. In general, no other function of the Senate is so completely delegated to its committees, which in turn act largely on the recommendations of individual Senators with regard to federal appointments within their states.

By well established custom, rarely departed from, the Senate accords the President a free hand in the selection of the members of his cabinet. Only four Presidents—Jackson, Tyler, Johnson, and Coolidge—have had a nomination to the cabinet rejected, although James Madison was prevented by the opposition of a small group of Senators from nominating Albert Gallatin to be his Secretary of State. In view of the fact that the members of the cabinet are the chief policy-determining officials under the President, it is somewhat anomalous that their nomi-

[1] These statistics appear in the *Congressional Record,* 81st Cong., 2nd sess., p. D1009 (daily ed.; Oct. 20, 1950).

nations are usually approved by the Senate with little question or inquiry, while nominations to lesser offices are often the occasion of bitter contests. In justification of the special practice, it is frequently said that the President should be permitted to select the persons who are regarded as his official family and who serve as his immediate advisers and chief assistants.

Another group of federal officials whose nominations must be approved by the Senate are those serving within individual states, that is, district judges, district attorneys, marshals, collectors of internal revenue and customs, postmasters, and some others. These offices are by long tradition regarded as the patronage of the party in power, and the President customarily accepts the recommendation of the Senators from the state where the office is located, if they belong to his party. (The appointment of postmasters, however, has always been regarded as the special patronage of members of the House of Representatives, except in the home towns of Senators, though their selection has been modified to some extent by the law establishing a form of civil service examination.) Unless an objection is raised against a nominee, the Senate committees do not ordinarily conduct hearings or make any investigation of any of the nominees to federal offices in this group, with the exception of candidates for district judges. The fact that they are sponsored by one or both Senators from the state, or by the party organization in states represented by Senators of the opposition party, and that their qualifications and records have been investigated by the department concerned before they are nominated, is ordinarily taken as sufficient indication of their fitness for the office.

The role of the Senate in passing upon nominations to offices in this group is acquiescent unless there is a contest, which rarely occurs unless a member of the Senate enters an objection to a nominee. If the administration fails to consult a Senator of the majority party about a nomination to an office in his state, or, having consulted him, fails to name his candidate, it is his privilege, under the well-established custom of senatorial courtesy, to enter a personal objection to the person nominated, alleging that the nominee is "personally offensive and obnoxious" to him. In such case the Senate almost invariably honors the objection and rejects the nomination. A personal objection need have nothing to do with the qualifications of the nominee (the objecting Senator often concedes that he is fully qualified) and, as a rule, it is not grounded on any personal considerations or genuine animus against the nominee by the Senator making the objection. It is usually made simply because the Senator has another candidate who was not accepted by the President.

The effect of the unwritten rule of senatorial courtesy has been virtually to transfer the nominating function for many of the federal field officers from the President to the Senators of each state, provided they are of the same party as the President. Senators of the opposition party are also free to enter a personal objection to a presidential nominee to office in their states, but rarely do so since they are not accorded the federal patronage and have little incentive to block the approval of such persons. Thus senatorial courtesy is usually invoked when the President attempts to cut off the patronage of a Senator of his party who has not supported his legislative program or when the two Senators from a state have a dispute over the distribution of federal patronage. To sum it up, presidential appointment and senatorial confirmation of the group of officers under consideration, many of whom hold distinctly minor administrative posts, is a political anachronism, and serves to retain under the patronage system many offices which should be placed under the civil service. Fortunately the practice is limited to the older civilian departments with field services—Treasury, Post Office, and Justice—and has not been extended to the field services of other departments.

The nominations which the Senate scrutinizes with greatest care are those of members of the federal judiciary, particularly members of the Supreme Court and circuit courts of appeals, and of members of independent boards and commissions. The contest over the confirmation of Leland Olds, nominated for a third term to the Federal Power Commission in 1949 and rejected by a vote of 53 to 13, affords a striking illustration of the forces which may influence the Senate in passing upon nominations to independent regulatory bodies, as well as the close relation between appointments and legislative policies.

The confirmation of presidential nominations is always of especial importance with regard to the members of independent regulatory commissions, which are regarded as having a special relationship to Congress. The function of the Senate in passing upon the nominations is not limited to the technical qualifications of the nominee and his fitness for the office, it is appropriately concerned with his stand on broad policies and the effect which his appointment may have upon the functioning of the commission. Often the character and attitude of the officers who head an agency have as much to do with its policies as the legislation under which it operates. The Senate must therefore consider whether a nominee to a regulatory commission is in sympathy with the objectives of the laws which he will be called upon to administer, and whether he will support policies which are agreeable to the majority of the Senate. Legislative battles over governmental policies may arise not only when new legislation is under consideration, but equally well when appointments or appropriations are being considered; contests won at one stage are often lost at another.

I. THE CONTESTANTS AND THE ISSUES

Early in June, 1949, President Truman submitted the nomination of Leland Olds for a third term as member of the Federal Power Commission. His nomination was not proposed until nearly the end of his term of office because another nomination to the Commission, that of Thomas Buchanan, had been held up in the Senate for about a year and the President desired to have it acted upon before submitting that of Olds. Both men were known for their support of effective public regulation of utilities and were opposed by the public utility, oil and natural gas interests which were regulated by the Commission.

Leland Olds had served for ten years on the Federal Power Commission, was for several years its chairman, and was widely recognized as one of its most able and effective members. His professional standing in the public utility regulation field was attested to in the hearings by Professor James C. Bonbright of Columbia University, who said:

> Leland Olds, in my opinion, is one of the country's most distinguished and most outstanding figures in the field of public utility regulation. . . . In Leland Olds, the Federal Power Commission has enjoyed the services of a man who has devoted almost his entire professional life to becoming an expert in the exceedingly complex problems of utility regulation. Were it to lose these services, the Commission would lose a good part of the distinction that it now enjoys as a guardian of the public interest . . . in my opinion, millions of people in this country today are presently paying lower utility rates than they would be paying but for the presence of Leland Olds on the Federal Power Commission, and that has taken place along with not a deterioration but a positive improvement of the financial standing and soundness of the private-utility industry.[2]

During the ten years that he served as a member of the FPC, Mr. Olds took a leading part in the development of federal regulation of electric power, hydroelectric developments, and natural gas moving in interstate commerce. When his nomination came up for a second term, he was opposed by the electric power group; but the charges against him were adequately answered. A number of state public utility commissioners whose close relations with the industry were well known testified against him, alleging that he favored federal centralization of utility regulation at the expense of the state utility commissions; but public utility commissioners from other states who favored effective regulation came to his defense, testifying that the FPC had been most helpful to the state commissions. In an attempt to charge him with communist leanings, some references were made then to his earlier writings, which were to play such a prominent part in the 1949 contest; but neither

[2] *Reappointment of Leland Olds to Federal Power Commission,* Hearings before a Sub-committee of the Committee on Interstate and Foreign Commerce, U.S. Senate, 81st Cong., 1st sess. (Washington, 1949), p. 13. Hereafter cited as *Hearings (1949).*

the committee nor the Senate took any stock in such charges, and he was readily confirmed.

Because of the prominent part which he had played in the development of federal regulation of the natural gas industry and his leadership in the opposition to the Kerr bill and earlier bills designed to cripple federal regulation, the reappointment of Leland Olds in 1949 was vigorously opposed by the oil and natural gas interests. The electric utility interests publicly took no part in the opposition, although it was generally assumed that they also opposed him. All of the witnesses testifying against the appointment of Olds, as will appear below, were directly or indirectly connected with the oil and gas industry, and most of them came from the great natural gas producing area of the Southwest. The members of Congress from both houses who had spearheaded the drives to pass the Kerr bill or similar measures, now led the opposition to Leland Olds. Indeed, his principal opponent was Senator Kerr of Oklahoma, wealthy oil man and author of the bill which Olds had effectively opposed just before his nomination went to the Senate. Senator Kerr did not appear as a witness before the Senate committee, and did not participate prominently in the Senate debate on the nomination; but he was generally credited with being the leading member of the group determined to block the reappointment. Senator Lyndon Johnson, chairman of the subcommittee which considered the nomination and leader of the fight against Olds in the Senate debate, came from Texas, the leading oil and natural gas producing state. Representative Lyle, also from Texas and the author of a bill in the Eightieth Congress to exempt the natural gas industry from effective federal supervision of prices, led the attack on Olds at the hearings, where he introduced the charges of Communism.

While the opposition to Olds centered in the delegations from the oil and gas producing states of the Southwest, his support came principally from the states which are consumers of natural gas, and hence desirous of maintaining effective federal regulation of prices. Those favoring his confirmation were principally representatives of consumer groups, public officials of cities which had received lowered gas rates, and several distinguished authorities in the field of public utilities. "Clearly the battle over the confirmation of Leland Olds as a member of the Federal Power Commission," declared Morris L. Cooke at the hearing, "is a battle between the great body of people who are consumers, on the one side, and the monopolistic power and oil-gas interests on the other. It is a part of the battle which has been going on for years to bring these vital interests under some measure of public control. This battle must go on if democracy itself is to survive."

The real issue in the Olds case was the Kerr bill. For several years the natural gas industry, joined by the oil industry which produces natural gas as a by-product, had made a determined effort to amend the Natural Gas Act of 1938 to remove any effective federal regulation of the price of gas moving in interstate commerce. In 1948 and again in 1949 such measures had passed the House by large majorities, but had been defeated in the Senate Committee on Interstate and Foreign Commerce by a divided vote. Mr. Olds, speaking as chairman of the Federal Power Commission, had been the outstanding opponent of these proposals before the committee. And despite the powerful backing of the Kerr bill, Olds courageously opposed it in the spring of 1949, just three months before his renomination came before this same committee. The supporters of the Kerr bill accordingly believed that his removal from the Federal Power Commission was essential to the passage of the measure.

II. BACKGROUND: THE DRIVE TO AMEND THE NATURAL GAS ACT OF 1938

In order to understand the Olds case, some knowledge of the background of the development of federal regulation of the natural gas industry, including the efforts of the industry to avoid federal price control, is essential. Under the Natural Gas Act of 1938, the Federal Power Commission was authorized to regulate the movement of natural gas in interstate commerce. This jurisdiction included the granting of certificates of convenience and necessity for the laying of new interstate pipe lines and the regulation of sales in interstate commerce. The production of natural gas was specifically exempted from federal regulation, as was local distribution to consumers, both of which were subject to regulation under state laws. Local officials and state utility commissions, however, had found that they were unable to secure rate reductions so long as the wholesale rates charged by interstate pipe companies to local distributing companies were unregulated; and it was to correct this situation that the Natural Gas Act had been passed.

Acting on complaints lodged by local officials and state utility commissions, the Federal Power Commission, starting about 1940, undertook to regulate the prices charged local distributors by interstate pipe line companies. In determining what were reasonable rates, the Commission allowed the price paid for gas in the field, plus a reasonable charge for its transportation to the market. In 1940, however, the large interstate pipe line companies were also large natural gas producers, drawing forty per cent of their gas from their own wells. The Commission found it necessary to determine not only what were reasonable charges for transporting the gas, but also the prices which these companies could pay to themselves for gas at the well mouth; for if they had been free to fix the production price, regulation of transportation charges alone would have had virtually no effect in protecting the consumer. By similar reasoning the FPC ruled that sales by subsidiary and affiliated companies to a parent pipe line company were subject to federal regulation.

The field prices paid by interstate pipe line companies to so-called "independent" or nontransporting producers for natural gas have not been regulated by the FPC. Prior to the decision of the Supreme Court in *Interstate Natural Gas Company* v. *Federal Power Commission*[3] in 1947, it had been assumed that the provision of the Natural Gas Act exempting local production and the gathering of natural gas from federal regulation prohibited the FPC from regulating the field prices paid to independent producers. But in this case the Supreme Court held,

[3] 331 U.S. 682 (1947).

in a unanimous decision, that all sales in interstate commerce were subject to federal regulation. At each step federal regulation has been contested in the courts, but in a series of decisions the Supreme Court has upheld the authority of the Commission.

Until recently the market for natural gas in the field was decidedly a buyer's market. The production greatly exceeded the available market, and small producers were virtually forced to sell at whatever price they could get from interstate pipe line companies. However, during and following World War II, with the laying of great pipe lines to tap the urban and industrial markets of the East and Midwest, the situation changed rapidly. The demand by interstate pipe line companies now exceeded available supplies, and the field prices steadily mounted. Although the FPC did not regulate field sales by independent producers, its regulation of the prices which interstate pipe lines could pay for gas from their own wells proved to be an effective bar against runaway prices.

The FPC has ordered reductions in the rates for natural gas totaling approximately $40,000,000 annually, reductions which have been passed on to the consumer. Although field prices rose rapidly in the years following the war, they did not rise so rapidly as the prices of competing fuels—oil and coal. And although the industry has experienced great prosperity, including both high profits and a tremendous expansion with the opening up of new markets and the laying of giant pipe lines, it would reap far greater profits if the threat of federal regulation were removed.

Evidence submitted in the Senate hearings on the Kerr bill also indicates a high degree of concentration of gas production in the hands of a relatively few large producers. Three companies (Phillips Petroleum, Shamrock Oil and Gas, and Canadian River Gas) own one-half of the great Texas Panhandle field, which contains one-seventh of all known reserves in this country, and the 33 largest companies own 62.2 per cent of all known reserves. These large companies would receive tremendous profits if federal control were removed from the price of gas, and prices rose. It has been estimated that an increase of five cents per thousand cubic feet in the field price of natural gas would increase the value of the holdings of the Phillips Petroleum Company alone in the Texas Panhandle and Hugoton fields by $389,000,000.

In view of these tremendous stakes, it is not surprising that the large natural gas companies strongly opposed the confirmation of Leland Olds. Failing in their fight to invalidate federal regulation in the courts, and unable to obtain the passage of legislation which would cripple or remove federal control over prices, they were anxious to secure a Commission which was more sympathetic to their position than the previous one. Two members of the Commission had come around to the industry point of view; the appointment of a third member, Mr. Buchanan, who favored federal regulation, was held up by the Senate Committee for a year, but finally had been approved. If Mr. Olds could be rejected and a person who was sympathetic to the industry's point of view appointed, the way would be paved to secure the enactment of the desired amendments to the Natural Gas Act to remove federal regulation of the field price of gas.

III. THE HEARINGS ON THE NOMINATION

On September 27, 1949, approximately four months after the nomination was submitted and three months after the term of Mr. Olds had expired, the subcommittee of the Senate Committee on Interstate and Foreign Commerce opened its hearings. Normally Congress would have adjourned before this date; but when the session dragged on, and after a good many columnists and editorial writers had criticized the subcommittee for its evident intention of bottling up the nomination without any action, it was finally decided to hold hearings. Chairman Lyndon Johnson announced at the opening session that it was definitely planned to report the nomination to the Senate, even if the committee recommendation was unfavorable.

Other members of the subcommittee were McFarland, O'-Conor, and Edwin Johnson (Democrats), and Bricker, Capehart, and Reed (Republicans). To persons familiar with their records, it was apparent that the Committee began its hearings unfriendly toward Olds and opposed to the policies which he advocated. Every member of the subcommittee (with the exception of Senator Reed of Kansas, who died in the autumn of 1949) voted for the Kerr bill when it came before the Senate the following year. The composition of the subcommittee, of course, greatly affected the course of its hearings. While opposing witnesses were aided in their testimony and asked leading questions, witnesses favoring the nomination were treated politely, but were usually asked no questions. Quite a different public impression would have been made had there been a single member of the subcommittee to ask searching questions of both sides. In attempting to refute the charges which were made against him, Olds always faced a hostile committee whose intention to reject his nomination was apparent.

A number of nationally prominent witnesses appeared in support of the nominee, including Professor James C. Bonbright of Columbia University and Morris L. Cooke, whose testimony has been referred to above, Adolph A. Berle, Ordway Tead, and Charles M. LaFollette. They reviewed Olds' record in public utility work in the State of New York and as a member of the Federal Power Commission and urged his confirmation because of his distinguished record, his devotion to the public interest, his technical qualifications in the public utility field, and his courage as a public official. All stated that he was needed on the Commission to carry out policies to protect the consumer.

Miss Anne K. Alpern, city solicitor of Pittsburgh and past president of the National Institute of Municipal Law Officers, was one of a group of municipal officials who appeared in behalf of Olds. In her testimony before the subcommittee, she declared that "consumers of this country have a very vital interest in men like Leland Olds, and in seeing that he is retained in public service. . . . Democracy flourishes when men of this caliber are in high administrative positions and administer the law of our country so that capital may prosper and so that consumers can be protected." She also praised Olds for the courage which he had displayed as a member of the Commission in protecting the consumer by taking the leadership for effective public regulation of utilities.

Other groups whose representatives appeared in support of Olds included the CIO, several other labor organizations, the National Grange, Americans for Democratic Action, and associations of cooperatives. The same groups and the same witnesses had appeared earlier in the opposition to the Kerr bill, and their testimony was very similar at both hearings. They regarded the fight over the confirmation of Leland Olds as a part of the struggle to end federal regulation of the price of natural gas, which they contended would increase the cost to the consumer by over a hundred million dollars annually.

Those columnists and editorial writers who had earlier condemned the Kerr bill as a "gas grab" to benefit the oil and natural gas companies at the expense of the consumer, now denounced the opposition to Olds as coming from the same interests. The members of the Senate subcommittee quite naturally smarted under the accusation that they were the willing tools of the public utility, oil, and natural gas lobby, and that they were about to reject an able and courageous public servant to serve the ends of these selfish interests; and their hostility to Leland Olds was due in part to the fact that they considered him responsible for this attack upon them.

IV. THE COMMUNIST SMEAR

The opposition to Mr. Olds was begun by Representative John E. Lyle of Corpus Christi, Texas, who based his attack on certain writings of Olds, prepared twenty-five years earlier when he was industrial editor of the Federated Press, a news service sold to the labor press and to labor unions. Selections from these writings in the 1920's were introduced to support the charge that Olds was either a Communist or a fellow traveler, and that he had bitterly attacked various aspects of the American capitalistic system. The real reason for Representative Lyle's attack, however, as he made clear at the outset, was the fact that Olds had led the opposition to the Kerr and similar bills. At the opening of the Eighty-first Congress, Lyle had introduced such a bill (H.R. 79), and a similar bill introduced by Representative Harris (H.R. 1758) passed the House by a large majority. These bills had the active support of the oil and natural gas interests. Representative Lyle, who comes from a district in which oil and natural gas are the leading industry, and whose law firm, according to reports, represents large oil and gas companies, accused Olds of having presented "misleading statements, half truths, distorted statistics, and a multitude of devices designed and utilized to obscure the issue at hand." Mr. Olds, he declared, had "launched a bitter and vicious attack on these bills and those proposing them, inferentially characterizing the bills as an attempt to mulct ultimate consumers of millions of dollars."

With respect to the writings of Olds during the period from 1922 to 1929, Representative Lyle made twenty-four charges against him and submitted fifty-four photostatic copies of the articles to support these charges. "I am here to oppose Mr. Olds," he said, "because he has—through a long and prolific career—attacked the church; he has attacked our schools; he has ridiculed the symbols of patriotism and loyalty such as the Fourth of July; he has advocated public ownership: he has reserved his applause for Lenin and Lenin's system; and he has found few words of praise for our American system; and, yes, gentlemen, he has seen fit to attack the men who serve as elected representatives in our Government—men such as you. He has characterized you as mere administrative clerks handling administrative details for 'an immensely powerful ruling class.'"

Throughout his testimony Representative Lyle endeavored to establish that Olds was a Communist, or at any event followed the communist line. The Federated Press was labeled a "left-wing labor press service, closely identified with communist movements and groups." Most of the articles which he placed in the record were taken from the *Daily Worker* or *Industrial Solidarity*, communist publications, though they had appeared in about seventy-five other publications. The impression was created that Olds had been a writer for the *Daily Worker*, which he took pains to deny. In one of these articles Olds had advocated paid vacations for workers and praised the practice in Russia, widely commented on at the time, of setting aside large estates as rest and recreation centers for workers. In several other articles Olds had made favorable comments about certain developments in Soviet Russia, and they were cited by Lyle to show that he had favored the communist system.[4]

The articles which Olds wrote for the Federated Press dealt with economic problems during the period of the 1920's. For the most part, they summarized and interpreted studies and reports of government and private research agencies, even including summaries of articles appearing in the *Wall Street Journal*. Those placed in the record by Representative Lyle were highly critical of economic policies and practices of the time. A number dealt with the sick coal industry, suggesting, but not actually advocating, some form of public ownership or nationalization. Others criticized the railroads for their anti-union policies, and included some statements favorable to public ownership. On the basis of these articles, Representative Lyle accused Olds of advocating not only public ownership of railroads and coal mines, but of all private industry.

In another article Olds had attacked the keynote speech of Senator Fess at the Republican national convention of 1928, a speech which cited, with approval, statistics to prove that industrial production had increased while labor costs had declined. Referring in the article to Andrew Mellon, Olds attacked the Republican party for its close association with big business and asserted that the policies of the government were being dictated by the "immensely powerful ruling group," while government officials merely carried out the administrative details.

[4] One article, which has appeared in the *Daily Worker* under Mr. Olds' name and to which Mr. Lyle drew particular attention, gave an account of communist classes which were starting, and urged comrades to enroll. In his rebuttal testimony, Olds categorically denied that he had ever written the article and offered the explanation that it was a case of a misplaced byline.

Representative Lyle charged Olds with attacking the government as being the servant of business, and with accusing the legislature (whom Olds had not mentioned) of merely handling administrative details for an immensely powerful ruling group.

In another article Olds had maintained that the policies of certain endowed universities were dictated by wealthy donors and trustees, which was interpreted by Mr. Lyle as a blanket attack on all universities, and, indeed, on all education. Still another article concerning Bishop Cannon's reported speculations in the stock market, criticized the church for passively accepting social and economic injustices and for not taking a more aggressive stand for economic reforms. On the basis of this, Mr. Olds, a deeply religious man, was accused of attacking all churches and all religion.

All of the articles, written in the intellectual climate of the 1920's and dealing with financial, economic, and labor problems and abuses of the time, were made to appear extremely radical. It should be borne in mind that they were written for a labor audience, to which they probably appeared entirely appropriate, and that similar criticisms of economic abuses were voiced by many prominent persons of the period, though not in so pungent a manner. Many of Olds' articles carried a punch sentence, which taken out of context appeared much more radical than the entire article. Only by the most flagrant distortion, by lifting sentences out of context and by actual misquotation, was Representative Lyle able to support his contention that Leland Olds was a Communist at heart, one who was opposed to private ownership and to the entire capitalistic system, and who had condemned the church, sneered at the flag, and looked with scorn upon government, particularly the legislative body, as the tool of big business.

Senator McFarland said that he was shocked by the charges and that they were the most serious he had ever heard in Congress. During Representative Lyle's testimony, Senator Reed broke in to say that here was a man whose writings showed him to be a "full-fledged, regular Communist."

Anticipating the attack which would be made upon him, Olds

obtained permission to appear before the subcommittee and read a lengthy statement covering his entire career. In this statement he attempted to explain the philosophy which led him to produce what he admitted were "radical writings," but it did not meet the charges and it did not deal directly with the real issue at stake—the Kerr bill and federal regulation of the price of gas. It included a brief review of the record of the Federal Power Commission during the preceding ten years, but for this account Olds was criticized by the chairman of the subcommittee on the ground that he claimed the credit for all of the accomplishments of the commission.

During his testimony Olds was frequently interrogated by members of the subcommittee concerning his writings, and especially was asked to explain and defend key sentences which were objectionable. His favorable references to Russia came in for a good deal of comment and questioning, although Olds categorically denied that he had ever favored Communism. In fact, Olds denied each of the Lyle charges and asked the subcommittee to judge the articles in their entirety, rather than on the basis of single sentences or parts of sentences lifted out of context. When asked whether he still held the same beliefs, he replied that the New Deal legislation had corrected many of the social and economic ills of the 1920's which he had described, and that on some subjects, particularly Russia, he had changed his mind.[5]

[5] During his testimony Olds was asked by Senator Lyndon Johnson whether he had ever addressed the Trade Union and Educational League, sharing the platform with Earl Browder, to which he replied that he remembered once speaking before this organization, but could not recall where the meeting was held or who the other speakers were. Senator Johnson thereupon inserted in the record a copy of the *Daily Worker* of March 29, 1924, which he had at hand, giving an account of the meeting, at which Browder and Olds were the principal speakers. The appearance of Mr. Olds on the same platform, twenty-five years earlier, with Earl Browder was shocking to the Senators. Lowell Mellett pointed out, in his column on October 1, that the Senators might have been shocked even more had they examined Elizabeth Dilling's book, *The Roosevelt Red Record,* for on page 59 appears the smiling picture of Senator Taft with Earl Browder and two others just after they had addressed a National Youth Congress.

The charges of communism and radicalism against Leland Olds were not new. Some of the same articles had been used to oppose him in 1944, but the charges then were not taken seriously. The chairman of the subcommittee which conducted the hearings on his nomination for a second term stated in reply to these charges: "I do not think that anyone believed that Mr. Olds was a Communist. I do not think that the Senator from Oklahoma believes that Mr. Olds is a Communist. I do not think anyone believed that."[6]

V. THE OPPOSITION OF THE OIL AND GAS INTERESTS

Of the fifteen opposing witnesses, all came from gas-producing areas, and all were directly connected with the gas industry. Seven represented gas-producing companies or associations of producers, and the connection of the other eight opposing witnesses with the gas interests was readily apparent, though not always stated.[7] Most of the industry spokesmen represented small producers; representatives of the largest gas companies were significantly absent in the line-up of opposing witnesses.

[6] *Congressional Record*, 78th Cong., 2nd sess., Vol. 90, pt. 6, p. 7692 (Sept. 12, 1944). The same charges of communistic associations and leanings were also made on the floor of the Senate on May 27, 1943, by Senator Bridges, with quotations from some of the writings later used by Representative Lyle. At that time Senator Aiken stated in defense of Mr. Olds: "I wish to say to the Members of the Senate today that of the Federal officials who have impressed me as being conscientious, honest, hard-working and sincere, one of the foremost of them all is Leland Olds, Chairman of the Federal Power Commission. He did have work to do in my state. . . . I think he did it well by forcing down some of the outrageous write-ups in utility values which existed in Vermont and in other States. I know of one single instance where property valued at $50,000 for the purposes of assessment was written on the books of the utility company at a million and a quarter dollars; and that was not an isolated instance. . . . I believe him to be one of the most honest, courageous and hard-working public servants we have today" (*ibid.*, 78th Cong., 1st sess., Vol. 89, pt. 4, p. 4942 [May 27, 1943]).

[7] The opposing witnesses who were not directly connected with the gas and oil industry included a representative of the East Texas Chamber of Commerce, an attorney representing the association of county commissioners of Texas, three representatives from colleges located in Texas and Arkansas, the chairman of the Arkansas Oil and Gas Commission, and two members of Congress from the Southwest.

The opposing witnesses offered the following three major arguments against the confirmation of Leland Olds: (1) he stood for the regulatory policies which were harmful to the gas industry; (2) his writings indicated that he was a Communist and unfit for office; and (3) the nominee was personally unfit for the office. "We believe that his confirmation would be against the best interests of the producers of gas and also of oil," said Russell B. Brown, General Counsel of the Independent Petroleum Association of America. "If Mr. Olds is reappointed," stated James A. Upham, President of the Ohio Oil and Gas Association, "we face but one destiny—full extinction. . . . So, our earnest prayer presented to you now is to give us some new Commissioner, not Mr. Olds, as we deeply feel the retention of Mr. Olds as a member of the FPC is a full threat to the free-enterprise system of this life in these United States."

Most of the witnesses who appeared to oppose Olds repeated the charges of Representative Lyle that the nominee was a Communist, a radical, and unfit for office because of his opposition to the free enterprise system. Several were unwilling to rest their opposition on these grounds and went on to abuse and vilify the nominee in language seldom heard in nomination hearings. One witness, who represented the Southern Minerals Association, declared: "Mr. Olds is boring from within; Mr. Olds is a termite; Mr. Olds is gnawing away the very foundations upon which this Government exists."

VI. OBSERVATIONS ON THE HEARINGS

From the outset it was apparent that the subcommittee was opposed to Olds, and it is doubtful that the public hearings altered their opinions; but the communist charges made by Representative Lyle, which were characterized by the *Washington Post* as "preposterous and despicable," undoubtedly influenced the vote of the Senate. Even though they were based upon gross misrepresentations of the writings of Olds, nevertheless there was enough partial truth in them to cause some members to change their votes. They also afforded those who were opposed to Olds because of his record and his fight against the Kerr bill with other grounds on which to justify their votes. The communist smear had nothing to do with the real issue—federal regulation of the price of natural gas—or with Leland Olds' qualifications and record for ten years as a commissioner.

In the hearings little or no attention was given to the record Olds made as a member (for several years chairman) of the FPC during the preceding ten years, or to his stand on policies affecting federal regulation of the natural gas industry. The hearings were devoted instead almost entirely to consideration of his writings twenty years earlier. Under the circumstances, it would appear that these earlier writings were largely irrelevant, or at least of little importance, in comparison with his long record as a member of the commission to which he was now renominated. No question was raised by any member of the subcommittee concerning the relevance of these writings; on the contrary, they were cited by the committee to justify its vote against confirmation. There was little in Olds' record which the committee could openly attack. He was known for his able and courageous administration of the federal laws under the jurisdiction of the FPC, and he could not be criticized for defending the legislative policies which Congress had passed and which the Supreme Court had upheld in a unanimous decision.

The defense of Olds in the hearings was relatively weak and ineffective, although with such a hostile committee an effective defense would have been difficult. The communist smear, which had been anticipated, might have been answered more forcefully. Too much of the defense was carried by Olds himself, despite the fact that others would have been better able to answer the unjust accusations made against him, and to have forced the hearings back to the real issues involved. Apparently no attempt was made to line up favorable witnesses from the natural gas industry, who would have carried great weight.

VII. PRESIDENT TRUMAN'S INTERVENTION

Early in October, while the nomination was before the Committee on Interstate and Foreign Commerce, President Truman wrote to Chairman Edwin Johnson, urging the confirmation of Olds. "Mr. Olds," the President wrote, "is a nationally recognized champion of effective utility regulation; his record shows that he is also a champion of fair regulation. . . . The powerful corporations subject to regulation by the Commission have not been pleased with Mr. Olds. They now seek to prevent his confirmation for another term. It will be most unfortunate if they should succeed. We cannot allow great corporations to dominate the commissions which have been created to regulate them."[8]

Senator Johnson replied that the subcommittee "was shocked beyond description by the political and economic views expressed by Mr. Olds some years ago. We cannot believe that a person under our democratic capitalistic system holding such views is qualified to act in a quasi-judicial capacity in the regulation of industry."[9] Despite the President's support, the subcommittee voted unanimously to reject the nomination; and the vote of the full committee was two for and ten against confirmation.

After the full committee made its report to the Senate, President Truman, undaunted, took the extraordinary step of calling upon the Democratic Party to support the nomination. On October 5, Chairman Boyle of the Democratic National Committee, acting on instructions from the President, sent a telegram to all state chairmen, requesting them to urge their Senators to vote for the confirmation of Mr. Olds. His defeat, it was stated in the telegram, "would be a defeat for the millions of Americans who are entitled to fair power rates, and a victory for the power lobbyists and the Republican Party."

At his press conference on the same date the President defended his action in making a party issue of the appointment on the ground that party discipline was essential to party responsibility. Two days later Senator Byrd placed the Boyle telegram in the *Congressional Record*, declaring that he was "shocked that the President of the United States would attempt to coerce

[8] Reprinted in *Congressional Record,* 81st Cong., 1st sess., Vol. 95, pt. 10, p. 13759 (Oct. 4, 1949).
[9] *Ibid.,* p. 13760.

the Members of the United States Senate in the exercise of their function in the confirmation of an appointment. . . . By implication, at least, Chairman Boyle threatens every Member of the United States Senate with the loss of patronage if the orders given in this telegram are not obeyed."

Editorial comments were generally unfavorable to the Boyle telegram and to the attempt of the President to make a party issue of the appointment. The telegram, it may be noted, contained no threat or intimation that patronage would be withdrawn from Senators who did not vote for confirmation. The final vote of the Senate, rejecting the nomination by 53 to 15, indicated that the President's appeal had little effect on the Democratic Senators, though it may have contributed to the practically unanimous vote of Republican members against confirmation.

VIII. THE SENATE DEBATE

The renomination of Leland Olds came before the Senate on October 12, 1949, but Senator Murray, who was unable to be present on that day, spoke in behalf of Mr. Olds on October 11. He maintained that the real issue was federal regulation of the price of natural gas, and placed in the record a series of statistical tables taken from the reports of the FPC showing the huge profits of the natural gas industry since the end of World War II, the high degree of concentration of gas holdings by a few large companies, and the estimates of the profits of these companies if federal regulation were removed. He asserted that the large companies might well have the value of their holdings enhanced by over sixteen billion dollars if federal control over fields prices were removed. The thesis that natural gas was a public utility, and as such subject to public regulation, was sharply challenged by Senator Kerr, who inquired why the price of natural gas should be regulated if the price of copper produced in Montana, or of coal, is not regulated.

The Senate debate was opened on October 12 by Senator Johnson of Colorado, speaking in opposition to the appointment. He charged Olds with Communism and radicalism, as well as with association with leading Communists when he was the industrial editor of the Federal Press. As a feature writer on the Federal Press, the Senator said Olds had stooped to the vilest kind of rabble rousing. Senator Johnson also stated that Olds was "slippery and evasive," that he "hedged and quibbled, but that he was not repentant." He went on to declare that, in his judgment, "Mr. Olds has not changed his offensive views regarding capital one iota, and . . . today, as when he was forty years of age, he believes capital should be confiscated and the profit system destroyed. A man having this kind of a warped mind is so far out of step with America that he is not qualified to sit in the seat of judgment and regulate our great utility industries."

The most able statement in behalf of Olds was made by Senator Morse, who asserted that Olds and the two other members of the FPC who joined with him in policies were only attempting to carry out the provisions of the Natural Gas Act for the regulation of the sale of natural gas in interstate commerce. The authority of the Commission under the Act to do this, he pointed out, had been upheld by the Supreme Court in the *Interstate* case. "The oil and gas interests," said Senator Morse, "have tried unsuccessfully to have the law amended so that the Commission can not regulate their sales of gas to interstate pipe lines. They know that they can not get such legislation enacted, so I believe that they are now engaged in a last-ditch effort to accomplish the same purpose by opposing the reappointment of a Commissioner who refuses to interpret the act and circumscribe his powers and obligations to the public in accordance with the purposes of those interests." The real test which should be applied in passing upon the renomination of Leland Olds, Senator Morse contended, was his record during two terms as a member of the Federal Power Commission. On this test he declared that Olds ranked with the ablest public utility commissioners in the country, and was so regarded by many businessmen who appeared before the FPC while he was a member. His rejection, the Senator concluded, "will discourage other men, devoted to the public interests, from running the risks of entering Government service."

Also speaking in defense of the nominee, Senator Langer reviewed the debate in 1944 when Olds' nomination came before the Senate, and pointed out that the identical charges of radical and communist leanings then made by Senator Moore were dismissed as unfounded. "These 25-year-old charges," said Senator Langer, ". . . are now dug up and dusted off again in the attempt to discredit an honest, sincere and capable public servant who has given the best years of his life in attempting to bring about an equitable regulation of public-utility rates in the interest of the common people. . . ." The Senator also maintained that "the case against Leland Olds smells strongly of oil," and that "during the extensive hearings . . . not one iota of information was brought out which reflected on the record of this man as a public-power commissioner."

Senator Humphrey placed in the record a number of editorials from newspapers throughout the country, many of them Republican, commenting on the case and supporting the confirmation of Olds. Practically all of these editorials pointed out that the real issue involved was the regulation of the price of gas. Senator Humphrey also defended Olds for his writings, criticizing the economic conditions and practices which prevailed in the 1920's.

The principal speech in opposition to Leland Olds was made by Senator Lyndon Johnson of Texas, chairman of the subcommittee which had considered the nomination. In his opening remarks he declared that the reputation of Leland Olds was a myth, "a clever, appealing fiction, which is not supported by the record. It is a fiction which the man himself has labored skillfully and tirelessly through ten years in public office to impress on the public mind." Senator Johnson stated that he proposed to reveal the record of Olds, which he said was almost unnoticed and unknown, in order to disprove "the myth of Leland Olds, the knight in shining armor, doing tireless battle with the dragons of 'special privilege.'" The first myth to be exposed, said Senator Johnson, was that Olds was being opposed by the power lobby. He reported that not a single representative of the power interests had appeared in opposition to Olds, and that not one of the hundreds of letters and telegrams which he had received opposing confirmation had come from a representative of an electric utility. What Senator Johnson did not point out was that the opposition to Olds had come from the oil and natural gas interests, and that the electric utilities, while not openly opposing him, had quietly but none the less effectively thrown their influence against him.

Despite the fact that Leland Olds had had twenty years of experience in the public utility field, ten years as a commissioner of the FPC, Senator Johnson asserted that he lacked practical experience, and accused him of prejudice and bias against the utilities which he regulated. In his words, "Leland Olds' record is an uninterrupted tale of bias, prejudice, and hostility, directed against the industry over which he now seeks to assume the powers of life and death. Never once in his long career has Leland Olds experienced, first-hand, the industries' side of the regulatory picture."

Senator Johnson accused Olds of conducting an "insidious campaign of slander," of directing public criticism, of making "vile and snide remarks" to "undermine and discredit" the members of the Commission who did not agree with him. This accusation that Olds had also "forced the Commission staff into a goose-step march under the whip of his deliberate public abuse" appears equally unfounded. Finally, Senator Johnson charged Mr. Olds with building a political empire for his own insidious purposes. He then summed up his argument in the following words: "In the twenties he scoffed at private property as just another myth; in the thirties he said our democracy had been made a sham; in the forties he has intimidated his staff, discredited his fellow Commissioners, fostered a smear on Congress, and taken the law into his own hands to substitute irresponsible confiscation for responsible regulation."

The intemperateness of the attack on Olds in the Senate debate may be attributed largely to the fact that those who opposed him were smarting under the blistering criticism which they had received at the hands of editorial writers and columnists. Olds' record was that of an able, intelligent and scrupulously fair public official. His ability and effectiveness as a commissioner and his devotion to the public interest, rather than his radicalism, caused him to incur the bitter enmity of the natural gas and oil industry. In the Senate debate, as in the hearings, those who opposed Olds were not content to rest their case with smearing him as a Communist and a radical, but engaged in personal abuse as well.

IX. CONCLUSION

The contest over the nomination of Leland Olds for a third term as a member of the Federal Power Commission affords a striking illustration of the importance of the confirmation of appointments in the determination of governmental policies. He was rejected not because of his radical writings some twenty-five years earlier, or the charge of Communism, although these caused some newspaper support to be withdrawn and made it easier for his opponents to bring about his defeat. The real issue was federal regulation of the price of natural gas, and his rejection was a victory for the gas and oil interests. Their opposition to Olds was due to the vigorous and effective role which he had played in the development of federal regulation and to his determined opposition to the Moore-Rizley bill, the Kerr bill, and similar ones for which they had pressed in Congress.

The rejection of the nomination of Leland Olds was similar in many respects to the refusal of the Senate in 1834 to confirm the nomination of Roger Taney as Secretary of the Treasury. Both were bitterly opposed by a strong business group because of the policies which they had carried out. Taney had incurred the wrath of Nicholas Biddle when, acting under instructions from President Jackson, he had withdrawn federal deposits from the Bank; and his defeat was regarded by the Bank and its supporters as essential to the renewal of its charter. Similarly, the defeat of Olds was regarded by the oil and gas industry as essential in its fight for the removal of federal regulation of the price of natural gas. It is highly significant that after Olds was defeated for a third term, the oil and natural gas forces were able to push the Kerr bill through Congress the following year.

The opposition of the oil and gas interests to the reappointment of Olds is understandable; and Senators identified with the industry doubtless had warned the President that he would be unable to secure Senate approval of Olds, and had recommended others for the position. His rejection by such an overwhelming vote of the Senate is not so readily explained, although the vote in favor of the Kerr bill the following year indicated that the policies which Olds advocated were not agreeable to a majority of the Senate. In addition, he was pictured in the senate debate, as well as in private discussions, as a fanatical zealot with pronounced radical ideas. In a period of nation-wide hysteria over Communism, perhaps it is not surprising that he was unable to withstand the attack which was made on him. The Senate vote also indicates that it is much easier for a determined and well-financed interest group to block the reappointment of an official who stands in its way than to secure a revision of federal law. As the city attorney of Pittsburgh declared in the hearings, his defeat serves as a warning to members of regulatory commissions not to incur the hostility of the interests which they regulate, if they value their jobs.

An especially unfortunate aspect of the fight over Olds was that an able, intelligent, and courageous public servant, devoted in an extraordinary degree to the public interests, was forced to submit to public abuse and vilification of a kind which makes public service unattractive to men and women of the highest ability. In appraising the consequences, Senator Aiken declared during the Senate debate: "Certain public utilities of the country are out to destroy a man for performing his duty. I do not know of anything worse than that. I do not know of anything more detrimental to good government. I do not know of anything to make it more difficult to get men and women to perform the duties of public office.

III. The President and the Bureaucracy

EDITORIAL NOTE. Should the President be Chief Administrator? What tools are at his disposal for this purpose? What changes should be made in the Executive Office of the President to increase his ability to control the sprawling administrative process? The following selections deal with these questions.

5. THE PRESIDENT AS ADMINISTRATOR

Herman M. Somers

It may be that full performance of the duties which have accrued to the President is impossible. William Allen White, who knew the job in less frenetic days, thought "the devil invented the Presidency by combining all the futile despairs of Sisyphus with the agony of Tantalus and shaking in a jigger of the nervous irritation of a man with ants in his pants."

TOO BIG A JOB?

Even in days when the nation and its government were smaller and simpler, Presidents cried for help. Almost every President in this century has publicly complained that he could not fully cope with his administrative responsibilities. More than fifteen years ago, President Roosevelt transmitted to Congress the historic study of the Federal Government made by the Committee on Administrative Management, and added:

> . . . they say, what has been common knowledge for twenty years, that the President cannot adequately handle his responsibilities, that he is overworked; that it is humanly impossible, under the system which we have, for him fully to carry out his Constitutional duty as Chief

> Executive, because he is overwhelmed with minor details and needless contacts arising directly from the bad organization and equipment of the Government. I can testify to this. With my predecessors who have said the same thing over and over, I plead guilty.[1]

Twelve years later, the celebrated Hoover Commission reported as its first findings: (1) "The executive branch is not organized into a workable number of major departments and agencies which the President can effectively direct. . . ." (2) "The line of command and supervision from the President down through his department heads to every employee . . . has been weakened, or actually broken, in many places and in many ways." (3) "The President and the heads of departments lack the tools to frame programs and policies and to supervise their execution."[2]

More recently *Fortune* reported that "according to old hands around the White House, the job of the Presidency has doubled in scope even since the peak effort of World War II."[3]

Under the best of circumstances, the proper management of the executive branch alone, now numbering 2,500,000 civil servants, plus the military organization of which the President is also administrative chief, would be a backbreaking ordeal (quite aside from the President's other full-time jobs); but neither the Congress nor the American people seem interested in helping to create the best of circumstances. On the contrary, a formidable array of obstacles, nettles, and mousetraps has been thrown in the President's path. These are frequently called "safeguards"; but just what or how they guard has never been made clear. In fact, they are in part the painful expression by Congress of its own frustrations. In part they represent the

[1] The President's Committee on Administrative Management, *Report* (Washington, 1937), p. iv.

[2] Commission on Organization of the Executive Branch of the Government, *General Management of the Executive Branch* (Washington, February 1949), pp. 3–5. All subsequent quotations from the Hoover Commission relate to this volume.

[3] *Fortune*, February 1952, p. 76.

normal compromises, concessions, and contradictions of conflicting forces in a highly pluralistic society.

This discussion attempts to: (1) enumerate some of the impediments unnecessarily hampering the President, (2) appraise the internal co-ordinating machinery available to him, (3) describe the difficulties in departmental organization, (4) suggest the manner of man who might best meet the challenges of the job, and (5) suggest some initial and practicable reforms. . . .

IMPEDIMENTS

A legislative assembly cannot govern. Consequently, the Constitution wisely gives the President indivisible executive authority. "The unity of the executive," advocated in *The Federalist* papers, remains a cardinal principle of the formal Constitution (and of most theories of organization), but has never been achieved in practice. Congress and the courts have diffused executive authority and fragmented the executive branch into relatively autonomous units at several levels. The pressure groups also promote an atomized bureaucracy, which, like a disorganized Congress, they find much easier to manipulate.

The Constitution charges the President with the responsibility "that the Laws be faithfully executed," but the doctrine is not supported by the necessary machinery.

1. The President is denied authority to determine the organization and structure of the executive branch for which he is responsible. The first recommendation the Hoover Commission made to Congress was that the President be given authority to initiate reorganization plans, subject to veto by joint resolution of Congress. This [has] resulted in grants of authority [under successive reorganization acts].

2. A substantial portion of the executive functions of government has been placed completely out of the reach of the President in a category often referred to as a "headless fourth branch of government."

3. Committees of Congress, themselves fairly independent of Congress, have undertaken to direct the affairs of individual departments or bureaus through direct relations with them. The

United States Corps of Engineers, for example, which neither the Secretary of the Army nor the President of the United States has been able to control, likes to refer to itself as "the engineer consultants to, and contractors for, the Congress of the United States."[4] As far back as Jefferson's administration, Fisher Ames complained that congressional committees had become "ministers."[5]

Because of its internal anarchy, the Congress has itself become imprisoned by the usurpation of power by individual committees. Agency officials, trained to smell the sources of power, sometimes form alliances with congressional committees against the fulfillment of portions of the President's program. This has led one of our most acute students of government to observe that "the real issue is then between the executive bureau and the congressional committee, on the one hand, and on the other hand, the Congress as a whole and the President."[6]

4. Personnel policy and personnel administration lie at the very heart of top executive management. This indispensable tool has been denied to the nation's Chief Executive, despite the urging of every important study of the Federal Government. The Committee on Administrative Management charged that the United States Civil Service Commission was no exception to the rule that "board administration tends to diffuse responsibility, to produce delays, and to make effective co-operation or vigorous leadership impossible." It recommended unification of responsibility in a Civil Service Administrator. Congress refused. The recommendations of the Hoover Commission twelve years later did result in the allocation of administrative authority to the Chairman of the Commission, but the recommendation that he become part of the President's Office was not followed.

5. Although the executive budget is almost universally ac-

[4] For an able account of this unofficial revision of Constitutional doctrine, see Arthur Maass, *Muddy Waters: the Army Engineers and the Nation's Rivers* (Cambridge, Mass., 1951).

[5] Leonard D. White, *The Jeffersonians* (New York, 1951), p. 29.

[6] Don K. Price, *The New Dimension of Diplomacy* (New York, 1951), p. 13.

cepted as a sine qua non of effective administration, the President does not have the power of "item veto," which has been demonstrated to be a primary source of economy and good management in many state governments. Also, appropriations are often made in such great detail that administrative form and process are strait-jacketed.

6. In practice, Presidents have found that their ability to handle the most difficult administrative job in the world depends, in large degree, upon the same factor conditioning their capacity to cope with the "built-in" rivalry of Congress: political strength, based on popular and party authority. Recently even this resource of popular Presidents has been abridged. The Twenty-second Amendment to the Constitution assures sharp curtailment of Presidential leadership, at least during the latter half of a second term.

The word and intent of the Constitution notwithstanding, without adequate control of the bureaucracy the President cannot meet his administrative responsibilities. Administrative integrity cannot be achieved without Presidential control of the organization and personnel of the government and its internal co-ordinating machinery.

Clearly, the problems of Presidential administration go far beyond legal authority and procedural mechanics. Perspective requires that the issues be recognized as reflecting the composite of political, social, and economic relations of our society. And much depends on the caliber of the man. But the *possibility* at least of securing co-ordinated and responsible administration rests in giving adequate administrative authority to the Chief Executive.

CO-ORDINATING MACHINERY

Only recently have we recognized that while executive accountability is ultimately centered in a solitary individual, the *Presidency* is an institution. It is an organization, a group enterprise, of which the President is in charge, setting the pace and determining its character. Only through the effective operation of this institution, which furnishes the staff tools of executive co-ordination and control, can the President be expected even to approximate his Constitutional obligations. Were it not for some structural continuity in the institution, a new President would hardly stand a chance.

The issue of staffing the Presidency is old (Congress resisted importunities for assistance made by Presidents in the early nineteenth century); but the modern conception of an Executive Office of the President dates back only to 1937 and the Report of the Committee on Administrative Management, though in a germinal sense one might look to the discussions surrounding the Budget and Accounting Act of 1921. The Committee's signal contribution was its sharp portrayal of the Presidency as the pivot of federal administration, all other aspects being secondary. As a consequence, the Executive Office of the President was formally established in September 1939, one of the great landmarks in the administrative history of this nation.

Structural weakness and changes

The passage of years, however, revealed some impressive shortcomings in the original structure as well as in the Committee's recommendations. By present-day standards, the Committee construed "administrative management" narrowly. It concentrated upon personnel management, fiscal management, planning management, and administrative reorganization of the government. Little consideration was given to the broader administrative responsibility for program and policy co-ordination on a systematic basis. Partly because of this omission, no provision was made in the Executive Office for any form of staff integration or internal co-ordination. The Office was an amorphous array of separate units.

It may be that the Committee was placing reliance on the Cabinet for such policy coordination. It is, however, the uniform judgment of close observers and the testimony of former Cabinet officials that the Cabinet has never been an effective instrument for formulating policy or for co-ordination. In its present form, it is unlikely so to develop.

World War II dramatized both the tremendous assets of an

organized Presidency and the shortcomings of existing arrangements. Throughout the period of defense preparation and the early part of the war, there were widespread demands for an "over-all czar" to cope with the apparent lack of adequate machinery for central policy and program co-ordination. A series of improvisations culminated in creation of the Office of War Mobilization in 1943, which satisfied immediate needs and, in large degree, furnished necessary staff leadership in the Executive Office.

Since that time, important changes have been made in the design of the Executive Office. The postwar additions reflected the growing recognition of the need for better facilities for policy and planning control at the pinnacle.

The Council of Economic Advisers (1946) may be broadly construed as [a partial] replacement for the ill-fated National Resources Planning Board (eliminated by Congress in 1943). The National Security Council (1947) was created in an attempt to obtain better policy and program co-ordination of military and diplomatic goals, through the long-advocated device of an active Cabinet-level committee with a secretariat. . . .

Within a few months after the outbreak of hostilities in Korea, the President created the Office of Defense Mobilization (December 1950) in the Executive Office, with direct authority over all phases of governmental activity related to economic mobilization.

Present setup

At the present time [updated by editor to 1966] the Executive Office is composed of the following units:

1. The White House Office (includes the President's secretaries, aides, and administrative assistants);

2. Bureau of the Budget (the oldest and largest unit in the Executive Office, and its institutional core);

3. Council of Economic Advisers;

4. National Security Council (whether it is, in fact, the Council or its secretariat that is in the Executive Office might be argued);

5. Central Intelligence Agency (operates under the direction of National Security Council and therefore is perhaps improperly shown as a separate unit);
6. National Aeronautics and Space Council;
7. Office of Emergency Planning;
8. Office of Science and Technology;
9. Office of the Special Representative for Trade Negotiations;
10. Office of Economic Opportunity.

Hoover Commission's findings

The Hoover Commission's approach to problems of the Executive Office was generally similar to that of the Committee on Administrative Management. It too recognized that the effectiveness of the Government of the United States rested on the ability of the Chief Executive to provide "firm direction to the departments and agencies" and orderly "organization for development and execution of policy." It found the President still dangerously "handicapped" for the performance of his responsibilities. In its first report the Commission submitted specific recommendations and valuable conceptual principles regarding the Office. It said that the President must be boss of his own office and "should be given complete freedom to adjust the internal relationships." It also said, "Statutory authority over the operating departments should not be vested in any staff or staff agency of the President's Office."

It appears that Congress does not intend to follow these recommendations. In 1951, for example, it legislated that a Director for Mutual Security, who would serve as co-ordinator in this entire field, should be located in the Executive Office and that the same man who held this post should be the administrator of a large operating agency, the Mutual Security Agency. Congress thereby flew in the face of the Hoover Commission precepts and violated other elementary principles of organization by making a single official both protagonist and umpire in interagency disputes.

The Hoover Commission enunciated the principles that multiheaded bodies, in the nature of full-time boards, could not serve effectively as Presidential staff, and that the heads of staff agencies in the President's Office "should be appointed by the President without confirmation by the Senate, except the Civil Service Commission." It specifically pointed to the Council of Economic Advisers as an example of violation of both principles, and recommended that it be replaced by an Office of the Economic Advisers with a single head. This was not done. . . .

The Commission took cognizance of the lack of organization within the Executive Office, pointing out especially that there is no place in the Office where the President can look for a current summary of principal issues on staff work or assignments to departments and agencies. Its recommendation to meet this deficiency indicated that it is much easier to determine what is wrong than to reach agreement upon a solution. The compromise proposal was a new staff secretary whose prescribed functions suggest a high-class clerk for clearing and assembling papers for the President. Some of the Commission's members apparently hoped that such a position, once established, might grow into a more affirmative and influential role of "staff leader."

Deficiencies and progress

Meanwhile, the crucial issues of coherent organization and internal staff relationships in the Executive Office remain unresolved. This affects more than the adequacy of assistance. A Chief Executive can become a prisoner of the imbalances in his own organization. Ultimate decisions must rest upon the solitary figure of the President. He must therefore be sure that when issues reach him for decision they have had staff appraisal from all the different aspects of Presidential responsibility, and that all viewpoints on vital controversies reach him through persons representing such different views. This protects the President's judgments and his position.

The present deficiencies of the Executive Office should not, however, becloud the remarkable progress made during the last decades. Large sectors are post-World War II developments. That it has not yet shaken down to a cohesive and orderly structure should not be discouraging. More informal coordination has been achieved internally than the formal structure suggests. In part, such institutions tend to achieve balance through an evolutionary process. For example, more and more of the legislative clearance function, basically located in the Bureau of the Budget, is passing into the hands of the White House staff without any formal ordering.

The general competence of the Executive Office is high. Acceptance of its Presidential functions are being achieved throughout the government. . . .

DEPARTMENTAL ORGANIZATION

Proper staffing of the Presidency will not alone provide a solution of the President's organization problems. Departmental organization is also vitally important. Three issues stand out:

1. The existence of commissions executing some of our most important statutes, claiming virtual independence of the Chief Executive, mocks attempts at meaningful co-ordination of government policy and administration. The independent agencies are regulatory in nature. Regulation is essentially political, concerned with the formulation of public policies. Independence of the Executive and, in some cases, even of the legislature, makes these agencies essentially irresponsible. There is indeed "very great danger in any doctrine that pretends we can preserve democracy and still vest economic powers in a governmental agency that is not clearly subject to officials who in turn are responsible to the people." [7]

2. There are entirely too many agencies for effective direction from the top. According to the Hoover Commission:

> At the present time there are 65 departments, administrations, agencies, boards and commissions engaged in executive work, all of which report directly to the President—if they report to anyone. This number does not include the "independent" regulatory agencies in their quasi-judicial or

[7] James W. Fesler, "Independent Regulatory Establishments," in F. Morstein Marx, Ed., *Elements of Public Administration* (New York, 1946), p. 228.

quasi-legislative functions. It is manifestly impossible for the President to give adequate supervision to so many agencies.

The Hoover Commission, like its predecessor Committee on Administrative Management, made useful recommendations for an orderly combining of agencies to reduce the total number. It is now clear that for the most part, Congress cannot heed such recommendations.

. . . [I]nteresting proposals have been made for creation of a new echelon of command, between the departmental and Executive Office levels, through grouping of departments and agencies with particularly related activities. If modeled after the integrated structure of the Department of Defense in which are combined three administrative departments, as distinguished from its predecessor the National Military Establishment which had statutory authority only of a holding-company character and proved to have no basis of strength, such redesigning may have administrative merit. But, in any event, it is unlikely to appeal to congressional committees.

3. Authority within departments is diffused and uncertain, partly because of statutes through which Congress has too frequently spelled out the internal organization of departments and agencies and has given authority directly to subordinate officers. In part, the situation is due to the informal power relationships which align bureaus and agencies more closely with congressional committees than with their organizational superiors.

In greater or less degree, all three of these impediments to unified executive administration reflect the congressional-Presidential rivalry within our system. Even more, they reflect the lack of organization within Congress. As long as Congress remains a congeries of warring factions, its committees are encouraged to usurp powers properly belonging to the whole of Congress, and to divide up the executive branch into colonial empires directly subject to committee domination.

The danger is great on many scores. As one distinguished scholar warned,

> It is extremely doubtful if government by congressional committees can be justified on either democratic or expediential grounds, because the standing committees of Congress are very nearly the *least representative* institutions in the government.[8]

It is insufficiently recognized that the proper organization and functioning of the executive branch is greatly dependent upon the internal organization and management of the legislature. As long as Congress is disorganized, it will continue to promote the disorganization of the executive branch. As long as the executive branch is fragmented, it will be difficult if not impossible for the Congress to hold it accountable. Only by strengthening the control of the Chief Executive, with whom it can deal in direct and unitary fashion, can the Congress ever assure to itself administrative accountability of the bureaucracy.

PRESIDENTIAL QUALIFICATIONS

Adequate administrative machinery is indispensable, but it will not do the job alone. The office of President properly remains flexible and keeps being recreated in the image of the man who occupies it. The character of the President will be foremost in determining the quality of leadership which will be exercised and the quality of personnel which will be attracted to and selected for key positions. The best of formal equipment can remain unused or misused. What manner of man appears most promising for the most complex administrative job in the world?

As White House correspondent Merriman Smith put it a few years ago, "A President is Many Men." Other aspects of the job are discussed in other essays in this volume. Although it is convenient for analysis to distinguish the facets of total responsibility, it would be an error to suppose that these can really be compartmentalized in practice. Long experience has demonstrated that a President is likely to succeed in most of his jobs or in none. They are mutually dependent. A President who is

[8] E. E. Schattschneider, "Congress in Conflict," *The Yale Review*, Winter, 1952, p. 189.

not a skillful political leader is not likely to be able to rise above his administrative handicaps. The President is not politician *and* administrator; he is rather a *political administrator*. His administrative success will depend not alone on management skills in the more conventional sense, but also on his skill in political manipulation and on his popular support.

The "pros" have done well

The task of the Chief Executive is thus essentially a job of good management made possible through political leadership and inspiration. It is therefore not surprising that, with few exceptions, the men who have most ably filled the job have had a long nurturing in party politics. Of the six American Presidents voted "great" by a poll of fifty-five scholars of American history and government,[9] four were professional politicians —Lincoln, Franklin Roosevelt, Jefferson, and Jackson. A fifth, Wilson, had served with distinction as Governor of New Jersey (and it is perhaps incorrect not to count his previous presidency of a university as toughening political experience). Only Washington falls in a special class. Of the four Presidents voted "near great"—Theodore Roosevelt, Cleveland, John Adams, Polk —all were professional politicians.

On the other hand, the men who were relative strangers to party politics and party leadership when they entered the Presidency have a much lower average. Grant, for example, strictly a military hero before his first nomination, is one of the two American Presidents acknowledged as "failures," while Zachary Taylor, who had never voted before he moved to the Presidency, is generously graded "below average."

The "great" Presidents were great leaders of their parties.

> Washington aside, all the titans had their hearts set upon becoming President and, defying the adage that the office should seek the man, spared no effort to bring it about. Elected as political chieftains, they continued, moreover, to function in that capacity in the White House, one

[9] See Arthur M. Schlesinger, *Paths to the Present* (New York, 1949), pp. 93–111.

badge of their greatness being the ability to advance their country's interest at the same time as their parties'. Scratch any of these demigods and you find a party man—a fact which tends to be forgotten in later years when the heat of partisan strife has cooled and the men themselves have become wax images in school histories.[10]

Former governors

Among the politicians, the tendency is for former governors to be most at home in the political administrative duties of the White House. The governorship of a large state is, on a smaller scale, the job most nearly resembling the Presidency. Although this is not the primary reason Americans have in this century chosen more Presidents and Presidential candidates from among state governors than from any other group (even though there are obviously twice as many Senators from whom to choose), this appears to have been a course of wisdom. There . . . [were] thirteen election campaigns [up to 1952] in this century. Fifteen of the twenty-six candidates of the two major parties were former governors (not including W. H. Taft, who was governor of the Philippines). Of the nine men who . . . occupied the office of President, five were former governors. Of the other four—Taft, Harding, Hoover, and Truman—only two had served in the Senate. Former governors . . . [were] in the Presidential seat more than thirty-four of the [first] fifty-two years in this century.

Type of leadership

The combination of training in the school of electoral politics and experience as political executive appears generally to work out best. The successful administrator in business enterprise or in military combat generally finds that his skills are not directly transferable or convertible to political administration. The different kinds of administration not only represent different habit patterns, but seem to require different types of personality The man accustomed to giving orders with the expectation that subordinates will automatically follow or bear the consequences

[10] *Ibid.*, p. 104.

will find the Presidency frustrating and baffling. The man who operates by making up his mind what is "right" and then driving ahead accordingly, irrespective of opposition, is likely to find the Presidency a strait jacket with taunting shackles.

The political administrator makes his leadership felt by media of persuasion, by winning wide public support, and by being a successful "lubricator of human relations." He cannot be doctrinaire or unyielding. He must be a man who can elevate compromise and draw out of it a creative principle. The necessity of harmonizing conflicting interests of functionally divergent groups in a pluralistic society is the most crucial task of top-level administration, just as it is of politics.

The President undertakes to co-ordinate not only the activities of an array of federal agencies but, through them, the conflicting tendencies and desires of our whole socioeconomic system. The basic conflicts cannot be "ordered" out of existence. Their reconciliation, issue by issue, is the keynote of democratic administration. And experience has taught us that "democracy is more efficient than efficiency."

Yet the great Presidents have also been strong and affirmative leaders. All were regarded as relatively "radical" in their own day. Each made the office as big as he could, and each left it more influential than he had found it.

A variable formula

However, it would be a mistake to attempt to fix the most desirable background for the Presidency into a mold, just as it is to fix the "right" procedures for him to follow. Human personality is flexible and unpredictable. Not every political background or business background or military background is the same as every other, nor does it have the same effect upon every man. For example, detractors of one of the possible candidates of 1952 (this is being written before either nominating convention), General Eisenhower, allege that he never was a real combat general, but rather a "chairman-of-the-board" commander of a political organizer in the military field. If true, this illustrates that intended derogation in one field may be commendation for another, as such talents are greater assets for the Presidency than those ordinarily associated with combat effectiveness.

Moreover, as President Franklin Roosevelt said of the Presidency, "It is pre-eminently a place of moral leadership." The consciousness of this fact and the searing responsibilities of the office have had a remarkable influence in molding the personality and the ability of men after they have assumed office. Presidents have often surprised themselves and their generations by their growth in office.

THE NEXT ADMINISTRATION

The Presidency is today the prime motive force in our Constitutional system. Our political and economic evolution and the nature of our party system have focused upon the President's responsibility for the origin of major policies and programs and for the implementation and effectuation of policies approved by Congress. The American system, in which the Presidency is a representative institution—elected by universal suffrage—emphasizes the fact that co-ordination of politics and administration is necessary in a democratic nation.

In our complex society, responsible leadership must have the means of ensuring that policy will not be distorted in its administration, and must have control of the ever broadening areas of decision-making and policy determination which are implicit in the administrative process.

Presidential administrative difficulties are intertwined with the fundamental issues of political organization facing American society, including the complex problems of deficient party organization and party discipline. The basic factors are the same as those which encourage increasingly dangerous stalemates between President and Congress, which make the legislature and the bureaucracy unduly vulnerable to powerful private interests, and which give to extremists in Congress a disproportionate influence. The fate of the largest share of even so popularly dramatized reforms as those proposed by the Hoover Commission and endorsed by the leadership of both parties illustrates the unreality of treating administrative revisions as things distinct from the political environment.

Suggested improvements

Nevertheless, there are several administrative improvements which, on the basis of precedent or related experience, appear to have a chance for practical achievement if demanded by a new and popular President during his "honeymoon period." Among them are four points which ought to be regarded as a minimum program for early achievement.

1. The President should be given permanent authority to initiate plans for internal reorganization of the executive branch, such plans to take effect unless rejected by joint resolution of both houses of Congress within a specified time. Presidents have already been given similar authority for temporary periods. Congress has demonstrated that its power of veto under such an arrangement is amply adequate. Such permanent executive initiative would go far toward correlating authority and responsibility and would offer some operational basis for workable reordering of the executive branch structure. Considerable useful reorganization has already been achieved in this manner which could never have been accomplished otherwise; for example, placing the collectors of internal revenue under the merit system.

2. The highly successful operation of the National Security Council has provided a case study of how the Cabinet may be made a viable instrument for executive policy co-ordination and how the Executive Office may be molded into a coherent organization without the monolithic dangers of a single "chief-of-staff" arrangement.

The NSC has demonstrated that Cabinet-level committees, given a circumscribed area of juristion and continuing responsibility, with members selected because of direct functional relationship to the committee's jurisdiction, can be effective instruments for Presidential counsel and co-ordination. One of the elements in its success has been the continuous efficient staff work of an able professional secretariat. The experience argues for similar Cabinet committees for other large areas of governmental responsibility which cut across departmental lines, each to be served by a full-time secretariat.

3. The various Cabinet committee secretariats should be interlocking and all attached to and assigned from the Executive Office, where they would be part of a central Presidential secretariat. The central secretariat would co-ordinate the work of the several committee secretariats, and, thereby, of the committees themselves. It should serve as a continuous channel of communication to the President, to whom it would be responsible. The Executive Office would thereby acquire the integrating amalgam it has long needed.

4. The administrative structure is composed of people. If the President cannot reasonably control, within the law, the personnel system of government, it is difficult to conceive how adequate democratic control can be achieved. The merit system, now covering over 90 per cent of federal personnel, can become a boomerang, and is itself endangered, if it is independent of the political officers of government. The objective must be a reconciliation of the principle of merit with the principle of administrative control. Progress toward such an objective can begin by creating a director of personnel, directly accountable to the President. A continuing civil service commission or board should act only in an advisory capacity.

Importance of reforms

Such reforms are within the realm of possible realization by a new administration. Important in themselves, they can also serve as a vehicle for Presidential leadership in continuous administrative reform, with the target of bringing the total job under control. We must all realize that "the reality of responsible government is dependent upon the ability of the President to control the executive branch."[11]

[11] Paul H. Appleby, "The Significance of the Hoover Commission Report," *The Yale Review, Autumn,* 1949,, p. 8.

> What I am placing before you is not a request for more power, but for the tools of management and the authority to distribute the work so that the President can effectively discharge those powers which the Constitution now places upon him.[12]

This is the type of plea the next President of the United States, whoever he is, is also likely to make. It would be well that he be heeded. It is tempting fate to continue to play the game of challenging greatness to surmount unnecessary and unreasonable barriers. The stakes of government are now too high!

[12] *Message,* The President of the United States to the Congress, January 12, 1937.

6. IN ACCORD WITH THE PROGRAM OF THE PRESIDENT?

An Essay on staffing the Presidency

Arthur Maass

The United States President needs staff to help develop the policies of the executive establishment and to insure unity in the pursuit of these policies—staff to develop "the program of the President" and to insure "accordance" therewith on the part of all executive agencies. This is obvious. To create this unity of program and action, however, the President needs diversity and, some would even suggest, a touch of discordance in staff. This has not been well understood by a great many students of government.

The President needs a small personal staff of top political and policy advisers—part of the White House staff. The President needs a permanent general staff to help implement policy decisions—the Budget Bureau staff. And between, or beside, or added to these the President needs staff or staffs either in the White House or elsewhere in the Executive Office to meet "the need for positive origination at the center of broad . . . objectives" and policies so that adequate "leadership and direction" are given to the development of the President's program.

The purposes of this short essay are to encourage further study of the precise requirements for this third type of staff—as I propose to demonstrate, the need for study is imperative; and to give direction to such study by interpreting certain experience of the existing staffs, particularly the Budget Bureau.

THE BUDGET STAFF

To begin with I shall consider the second type of staff. The President needs a group of assistants which has an *intimate technical knowledge of the structure and functioning of Government*—to help him put full body on the skeleton of policy decisions and to give full attention, in his name, to the day-to-day operations of the government bureaus. If such a staff is to contain the necessary qualifications in technical knowledge, then it needs be a career staff, a permanent staff, an institutional staff. At the same time, if such a staff is to act as the President's alter ego on implementing political decisions and supervising day-to-day operations, then its leaders should be the personal appointees of the President. The Budget Bureau is, of course, such a staff—a large institutional career bureaucracy, headed by a Director and Assistant Director, who are intended to be so peculiarly personal agents of the President that their appointments need not be confirmed by the Senate.

Because the Budget is a large career bureaucracy and must serve the President intimately as well as perform certain statutory duties, it has become a deceptively complex organization. In discussing its legislative clearance functions, Harold Stein has identified three different interests of the Budget Bureau staff:

> (1) It acts as spokesman for the President's over-all policy, as it understands that policy; (2) It acts as intermediary to secure agreement among the interested agencies when proposed legislation is of interest to more than one agency; and (3) It acts to represent its own interests . . . in those areas in which it has statutory responsibilities—particularly its responsibilities for the President's budget and its responsibilities for government organization.

If these three interests are present in most Budget Bureau work, and it is believed they are, then we can agree that the overriding interest at all times should be the first—spokesman for the President's policy—and that the other two interests should be operative only as they implement this primary one. Indeed, Stein, in mentioning the Budget's own interests, states parenthetically that they "are presumably consistent with the President's, or at least general rather than special." In Budget Bureau practice, however, the first interest has not always been overriding (unless one interprets very broadly the phrase, "as it [Budget] understands that policy"); and the reasons why it has not are of first importance in this analysis.

We have said that the President must depend upon the Budget Bureau to handle a great many of the day-to-day decisions which are made in the Executive Office, decisions arising from the process of piecemeal review, rejection, and modification of individual proposals flowing up from the administrative units to the office of the Chief Executive—new legislative proposals, reports on legislation prepared at the request of Congressional committees, estimates for appropriations, apportionments, and allotments. Inevitably a great many of these decisions have important policy implications. Where there has been clear general policy direction by the President, or by the White House, or by some top presidential policy staff—and remember the Budget Bureau is not such a staff—the role of the Budget Bureau in these day-to-day operations is clear. It can speak for the President and apply his general policies with technical expertise in a wide range of matters. Where such direction is not forthcoming—and this appears to be the case today in a great majority of issues—the Budget must either find some way of muddling through or go to the President for a decision on each day-to-day issue which involves important policy. The Bureau has chosen to muddle through for the most part, and in this process, as we shall see, its institutional interests have come alarmingly, if understandably, to the fore.

Without Presidential policy direction to guide it, then, the Budget Bureau is asked daily to inform departments and agencies whether or not their proposals are in accord with the program of the President. Often the proposals of one department are in direct conflict with those of another. If the Budget were to take a very positive stand for the President against the proposals of one department, it might be challenged by that department to prove that its position was in fact the President's, or the challenge might be taken directly to the White House. If there were many successful challenges of Budget decisions, then the Bureau might lose face as the institutional right arm of the President; to this threat a permanent career bureaucracy like Budget is peculiarly sensitive. Thus, there is every incentive not to take definite positions on important and controversial policy matters, but rather to avoid them, or to postpone them, or to mediate policy differences between departments so as to "settle" them.

SETTLEMENT BY MEDIATION IN BUDGET

To illustrate, let us assume an important difference of opinion between the Secretaries of Agriculture and Interior on agricultural land policy. The Budget Bureau is made aware of this when the Departments request it to clear conflicting reports to a Congressional committee on legislation. Budget decides that the matter is important, that there is no applicable policy directive, but that, rather than bother the President, it will make an effort to settle the matter. The Director asks the Secretaries of Agriculture and Interior to attend a conference in his office. Present at the conference in addition to the Secretaries and the Director are several Budget officials—the Executive Assistant Director and one officer from each the Divisions of Estimates and Administrative Management.[1] The Director emphasizes the desirability of settling the issues without bothering the President and presents a staff memo on the differences between the positions of the two Departments, as seen by the budget examiner or analyst who prepared the memo, and on possible reconciliation. After some discussion, which reveals a fundamental disagreement in the basic approach and principles applied by the two Secretaries—a disagreement which cannot be reconciled—the conference proceeds to the specific points of difference contained in the Budget memo. Each Secretary agrees to yield on certain points, to compromise on others, and to disagree on yet others which are then postponed for later determination. The Director declares the matter settled, directs action to "clear" appropriate letters to Congress on the legislation, and at a later time will report to the President that he has settled certain differences between the Departments of Agriculture and Interior on land legislation.

[1] The Bureau has been reorganized recently, and these Divisions no longer exist.

Budget conferences on important policy matters have become increasingly popular, at least at Budget, in recent years. A Budget employee said recently that what he likes most about his work is "attending those conferences where the Bureau leaders knock together the heads of Cabinet members, agency directors, and bureau chiefs."

There are certain characteristics of this type of activity that should be noted. The conferences usually do not settle basic policy questions. Instead they avoid the basic issues and compromise, through a game of give and take, certain specific manifestations of these issues. Each conference produces a Pick-Sloan plan; there is no agreement on fundamental policy for development of the valley, but specific projects are divided up between the departments in such a way that Budget can say it has settled the immediate differences. And the settlement often centers around what I shall call the "bureaucratic" or institutional aspects of the problem—those aspects that would assume importance for a budget examiner or an administrative analyst, rather than the program or policy aspects.

In summary, it can be said that "horse trading among subordinates is not a satisfactory substitute for a clear policy directive from their politically responsible superior." It must be remembered, however, that Budget has received no clear policy directive and has resorted to this version of the horse-trade as an alternative. It is interesting to note, nonetheless, that through this activity Budget has in fact come to assert authority *in its own right* over departments on issues of policy—however negative this authority may be.

Some will point out that the Budget activity is not determining, that if a Secretary feels strongly about the issues he can bring them to the President's attention. Certainly this is true, and we have already pointed out that the threat of an appeal to the President from a Budget decision reached without an initial policy direction from the President strongly conditions the Bureau's conduct. However, heads of agencies, especially in the domestic sphere, appear to have become increasingly reluctant to appeal to the President or the White House over the head of the Budget. They know, after all, that if Budget has not received policy direction from the President or a presidential policy staff, then in most cases they are not likely to obtain such direction. Furthermore, they are of the opinion that the President supports the Budget methods of operation.

This, then, is how the most important and long-standing staff in the Executive Office, the Budget staff, has developed under the influence of a frequent policy vacuum. Are there alternative courses which the Budget Bureau might have pursued under these conditions?

WEAKNESS OF POLICY FORMULATION BY A PERMANENT BUDGET STAFF

Faced with a policy vacuum, the Budget Bureau might have sought to become itself the top policy staff. But this it did not and should not have attempted for several reasons. Top policy formulation was not a function intended for the Budget by the drafters of the Budget and Accounting Act of 1921 or by the authors of the Report of the President's Committee on Administrative Management in 1937 and of the Executive Office Reorganization Plan of 1939. Apart from this, the Budget Bureau is to a considerable degree institutionally incapable of positive policy formulation. This is true for two reasons. First, the expenditure implications of so many policies are strictly counter to the Budget orientation of restricting expenditures wherever possible. Where the President directs a policy that involves great new expenditures, the Budget is capable of implementing this directive, and of doing so with economy. But it is quite another matter to expect the Budget itself to develop policy proposals and in doing so not to make its own statutory and institutional interests—the preparation of the Budget and in this task, the paring of departmental estimates of expenditures—the dominant consideration.

Second, the permanent and career nature of the Budget Bureau tends to make the organization overly cautious and thus not well-suited for making or proposing political decisions on important matters of policy. The man or institution that proposes key policy decisions must be prepared to pay a dear price, possibly his or its political life, if the proposals are rejected subsequently by Congress and the public. The Budget Bureau was not intended to be, and is not, so prepared. To the contrary, the Bureau's employees seek to protect and preserve "THE Bureau," as they are wont to call it, as an independent technical staff organization, ready to serve any President—a Dewey or a Truman in 1948, an Eisenhower or a Stevenson in 1952. To protect its institutional status and indeed to perform its institutional staff functions, the Bureau seeks above all to be neutral and impartial in policy controversies where the President has not stated his position or program. As such, the Bureau cannot become a top level policy staff for the President.

This Budget tendency to particularism and the promotion of its own parochial interests is characteristic of most career bureaucracies. In one respect the Budget Bureau is unique as such a bureaucracy, however. It has few outside contacts; it is insulated pretty well against pressure groups, Congress, and the courts and in consequence becomes a peculiarly introverted organization. This, of course, limits even further its capacity to serve as a policy staff.

The career bureaucracy of the Budget is headed, to be sure, by political appointees of the President. And it might be argued that this personal leadership should equip the Bureau to serve as the President's policy staff. Taking into account, however, the many other limitations noted above, it is doubtful that the Director and Assistant Director, if they are to be effective leaders of the Bureau in the performance of its technical staff functions, can at the same time turn that agency into a top level policy staff. Furthermore, the Bureau's leaders today are not political leaders; they are career civil servants who have risen to positions of control. Each of the three top leaders (as of July 1952) has spent the better part, if not all, of his government career in the Bureau, and each in the recent past has been Director of one of the important divisions of the Bureau. These men, as one should expect, have a strong loyalty to, and pride of service in, the Budget as an independent corporate organization.

THE POLICY DILEMMA ILLUSTRATED

Without policy direction from the President the Budget has tried to muddle through by "settling," mediating, and postponing policy decisions. This we have noted earlier. The natural tendency to self-protective bureaucratic conduct complements, in a sense, this same type of activity—to the extent that there is a danger that the "settling" of policy matters may become so fixed a pattern of Bureau conduct that it may stand in the way of the operation of a policy staff in the future. Lest this whole analysis be considered somewhat hypothetical, and to illustrate the danger, it is well at this point to introduce an example.

In March of 1949 the Hoover Commission proposed that the water resources functions of the Corps of Engineers and the Bureau of Reclamation and the power functions of the Interior Department be consolidated in a new Water Development Service to be organized in the Department of Interior or, as three members proposed, in a new Department of Natural Resources. This Hoover recommendation was discussed by the Director of the Budget and the President sometime in the Fall of 1949. Because the Secretary of the Army had put forth the claim that the conduct of river work by the Corps of Engineers was *essential to the military mission* of the Army Department, the President directed Budget to investigate this claim and to report back to him.

The Budget Bureau went to the Army files, conducted an extensive survey, and concluded that the conduct of river work by the Corps of Engineers is not important enough to the military mission of the Department to stand in the way of sound water resources organization. On the basis of this conclusion, members of the staff of the Bureau prepared reorganization plans and justifications for transferring all river work to a Water Development Service in the Department of Interior. These plans, it appears, did not get beyond the front office of the Budget Bureau; they were not presented to the President. Apparently the Bureau leaders decided that because the issue was controversial—the Secretary of the Army continued to insist upon the essentiality of the civil work to his Department, and it was known that any reorganization affecting the Army Engineers would be met by intense Congressional opposition—they would not refer it back to the President immediately. Perhaps they could "settle" the matter by working out a compromise. So the Budget leaders called a conference, themselves and leaders of the Army and Interior Departments attending. The compromise they proposed was a new twist on the old Pick-Sloan formula—the Department of Interior would plan and operate the projects and the Corps of Engineers would construct them. To those who had worked in the resources field this compromise appeared completely unworkable and undesirable, so that heads were knocked together with no avail. Still the matter was not referred to the White House as a completed piece of staff work.

On income tax day of 1951 the Citizens' Committee for the Hoover Report had bills introduced into Congress to carry out many of the Hoover proposals. One, S1143, 82nd Congress, would have created the Water Development Service. Senator McClellan, as Chairman of the Senate Committee on Expenditures, referred all of these bills to the Budget Bureau, among other agencies, for advice. The reply of the Director of the Budget on S1143 was entirely noncommital. It stated arguments for and against transfer of Corps river functions and included the following sentence: "In my opinion many of the factors involved in both of these positions [that the conduct of river functions is, or is not, essential to conduct of the military mission of the Army Department] rest so directly on policies and relationships established by the Congress that a fact-finding inquiry into these subjects by a Congressional committee would be both an appropriate and a necessary action to solution of the organizational issues involved."

The letter and especially the quoted sentence are noted for several reasons. First, it is obviously an effort to pass the buck to Congress and to defer any decision by Budget. And, incidentally, a somewhat disingenuous effort. Was not the Hoover Commission a fact-finding body established by Congress? Had not the Budget Bureau just recently completed an extensive survey into the military mission aspect of the problem? Do not all major reorganization problems "rest directly on policies and relationships established by the Congress?" How did this one differ? Second, the Director of the Budget in communications to Congress presumably speaks for the President. Yet it appears that this specific issue, like the results of the earlier survey into military mission and the reorganization plans drawn on the basis of that survey, was not presented in full to the President.

In the meantime the President's Water Resources Policy Commission had submitted its final report in December 1950. This Commission had been established by President Truman in January to consider major policy problems in the water field —such, for example, as standards for evaluating the feasibility of water projects. Under the President's Executive Order the Commission was not to consider matters of organization, as these had been studied extensively by the Hoover Commission and were then under active consideration in the Executive branch. The PWRPC, however, failed to abide by the limitations of its instructions from the President. It proceeded to consider and make recommendations on organization. The Commission proposed that: "If the recommended changes [those of the Hoover Commission] are not carried into effect, then, as an absolute minimum, it would seem necessary to utilize the present voluntary Inter-Agency River Basin Committee approach through Congressional approval of river basin commissions, set up on an inter-agency basis."

In June 1951 the Budget Bureau undertook to review for the President the report of the Water Resources Policy Commission. To conduct the review it organized a large inter-agency committee, consisting of representatives of all federal agencies interested in water resources development, supported by a series of task forces with the same members. At the time this review machinery was being established, representations were made to Budget that organization matters should not be handled in this way, that they had already been given exhaustive study by the Hoover Commission and the Budget Bureau, that it was futile to ask an inter-agency committee of the affected agencies to draw up a proposal for their own reorganization, and that this futile effort would provide another excuse for delaying an important policy decision that could be referred to the President immediately. Nonetheless, the Budget Bureau did refer organization matters to the inter-agency review committee and to one of its task forces. A majority of the task force on planning procedures of the inter-agency committee to review the report of the President's *ad hoc* Commission on Water Policy recommended, in late winter of 1952, after due deliberation, that river commissions be established with Presidentially appointed chairmen, but with no basic reorganization affecting the Engineers and Interior. The Budget Bureau accepted tentatively this alternative to the more controversial reorganization proposal, and commenced drafting legislation to effect it, although concurrently, it appears, the Budget staff were conducting certain conferences to take yet another look at the organization problem.

The Department of Interior opposed river commissions as an alternative to a consolidated Water Development Service. As April 1952 approached, the leaders in the Department realized that the deadline for submitting reorganization plans to Congress under the Reorganization Act of 1949 would be passed very soon. The 82nd Congress was expected to adjourn on July 1 for the political conventions, and according to law plans can become effective only if they have been before Congress for 60 calendar days of continuous session during which period either House can kill them by a constitutional majority vote. Furthermore, the Reorganization Act was to expire on April 1, 1953, and it was doubted that a new President would be likely to submit plans under an expiring Act so soon after his inauguration in late January. The 1st of May seemed like the last chance for reorganization; and the Budget Bureau had taken no action leading to a Presidential decision in the two years since the Director had been instructed to conduct the study on military necessity. Thus, the Secretary of Interior went over the head of the Bureau in a sense and presented the matter personally to the President. As reported, the President said he was prepared to submit a reorganization plan for a Water Development Service in the Interior Department, and the White House informed the Budget of this decision. Finally, about three weeks later, while work on the final draft of the plan was underway in Budget and Interior, the President announced at a press conference that the plan was to be dropped. He did not give the reason. At this writing (July 1952) it is reported that the Budget Bureau is again working on legislation for river commissions, but that some staff officers at Interior hold out hope for a reorganization plan after the election.

This story is not a simple one. A full length essay could, and perhaps should, be written to interpret it. It is used here, however, to illustrate the nature of Budget Bureau operations on an important policy question and how these operations of necessity limit the Bureau's capacity to serve as an effective policy staff for the President.

HURDLES ON THE PATH OF ALTERNATIVE STAFFING

Faced with a policy vacuum, the Budget Bureau, as an alternative to muddling through or to seeking to become itself a policy staff, might have encouraged and promoted the development of adequate policy staff or staffs in the Executive Office. In this way it could have obtained the Presidential policy direction it has needed so badly. But this it has not attempted for several reasons, though no doubt it should have done so. First, just as the Budget Bureau is itself poorly equipped to develop policies which have large expenditure implications, so is it somewhat loath to see other organizations in the Executive Office do this. In the early 1940's the President, the Budget Bureau, and the National Resources Planning Board, which for purposes of this example we shall call a top level policy staff agency, agreed to a general plan for presenting to Congress annually a long range program of resources development and public works expenditures and activities. On the basis of development programs prepared by Federal agencies, and through its elaborate project evaluation procedures, the Planning Board was to develop a six-year program, listing in order of priority the Federal development projects of each major category and detailing the expenditures proposed for each project in each of the six years and the total required to complete them after that time. This program would be sent to the President and the Bureau where it would become an important basis for decisions on the pending budget estimates. Once the President's Budget for the coming year had been agreed to, the first year of the Planning Board's six-year program would be revised to agree with the Budget, and the remaining five years modified accordingly. Then at the beginning of each year the President would submit two reports to Congress, his Budget and his Development Report. The Budget would contain the recommendations of the Chief Executive for the financial outlays to carry on a development program during the next fiscal year. The Deveolpment Report would place "these recommendations within the framework of a long range policy of intelligent planning for the future."[2]

The first such program was prepared by the NRPB for 1941, but the Budget Bureau opposed publication of the program. Budget did not wish to provide Congress and the public with an indication of the amount of resources development and public works appropriations to be expected in the budgets of later years for fear that such an indication might become embarrassingly binding. The Budget Bureau was not prepared for this innovation in development planning and programming. After considerable negotiation, the Planning Board agreed to limit to Executive Office use only the prepared program, and to publish in its place only a list of projects recommended for the ensuing fiscal year, with estimates for each project of expenditures proposed in the Budget and additional expenditures

[2] President, memo to Congress, March 17, 1941, in transmitting report of NRPB on *Development of Resources.*

required thereafter to complete it. These additional expenditures were not programmed over the succeeding five years nor were any projects included other than those for which expenditures were estimated in the Budget.

The Planning Board prepared three such annual reports prior to its abolition by Congress in 1943, at which time the entire project was dropped. The Budget Bureau had little sympathy for a Presidential staff activity which had significant expenditure implications.

A second reason why Budget has not encouraged the development of policy staffs is the almost inevitable bureaucratic tendency, however illogical in the broad picture, to fear that other staffs in the Executive Office may challenge the institutional status of the Bureau. Budget"s wary attitude towards, and conflicts with, the OWMR have been pointed up by Herman Somers.[3] When the Foreign Affairs and National Security Task Forces of the Hoover Commission were considering proposals for a full-fledged Cabinet Secretariat, they undertook discussions with the Bureau. Budget's opposition was very firm; and some of the Task Force members were convinced that this opposition was based not alone on principle, but significantly on fear of a challenge to Budget's independent status.

NEEDED: A STUDY OF PRECISE REQUIREMENTS FOR POLICY STAFF

How, in summary, does this analysis of certain operations of the President's Budget staff lead to realizing the purposes of this essay which are concerned with the President's policy staff needs? First, the analysis indicates the importance of policy staff for the President. V. O. Key has stated that "less and less can it be presumed that the negative process of piecemeal review, rejection, and modification of individual proposals flowing up from the administrative units to the office of the Chief Executive will eventuate in the sort of integrated program of objectives that evolving conditions seem certain to require. . . .

[3] Herman Somers, *Presidential Agency* (Cambridge, Harvard University Press, 1950), especially pp. 211–212.

Thus it may be expected that the need for positive origination at the center of broad but intelligible objectives will become more pressing." The truth of this has been demonstrated; but further, and no doubt implied in Key's statement, the process of piecemeal review itself cannot be conducted satisfactorily without policy direction, and this requires policy staff.

Second, the Budget Bureau was not intended to and is not capable of performing the policy staff functions; and this means that the President cannot depend on any one central institutional staff in the Executive Office to service him fully.

Third, the Budget Bureau, though it has a major responsibility for recommendations to the President on administrative organization, has not promoted the development of adequate policy staff in the Executive Office, nor is it likely to do so. Thus, there is an urgent need for study by students of administration of the precise requirements for organization of such policy staff. This study must include, among other factors, an evaluation of the operation of the National Security Council, its small staff, and its relations to the Budget Bureau to see if this model might meet the requirements for policy in the domestic sphere; of the role of the Council of Economic Advisors and particularly of the Nourse-Keyserling disagreements, which in many respects bear a close relation to the problems of the Budget Bureau as explained in this essay; of the effectiveness of the National Resources Planning Board as a Presidential staff; of the operation of the Cabinet and of various proposals for imparting to it new vigor and providing it the support of adequate staff; of other proposals for policy staff units in the Executive Office; and of the total complex of institutions and relations which President Roosevelt used to impart to his Administration the overall policy directives. These matters have not been given adequate attention largely because administrative experts have been absorbed so fully in the development of the President's institutional staff facility, is well-developed now; we must stimulate bold, new thinking on the subject of organizing policy leadership.

Some direction can be given the new study, it is hoped, by

the analysis of this essay. Two important yet tentative requirements for policy staff or staffs can be derived, though they must be examined further. First, the President must personally desire such facilities and must always be fully free to alter or abolish them. At the same time, the administrative experts should present to him as forcefully as they can the advantages of the types of policy staffs they find best suited.

Some will say that responsibility for those Budget difficulties of the last seven years which stem from policy vacuum must be laid squarely at the feet of President Truman; for if the President had desired and established a policy staff Budget would have received and applied policy direction. This is true. But it is believed to be equally true that those who should know most about organizing policy leadership—the administrative experts in and out of government—failed to impress upon the President the desirability of policy staff or even to point out clearly the distinction between policy staff and institutional staff and the limitations of the latter as policy advisers.

A second requirement is that to a considerable extent (the precise degree must be determined) the policy staff must be flexible as regards both its organization and the permanence of status of its personnel. Unless this is so, the staff is likely to acquire its own independent and parochial interests, as is the wont of most bureaucracies. As for flexibility in organization, it is clear that no one staff organization in the Executive Office can serve the President in *all* respects. It may well be that no one staff organization in the Executive Office can serve the President as policy staff, that several staffs of varying forms are required.

President Roosevelt carried the doctrine of flexibility quite far. At one point in the 1940's, for example, important policy in a wide area was set for the President's approval by a heterogeneous group of government officers, largely lawyers selected for their individual capacities and not as representatives of the agencies for which they worked, chaired by the Assistant Director of the Budget, who also was selected largely for this reason. In contrast, President Truman is reported to have taken some pride in the way he regularized the organization of the Executive Office; and officers of the Budget Bureau often express a fear of "cluttering up the Executive Office with too many units." The advantages of order and simplicity are not to be denied; but we must be wary that we do not use these to obscure, rather than highlight, the necessity of flexible organization for policy leadership.

As for flexibility in staff, those who hold important positions on policy staff cannot expect permanent career status there. To a significant degree those who help the President develop his important policy directives must be prepared to offer their necks on the political block.

IV. Congress, The Bureaucracy, and Law Making

EDITORIAL NOTE. Administrative agencies make law in many ways. They fill in the details of vague congressional statutes, and the volume of administrative rule making is truly momentous. This may be seen by brief reference to the voluminous code of federal regulations, which contains the law made by the agencies. Most congressional statutes are vague, leaving maximum discretion to administrators to implement whatever programs they see fit. In addition to making such rules, agencies influence the legislative process directly by swaying Congress. The advice and assistance of administrators often shapes statutes. The following selections illustrate this.

7. ADMINISTRATIVE AGENCIES AND STATUTE LAWMAKING

Edwin E. Witte

The role of administrative agencies in legislation has generally been discussed in terms of delegated legislation, the order-making powers vested in administrative departments. This is an important aspect of the relations between administration and legislation but by no means the entire relationship. The other part is the initiation within the administrative departments of bills considered and passed by the legislative bodies, and the influence which these departments exercise upon the action of the legislature.

The fine descriptions and interpretations which T. V. Smith has given us in recent years of "the legislative way of life" are something less than complete because they fail to assign sufficient importance to the activities of administrative departments in relation to statute lawmaking. The basic function of the legislature is seen by him to be the working out of an acceptable compromise between conflicting positions taken by different groups in our society on proposals for legislation originating outside the legislature, most commonly with private organizations. The function of administrative departments is chiefly to supply the legislature and the executive on their request with information they need for the efficient discharge of their duties in relation to legislation, and to initiate minor bills designed to correct defects which have shown up in the laws that these departments administer.

This description is very much an understatement of the role played by administrative departments in statute lawmaking today, particularly in the national government. Beyond question many important statutes enacted by Congress have their origin in administrative departments and congressional action is profoundly influenced by the wishes of these departments. To my personal knowledge this has been the situation as to substantially all social security legislation and also, I believe, as to most of the agricultural, banking, credit, defense, housing, insurance, public utility, securities, tax, and much other legislation of the last five or eight years.

As developed by Prof. O. Douglas Weeks in the only article dealing with this subject I have been able to find,[1] the present situation is not entirely new. Ever since Jackson's time there has been a close correspondence in the scope of many of the committees of Congress, particularly in the House, and the administrative departments of the government. McConachie, commenting upon this situation as long ago as 1898, said: "There is no suffrage for the administrative officer in a committee meeting, yet he has there the more important power which superior knowledge always gives."[2] In the middle twenties, Ex-Congress-

[1] "Initiation of Legislation by Administrative Agencies," 9 *Brooklyn Law Review* 117–131 (1940).

[2] *Congressional Committees* (Crowell, 1898), p. 236.

man Robert Luce, describing the functioning of Congress, said: "Probably more than half the business, measured by importance, comes directly or indirectly from the Departments or Bureaus of the government."[3]

In the first years of the New Deal the administrators played a much smaller role in congressional lawmaking than in the preceding period of Republican rule. Much of the important early New Deal legislation was prepared by "braintrusters" brought in from outside the government. The Democrats, distrusting the officeholders, went so far as to create many new, independent agencies to administer the laws they passed rather than to vest their administration in any of the established departments. This preference is probably a phenomenon to be expected whenever there is a complete turnover in the control of the government.

Within a few years most of the imported "braintrusters" disappeared from Washington and the rest were absorbed in the departments. With acquaintance, Congressmen, department heads, and apparently the President gained confidence in civil service administrators. In consequence, their influence in legislation grew and reached an importance unique in the history of this country.

INITIATION OF LEGISLATION

In this recent period a very large percentage of all public bills acted on in Congress have originated in the administrative agencies of the government. By no means all of these bills came to Congress with the approval of the President or were labeled as Administration measures; a not inconsiderable number of them did not even have the endorsement of the administrative departments in which the persons who concocted these measures were employed. Very generally in the latter cases but few members of Congress have known anything about the connection of bureaus or departments of the government or their executives or employees with the initiation of the measures in

[3] *Congress: an Explanation* (Harvard University Press, 1926), p. 3–4.

question. Most commonly in such cases their introduction was an outgrowth of a personal relationship between the author and the introducer. In at least some instances, however, bills having such an origin have made their appearance in Congress as measures sponsored by national organizations, without the slightest suggestion that they came from administrative departments of the government.

A large part of the energies of many of the ablest persons in the administrative agencies of the government have gone into the consideration and preparation of legislative bills to be presented to Congress and, less frequently, the state legislatures. Countless conferences have been devoted to this subject and much of the research of many government agencies has been directed to this end. Even more than the top executives of the administrative departments, their subordinates a little lower down have concerned themselves with legislative proposals. Bitter battles have been fought within the bureaucracy over such prenatal legislative proposals, which have centered in gaining the support of the department heads and ultimately of the President for the position taken by a particular group.

Many of the important bills acted on by Congress were under consideration for many months and even years in administrative circles before they saw the light of day. Most commonly the initial (informal) drafts of these measures were developed within the bureaus or departments which later were charged with their administration. Commonly, however, other interested departments have also been drawn into the consideration of these measures before their introduction in Congress, sometimes only through informal conferences, often through more or less formalized interdepartmental committees. At times, bills originating in administrative departments have gone to Congress without complete agreement between interested departments, with the result that interdepartmental conferences on these measures proceeded simultaneously with congressional consideration and often have had quite as great an influence on their final form as the congressional committees. Only seldom have departments disagreed publicly over legislative proposals, but behind the scenes there have been violent disagreements. These have been resolved through the processes of conference or by the decisions of higher officials in the administration, not a few of them by the President himself.

In addition to interested administrative departments, a considerable number of other organizations and individuals are usually consulted before legislative proposals originating within administrative circles are presented to Congress. Advance consultation with members of Congress is not widespread and is confined to the peculiar friends of the department in Congress and, at a later stage, to the chairman and perhaps other influential members of the congressional committee to which the measure will be referred. Some private individuals, not regular government employees but specialists in the subject matter, have quite often been brought in to give advice on important contemplated legislation and still more to try out on them the policy contemplated by bureaus or departments. Occasionally, also, advisory committees composed wholly or mainly of outsiders have been appointed to consider proposals for legislation, but this plan has been the exception rather than the rule. Where created, they have served primarily the purposes of publicity and of getting the reactions of peculiarly interested organizations and individuals.

Practice in relation to informal consultation with interested private organizations differs from department to department and, to a considerable extent, with the particular proposal which a department has under consideration. Some departments have such peculiarly close relations to particular interest groups that almost everything they propose by a way of legislation is certain to be "cleared" with these groups; in fact, they are likely to be "in" at every stage of the departmental legislative proposals to such an extent that it is difficult for an outsider to determine whether the initiative came from the department or the private organization, or to decide which had the greater influence on the recommendations finally made to the Congress. This statement is true especially of departments which public opinion regards as the spokesmen for particular interests, such as the Veterans Administration and the Departments of Agriculture, Commerce, and Labor; but a much larger number of agencies have one and usually more organizations that they consult in advance on every important legislative proposal they offer. Still other organizations are consulted on particular bills or types of bills. Often such consultation occurs at a late stage of the development of departmental bills, but there is no general rule in this respect.

The basic purpose of the consultation is to avoid opposition to the measure when it comes before Congress. So it is that the organizations consulted are almost exclusively pressure groups, i.e., organizations representative of special rather than general interests and usually also organizations active politically and with a substantial membership. Organizations representing general interests, particularly small groups, and organizations certain to be opposed to the proposal are not consulted.

Departmental regulations regarding unauthorized publicity usually are effective in preventing any reliable information regarding contemplated legislative proposals from reaching the public until they are about ready to be presented to Congress. Advance information has most frequently appeared in the stories of Washington columnists. On some occasions such items seem to have been inspired by the proponents of new legislation as a method of trying out public opinion or of preparing it for the forthcoming proposals. But usually not until the congressional hearings does the general public get any chance to present its views.

The initiation of legislation in administrative departments is by no means the same thing as executive leadership in legislation. Most bills which the President recommends to Congress originate in administrative departments. A considerable part of the importance of these departments in statute lawmaking today arises from the influence they exert upon the Chief Executive. As has been noted, much energy is devoted within administrative circles in trying to get the support of the President for the legislative proposals of the departments, often in competition with alternative suggestions also originating within the administration. But by no means all nor even a majority of such bills ever become a part of the legislative program of the President or get his endorsement in any form, although "cleared" with him, either personally or through the Bureau of the Budget.

Centralized clearance of proposals for legislation originating in administrative departments was first provided for in the Budget and Accounting Act of 1921, under which administrative departments were required to submit all proposals for legislation involving appropriations or finances to the Bureau of the Budget before presentation to Congress.[4] By executive orders issued principally between 1934 and 1937[5] this requirement has been expanded to include all recommendations or reports concerning proposed or pending legislation, other than private relief measures, to be presented to Congress or to any committee or member thereof. After such submission, the Bureau of the Budget advises the interested department of the relationship of its proposals or report "to the program of the President." Thereafter the department may do what it sees fit, but in any statement made regarding its proposals it must include the advice thus received from the Bureau of the Budget.

During the first years in which these requirements were in effect, the prescribed procedure was generally not followed in the case of the most important measures, but instead these were taken up directly with the President by department heads. Numerous less important measures were cleared in the same informal manner or not at all, although the number of proposed bills cleared regularly was fairly large.[6] What the situation in

[4] The history of the development of central clearance of legislative proposals originating in administrative departments is related in the author's report on "The Preparation of Proposed Legislative Measures by Administrative Departments," President's Committee on Administrative Management, *Studies,* No. V, (1937) pp. 53–55.

[5] The basic order governing the clearance of legislation initiated in administrative departments now in effect is Budget Circular No. 344, dated Nov. 15, 1937, which was reaffirmed in Executive Order No. 8248, Sept. 10, 1939. Closely related is Budget Circular No. 346, dated Jan. 19, 1939, and amended June 20, 1940, relating to departmental advice to the President on enrolled bills and resolutions.

[6] Witte, *op. cit.,* pp. 55–57.

this respect has been more recently the author does not know firsthand, but information from individuals in the government service is to the effect that since the Bureau of the Budget has been attached to the Executive Office of the President and has set up a Division of Legislative Reference, there is much more general compliance with the clearance requirements.

The clearance of departmental bills through the Bureau of the Budget is largely a formal requirement. The main purpose of clearance is the negative one of preventing departments from sponsoring legislation which is out of line with "the program of the President." The real consideration of legislative proposals in administrative circles precedes, rather than follows, compliance with the formal clearance requirements. And not every bill which is "cleared" becomes an Administration bill or gets any support from the President.

INFLUENCE UPON THE ACTION OF CONGRESS

The role of administrators and administrative agencies in statute lawmaking is not confined to the preparation of bills introduced in Congress. Their influence is important also in the congressional consideration of these measures. Administrators are constantly appearing before congressional committees to give testimony in public hearings both on measures which originated in their departments and on other bills. Many of these appearances are at the specific request of congressional committees. Frequently, also, departments are asked to express their views in writing on bills pending before committees.

These public appearances and reports are by no means the only influence which administrators exert on congressional action. Many times administrators are invited to appear before congressional committees in executive sessions to give their opinions on contemplated amendments or some particular aspect of pending bills. In many committees it is customary for representatives of the administrative department principally interested in the legislation under consideration to attend all of the executive sessions in order to be able to answer questions and to state the views of their departments on subjects upon which any member may request information. Departmental representatives work with legislative draftsmen and committee clerks in preparing committee amendments, substitute bills, and reports. Commonly also the interested departments supply the committee chairmen and other members who champion their bills with material for their speeches, and their representatives are within beck and call to supply needed information during the course of the debate in the houses themselves.[7] Almost always representatives of the interested departments work and sit with conference committees in the final stages of important congressional enactments. While Congress has before it bills in which administrative departments are vitally interested, a large part of the time of bureau chiefs and other top executives, as well as of many employees lower down in the public service, is devoted to pending legislation. Sometimes there are as many meetings and conferences in administrative circles on the progress of pending legislation and amendments as there are sessions of congressional committees.

Buttonholing and more questionable forms of lobbying appear to be resorted to but seldom by representatives of administrative agencies and when employed are likely to lead to repercussions unfavorable to the legislation in question. On the other hand, departmental executives and employees constantly meet members of Congress and informally discuss with them pending bills in which the departments are interested, often at the initiative of the members and nearly always without intent of lobbying. Administrative agencies usually also have particular friends among members of Congress, who are consulted freely and utilized to keep track of what is happening on the inside. Sometimes also departments are instrumental in getting private organizations to take up the cudgels for the bills they originated, utilizing the voters back home to bring pressure upon members of Congress. In such cases, the departments try to keep secret their part in these campaigns, although they may be directing

[7] In the Senate, departmental representatives are often on the floor during debates. In the House they are barred strictly from the floor but are in the galleries or in near-by rooms to be called for as needed.

them. On the whole, however, the methods used by administrative departments to induce Congress to act favorably upon their proposals are much more aboveboard and free from objectionable features than those employed by private interests and by opponents of departmental bills.

The natural result of all of the activities of administrative agencies devoted to legislation is that they very greatly influence the action of Congress. The members of Congress are far from being rubber stamps in the process of legislation. The congressional committees to which bills are referred still have the largest influence upon the legislation enacted by Congress, but they do not initiate the measures they recommend and, normally, they give much weight to the wishes of the departments to whom the administration is entrusted and in which, very often, the proposals originated.

The influence of administrative departments in statute lawmaking does not end with the action of Congress upon legislative proposals. It has another inning when measures passed by Congress reach the President. At this stage are included not only measures sponsored by these departments but all bills passed by Congress which affect them in any manner. The clearance orders now in effect make it the duty of the Division of Legislative Reference of the Bureau of the Budget to analyze the provisions of all enrolled bills at once after final action by Congress and to get reports and recommendations from all departments interested in the subject matter. The Director of the Budget is then to make recommendations to the President for approval or disapproval of these bills, taking into account the views expressed by the interested departments.

The total influence of administrative departments upon the President in the performance of his duties in relation to legislation is at most times even greater than upon the action of Congress. Normally the departments formulate much of the legislation which the President recommends to Congress. They prepare first drafts of his messages and speeches endorsing this legislation. They utilize him to bring pressure upon congressional leaders when measures in which they are interested and which he has endorsed are apparently stalled or in danger of being altered in respects which the interested departments do not like. Finally, they influence his action in relation to the approval or disapproval of all bills passed by Congress.

The reasons why the departments exert such very great influence in statute lawmaking are basically two: (1) the fact that administration is such a large part of present-day government; and (2) the superior knowledge which administrators have in their special fields. It is a commonplace but true observation that a large part of all legislation is concerned with the structure or functioning of administrative departments and the creation or modification of administrative powers. It is also true that the administrators have much to contribute which is of value in connection with legislation. Members of Congress who have served long on committees concerned with particular governmental problems often become real specialists in these fields, quite well able to hold their own with any one. On any particular measure, however, few members of Congress can become as expert as able civil servants who devote most of their lives to a narrow specialty.

Besides these two major reasons for the great influence of administrators in statute lawmaking, some other factors merit mention. As always, influence in this connection depends to a very large extent upon personal relationships. Members of Congress come to know and have confidence in the executives and specialists of the administrative departments; moreover, many times they are obligated for favors and are very conscious of the advisability of maintaining good relations with those departments.

Being a congressman or a senator is now a full-time job, requiring practically continuous attendance in Washington, except during political campaigns. The life of the members of Congress and that of their families is in the capital and the longer they remain the more this becomes true. Inevitably they meet many persons in the administrative departments, socially and otherwise. They like life in Washington and come to feel themselves a part of the community. They also come to think as does Washington, and Washington is predominantly composed of individuals who work in the administrative departments.

Probably on the whole less important, but in the aggregate very real, are considerations of a political character. A great many members of Congress, particularly those who serve on committees to which most of the bills in which a given department is interested are referred, have succeeded in finding places in these departments for friends and constituents.[8] I am satisfied that in most cases the pressure for such appointments comes from the members of Congress and arises from the fact that they are bedeviled by constituents for whom they must find jobs. Being politicians, members of Congress know that favors must be returned and that there are dividends in working closely with administrative departments. On the part of the departments there is an even more keen realization of the need of maintaining good relations with the members of committees who control appropriations or pass upon their legislative proposals. Such relationships go a long way in explaining the influence which administrators have come to exert in statute lawmaking.

THE SITUATION IN THE STATES

There are great differences among the states with respect to the activities of administrative departments in relation to legislation. In all states a considerable number of bills introduced in the legislatures originate in administrative departments. The heads of these departments frequently appear before legislative committees to give their views on bills under consideration, including many measures with whose introduction these departments have had nothing to do. Probably more frequently than

[8] There is evidence that similar relationships are being developed with the major national private organizations in the fields in which departments operate. A considerable number of administrative departments have placed persons on their pay rolls whose appointment was particularly desired by the executives of these private organizations and whose principal function is to serve as liaison officers between the departments and these organizations.

in the national government administrators buttonhole state legislators on pending measures and perform much like private lobbyists. Many state departments also have very close relations with which they cooperate in their legislative programs. In some states, for instance New York, administrative departments seem to play quite as important a role in statute lawmaking as in the national government. Viewed in its totality, however, their influence in statute lawmaking is much smaller in the states than in the national government.

The reasons for this situation are fairly clear. While the national government has been free from political turnover for nearly a decade, shifts between parties and factions have been exceedingly rapid in most states. In many if not most states, changes of governors have meant well-nigh a complete switch in all important departmental positions. In only a few states has anything like a career civil service developed. Under such circumstances state administrators have been afraid to do anything which might lead to criticism and everything they propose is discounted as being political. The state legislators also typically do not remain in office nearly as long as members of Congress. The legislative sessions are short and most of the members do not live at the capital. State legislation is quite as much concerned with administrative matters as is that of the national government, if not even more so. All other factors making for great influence in statute lawmaking on the part of administrative departments, however, if not entirely absent, are less powerful in most state governments. As a career civil service is developed in the state governments, the influence of administrators in statute lawmaking may be expected to grow as it has in the national government. Similarly, long terms of governors, legislators, and the heads of administrative departments are conducive to greater influence upon legislation by these departments. The existence of a genuine civil service system and longer periods of official service seem to be the major reasons why such influence is much greater in some than in most states.

A considerable part of the more important state legislation of recent years has come from administrative departments of the national government, directly or indirectly. Sometimes this trend has taken the form of model bills prepared in Washington or adaptations thereof. More commonly it has had its origin in the requirements of federal laws, in suggestion by federal agencies, or in assistance extended by their representatives in the preparation of bills or amendments offered in state legislatures. Much of the participation of administrative departments of the national government in state legislation has been in fields in which federal financial aid is extended to the states. Some of it has resulted from leadership given by federal departments in particular fields of legislation, such as defense, the war on organized crime, and labor legislation. Where federal aid has been at stake, the state legislatures have complied with every suggestion, although grumbling. In other cases the state legislature has adopted the suggestions of national agencies only when these proposals appealed to it, but there has been little resentment of federal leadership.

SIGNIFICANCE

These developments have given the experts an influence in government heretofore unknown in this country. The public service has come into its own in legislation. Career public servants, specialists in their fields, along with academic social scientists serving government departments as consultants, have come to influence profoundly the legislative output of Congress.

Hence it follows that the functions of Congress can no longer be fully stated in terms of arriving at compromises between conflicting private interests. While apparently as yet little appreciated by the members of Congress themselves, their function has become, to a very considerable extent, passing judgment as the representatives of "the folks back home" upon the proposals of administrators. Congress, and to a lesser extent the state legislatures, are the medium in which a reconciliation must be effected between the points of view of the experts and the mass of citizens, quite as much as between the differing views of citizen groups.

ADVANTAGES AND DISADVANTAGES

The primary purpose of this paper is to call attention to an important development rather than to appraise it critically. It will not be inappropriate, however, to set forth some of its advantages and disadvantages.

The great gain from the closer relations that have prevailed in recent years between the administrative and legislative branches of the national government has lain in the utilization to the full of the special knowledge of the experts. Beyond question the point of view of administrators and specialists merits consideration in statute lawmaking. They are persons of ability and good judgment, unusually disinterested and objective in their attitude and incorruptibly devoted to the public welfare. They have much to contribute to statute lawmaking, perhaps more than any other element in our society.

A considerable part of the credit for the forward-looking legislation of recent years clearly belongs to the individuals in administrative departments who initiated much of this legislation. It is probable that at all times governmental experts will have a better understanding of fundamental needs than the general public and their proposals will be progressive, in the best sense of that term.

Yet some disadvantages and dangers must be recognized. Foremost is the danger that too much weight will be given to the recommendations of the administrator and the specialist. The limitations of the expert have often been set forth.[9] He is likely to have a disproportionate view of values, grossly overrating the importance of his specialty. He lives in a narrow, sheltered world, pretty much out of touch with reality. He does not understand the point of view of people outside of the government, and, as Bagehot pointed out as long ago as 1867, is often contemptuous of public opinion.

[9] Among others by H. J. Laski, "The Limitations of the Expert," 162 *Harper's* 101–110 (1930); Sir Cecil Thomas Carr, *Concerning English Administrative Law* (Columbia University Press, 1941).

To these limitations of experts as individuals are added considerations arising from the conditions under which they must do their work. As T. V. Smith and Richard L. Neuberger have brought out, one of the strongest features of our legislatures is the fact that all of the members are on a basis of equality, none of them owing their office to other members or having to answer to them for anything they may do. A very different situation prevails in the administrative departments. Within those departments there is a rigid hierarchy. Everybody is answerable to some higher up and in many departments no greater offense can be committed than to try to by-pass an immediate superior. Despite civil service laws, there is also a pronounced tendency toward inbreeding in the selection of administrative personnel. The academic degree received, the college attended, and the economic views held all play their part in filling the more important positions in at least some of the administrative departments of the national government and in the selection of consultants and advisers. To this must be added the insistence of the unions of federal employees upon promotion from within, which further tends toward the development of patterns of thought and action peculiar to a closely knit bureaucracy—the sort of situation to which David E. Lilienthal has applied the picturesque phrase of "a kind of Phi Beta Kappa Tammany Hall." [10]

SUGGESTIONS FOR IMPROVEMENTS

During the war it is probable that administrative departments will devote less attention to statute lawmaking than in recent years. The reason is that congressional legislation in wartime will be less important than executive action. Administrative departments will prepare far more executive orders and fewer congressional bills, although many little heralded departmental measures will still be presented to Congress—some of them very important.

Assuming as I do that our democratic form of life will survive,

[10] In "Management–Responsible or Dominant?" 1 *Public Administration Review* 390–392(1941).

statute lawmaking will again come into its own after the war. If it does, the role of the departments will be at least as important as it has been in the recent past. This is a safe prediction because, as J. M. Clark has said, "The logic of events is on the side of the expert; the job of governing a complex and technical economy cannot be done without his services."[11] If this conclusion be true, the advice that Clark gives is also sound: ". . . the answer is neither to get rid of the expert nor to surrender to him unconditionally but to devote some real effort to devising ways of keeping track of him. The methods of democracy must be adjusted to the job that has to be done, and this job now requires the expert."

Most important for gaining to the full the potential advantages of participation of administrative departments in the process of statute lawmaking while guarding against the dangers involved is to bring into the open the present-day role of these departments in this process. It needs to be recognized that administrative departments must interest themselves in statute lawmaking in this day and age. They should be encouraged to do so openly and aboveboard.

Research studies are badly needed to bring out all discoverable facts about the activities and influence of administrative departments in statute lawmaking. When the facts are better known, we are likely to have much more publicity about their current legislative activities. With the limelight of publicity turned upon these activities, there is much less danger of legislation which will be out of line with current needs and opinions.

Improvement of the functioning of administrative departments in relation to statute lawmaking will depend, in part, upon their policies. Their main objective should not be to get their bills through Congress or the state legislatures with the least expenditure of effort but to develop the best possible proposals and to give genuine assistance to legislatures in their consideration of these measures. In developing their proposals, they should realize that the departmental experts are not the fount of all wisdom

[11] "The Relation of Government to the Economy of the Future," 49 *Journal of Political Economy* 797–816, at 805 (1941).

and that public opinion needs to be given quite as much weight as technical perfection. To overcome the inevitable tendency toward narrowness and provincialism in administrative circles, much is to be said for the wide use of something like the British commissions of inquiry which allow persons from all sections of the country and from all interested groups to participate in the development of departmental legislative proposals. In our national government it is desirable to give field employees a voice in the preparation of such proposals and not merely the Washington staffs, as now appears to be common practice. Where the proposed legislation requires state cooperation, state administrators should likewise be consulted; and they clearly should be given a part in the preparation of legislation which is to be put through legislatures. Consultation with other interested departments should be continued but brought out into the open. These suggestions will mean, of course, longer consideration of legislative proposals within administrative circles and increased work devoted to their development. They should serve, however, to lessen the very real danger of a strong reaction against the legislation finally enacted and against all active participation of departments in statute lawmaking.

The functions of Congress in statute lawmaking have not been rendered any the less important by the increased participation of administrative departments in this process. Congress must sit in judgment upon their legislative proposals in much the same way as it does upon those originating with private interests. It will have to pass on their practicality and, above all, on their feasibility in the light of prevailing public opinion. As with private proposals, it will often have to work out compromises, less perfect but more enduring. It should neither shy away from departmental proposals nor merely rubber-stamp them. It should make the fullest possible use of administrative wisdom and the experts' special knowledge but should also make certain that all other interests have full opportunity to present their views and that they are given real consideration in legislative deliberations.

Extensive participation by administrative departments is an

important characteristic of statute lawmaking today. It deserves more attention than it has received from students of administration and legislation. It is here to stay, because it has become a necessary part of the efficient functioning of democratic government. The basic problem is how to make it a more effective instrument for an improved democracy.

8. EXECUTIVE ASSISTANCE IN THE LEGISLATIVE PROCESS

Carl R. Sapp

Although a great deal has been written on the functions of the President in the legislative process, relatively little has been said about the vital role which the executive departments and the Bureau of the Budget play in connection with these responsibilities of the Executive. Yet their part is important, since in most cases the President has neither the time nor the detailed knowledge to perform his duties with respect to legislative proposals on a purely individualistic basis. He must base his decisions to a large extent upon information and advice from subordinates who enjoy his confidence. This necessity is clear when it is realized that, from the standpoint of numbers, most acts of Congress relate to technical administrative matters or to the detailed methods of carrying out existing policy rather than to the establishment of basic policy itself. Even Congress bases most of its decisions upon recommendations of its committees and passes the vast majority of statutes by unanimous consent.

In considering the functions of the operating agencies and the Bureau of the Budget in connection with proposed legislation, it should be remembered that the President has a responsibility for assisting in the legislative process from the following major standpoints:

1. The Constitution requires that he "from time to time give to the Congress information of the state of the Union, and recommend to their consideration such measures as he shall judge necessary and expedient."

2. The Constitution also states that "the executive power shall be vested in a President." Thus he is responsible for the general management of the government and is obligated to assure orderliness and a minimum of duplication, conflict, and confusion in the executive agencies, and for that reason he must be concerned with the legislative recommendations which the executive agencies make to Congress.

3. The President has the power to approve or veto bill passed by Congress.

4. As a leader of his political party, the President is expected to lead in the formulation of its legislative program.

5. To carry out the spirit of the Budget and Accounting Act of 1921, which provides for a system of coordination and review of departmental appropriation requests before they are submitted to Congress, the President must consider the recommendations of the executive branch concerning legislation which would result in appropriation estimates or which involves budgetary questions.

Under the Budget and Accounting Act great progress has been made toward systematizing the President's consideration of budget estimates and proposed appropriating legislation. But consideration of other legislative proposals in the executive branch is not so regularized, and even the arrangements which do exist have not generally been taken seriously by students of public administration.

ASSISTANCE OF THE DEPARTMENTS

Government departments and agencies provide information and advice concerning proposed legislation to both the President and Congress. They do this by testifying at committee hearings, providing technical drafting service, initiating legislative proposals, and submitting written reports on pending bills. Most of their activities in this regard consist of preparing written reports on legislative proposals.

Each year the departments receive from committees and members of Congress hundreds of requests for reports and recommendations on proposed legislation. Such requests are made not only to ascertain the personal views of the department heads but also to obtain information which is available from the subject-matter specialists within the departments. The replies are thus reports from the government agencies as institutions in addition to being personal letters from the department heads.

Importance and Uses of Reports on Bills. Departmental reports on bills are one of the most important links between the legislative and executive branches. They require the most thoughtful attention of the officials who prepare them. Congress desires that such reports contain the most accurate, reliable, and objective information and recommendations which the executive branch can furnish. Not only does Congress desire complete and useful reports, but as the major policy-forming organism in our government, it is entitled to receive them. This is in the interest of our system of government. Moreover, if departmental reports are poorly constructed, lack essential substance and information, are vague, draw unsupported conclusions, or are otherwise deficient, they not only fail to serve their purpose but also reflect adversely upon the executive agencies in which they originate.

Reports from the departments are often printed in the committee reports, the hearings, or the *Congressional Record.* Thus they frequently become a part of the printed record of the legislative process leading up to enactment. Occasionally situations arise in the administration or interpretation of a statute when the contents of a departmental report may assist in clarifying a confused point.

A legislative report from an executive agency usually begins with a concise statement of the purpose and principal provisions of the bill under discussion, for background and reference purposes. It sometime includes references to previous reports and bills on the same subject. A large portion of the report then discusses the policy and program phases of the proposal. Any amendments suggested by the department are set forth and explained. The financial aspects of the bill are ordinarily considered. Except in rare instances, the report concludes with the specific recommendation of the department as to whether the bill should be passed. The advice of the Bureau of the Budget as to the relationship of the bill or recommendation to the program of the President is included, usually at the end of the report.

How Reports Are Prepared. Obviously, it is often impossible for a department head personally to sift out the information available in his agency, discuss all the pertinent questions with the subject-matter specialists, and see that this information is written up in a form which will be most helpful to Congress. Much of that work is ordinarily assigned to a definite unit or person in the department in order that the reports which are prepared will contain, so far as practicable, the most valuable, accurate, and complete information which is in the possession of the department concerned. In some agencies the budget office performs this function. In others the responsibility is lodged in the legal office. In still others it is assigned to an official in the immediate office of the department head or to a departmental committee. There can be no definite standard as to which office should do this work. That depends upon the nature of the organization's programs and the preferences of its head. The important point is that a good job be done in coordinating all interests—operating, legal, personnel, budgetary, etc.—and there are logical reasons for the performance of this work by any one or more of these groups.

The designated office or individual (hereafter referred to as the "reporting unit") usually receives from the congressional committees and the Bureau of the Budget requests for reports on proposed legislation and assigns the requests to the appropriate subject-matter specialists within the department for preparation of drafts of reports. If no one agency in the department is appropriate in particular instances, the reporting unit obtains the comments of all the agencies involved and then prepares drafts of reports which include the information obtained from the various agencies. The reporting unit then reviews these proposed reports from the standpoints of administrative and general policy implications, clarity, completeness, etc., and clears them with the interested bureaus and appropriate staff offices. If there are differences of opinion, through this mechanism an attempt is made to get agreement between the agencies involved; if agreement cannot be obtained, the different viewpoints are presented to the department head for decision. In addition, the reporting unit provides the department head with background information concerning previous legislative proposals on the same subjects, the disposition of recommendations made on similar measures, and other factors. One of the major responsibilities of the reporting unit is to watch for major policy questions and to point them out for the special consideration of the department head when the reports are reviewed. Moreover, the reporting unit operates as a contact medium with the Bureau of the Budget and the congressional committees in order to assist them in obtaining all desired information from the department, and it may also provide a legislative-information service to department officials (a law enacted in 1895 [44 USC 215] requires that each agency review the *Congressional Record* daily).

Appraisal of Departmental Assistance. Departmental assistance in the consideration of proposed legislation has been the subject of relatively little discussion. From time to time, however, members of Congress have expressed concern at the tendency of committees to postpone action on bills until reports have been received from the departments. One Congressman stated, "I was a little surprised when I came to Congress; I could not get a bill enacted or even considered until I had a report from the department, and sometimes it was 6 months before they got it." [1] Some members also apparently feel that the recommendations of the departments are given more consideration than is proper. This thought was expressed by one Representative as follows: "The Congress has consistently depended upon the governmental departments to advise what course to pursue before giving serious consideration to legislation referred to committees. The practice has grown and grown to such an extent that it is almost an impossibility to pass a proposal through both Houses without the acquiescence of the executive department." [2]

These expressions, and others like them, do not necessarily imply criticism of the departments but, instead, emphasize the need for stronger committee staffs to enable Congress to have

[1] *Hearings before House Civil Service Committee Pursuant to H. Res. 16, 78th Congress,* p. 371.

[2] *Hearings before Joint Committee on Organization of Congress, 1945, 79th Congress,* pp. 262–63.

the technical information necessary to develop its own opinion on governmental issues rather than to depend upon the advice of executive agencies and outside groups. There is now sometimes a tendency to depend upon the departments for such advice when it is difficult to make a decision, since they are ordinarily more objective, from the standpoint of the nation as a whole, than the various special-interest groups. If the committee staffs were strengthened, the departmental reports would, of course, continue to be valuable and could be considered thoroughly together with information and recommendations which committees receive from other sources. Mr. Charles F. Boots, Senate legislative counsel, summed up the value of departmental reports to Congress in this fashion:

> A lot of proposed legislation that comes down here is the outgrowth of long study by administrative agencies over a long period, possibly years; it is the result of an evolutionary process that would be particularly difficult to handle if there were a rule that all legislation had to originate, as it were, with Congress. And of course it needs no statement on my part that the Congress is under no obligation at all to accept that proposed legislation, either in form or in substance, and perhaps bills that have originated in the executive departments should be subjected to particularly careful scrutiny, having in mind that the administrators of the law might have an over-zealous approach to the subject.[3]

The legitimate assistance of executive agencies in the consideration of proposed legislation should not be confused with "lobbying." Most of the departmental legislative activities are in response to congressional requests. Although there may be exceptional cases when irresponsible departmental officials overstep their rightful functions and try to bring pressure upon Congress, probably more agencies are so afraid of the "lobbying" charge that they fail to provide Congress with information it would welcome and find helpful.

[3] *Ibid.*, p. 461.

ASSISTANCE BY THE BUREAU OF THE BUDGET

Why the Bureau Is Involved. Obviously the Bureau of the Budget is concerned with appropriating legislation. But why should it have anything to do with substantive legislation? The answer is that most substantive legislation involves budgetary questions. It generally authorizes appropriations, either specifically or inferentially. Many substantive laws actually specify amounts of money, and although these amounts are usually ceilings, they are often construed as indications of congressional intent regarding the size of the appropriations to be made. Some laws, such as those authorizing grants to states, include provisions which govern the use of funds by setting up formulas to be used in incurring obligations. Other legislation, while not authorizing appropriations as such, enables the executive departments to enter into contracts which bind the government to practically the same extent as appropriations. Some laws authorize government agencies to borrow money that is then used for such purposes as subsidies or loans. Enabling legislation may also contain limitations on the expenditures which may be made for various purposes in carrying out a program. Frequently legislation limits the amounts which may be used for administrative expenses. Several laws make permanent appropriations which become available without being renewed periodically. Other legislation authorizes trust funds to be set up, without specific appropriation, for the expenditure of money deposited by persons or firms that cooperate with the government in various activities. Occasionally laws are passed which provide for revolving funds that can be used and replenished repeatedly without being appropriated each time.

Such substantive legislation is as truly budgetary in character as the annual appropriation acts. In effect, it limits the scope of questions that have to be decided at the time the appropriating legislation is considered. The budget is a program of work which must be fitted into the pattern formed by substantive law. Thus budgetary planning involves authorizing, as well as appropriating legislation.

Moreover, there is a close relationship between budgetary problems and those of a general administrative nature. This is shown by the recent trend toward combining budgetary and administrative-management work. Many legislative proposals that are not strictly financial have management implications. Legislators are confronted with such questions as: "Is the objective of this bill carefully defined and clearly limited in relation to existing related legislation?" "What should be the basic method of administration and operation?" "Does the bill provide the necessary authorities for practical, efficient administration?" "Does it propose a basic organizational pattern which is simple but adequate?" "Does it contain provisions which would result in unnecessary red tape?" There are also questions relating to such specific matters as administrative promotion, overtime pay, personnel ceilings, competitive purchasing, and job classification. Although many of these problems are interrelated and must have coordinated study by the offices concerned with the specific subjects, all of them have budgetary and administrative-management aspects.

In recognition of this relationship of substantive legislation to budgetary administration, the Bureau of the Budget, at the direction of the President, has issued a circular requiring all departments and agencies to submit each of their reports and recommendations concerning proposed legislation to that bureau for advice as to the relationship of the proposed legislation and the reports thereon to the program of the President. The departments are required to include a statement of the advice from the Bureau of the Budget in each report to Congress on such proposed legislation.[4]

History of the Central Clearance Procedure. The Budget and Accounting Act of 1921 prohibited the departments from submitting directly to Congress their requests for appropriations, but it did not prohibit them from submitting recommendations on proposed substantive legislation which, although not actually appropriating money, to carry out its provisions. It was soon

[4] See Budget Circular No. A-19 (August 1, 1944), as amended.

realized that the new budgetary system was thus not preventing the departments from making indirect requests for funds and that, as a result, the effects of the budget procedure were being limited. General Charles G. Dawes, the first director of the Bureau of the Budget, stated in his report on the first year of the Budget Bureau that it became the practice of the chairman of the House committee on appropriations to refer proposed legislation involving subsequent appropriation of funds to the Bureau of the Budget for information as to the relation of such proposals to the policy of the President.

It seemed desirable to clarify this situation and to give the President control over all departmental requests involving subsequent appropriations. Early in General Dawes' term of office, therefore, Budget Circular No. 49 was issued requiring that all departments submit to the Bureau of the Budget, for advice as to their relationship to the President's program, all reports which they planned to send to Congress on proposed legislation authorizing additional appropriations. This order stated that the Bureau of the Budget would clear each case with the President and required the departments to pass on to Congress the advice which they received from the bureau. In 1929 the order was amended so as (1) to exempt from the clearance procedure the reports on private-relief measures and reports making recommendations against legislative proposals and (2) to remove the specific requirement that the Bureau of the Budget clear all cases with the President personally.

In 1934 the legislative-clearance function was expanded to require the departments to submit legislative reports dealing with financial matters to the Bureau of the Budget and those dealing with policy matters to the National Emergency Council. This requirement applied to unfavorable as well as favorable reports. Apparently because confusion arose regarding the meanings of "financial" and "policy," the President in 1935 directed (Budget Circular No. 336) that all reports on legislation be submitted to the Bureau of the Budget, which would clear those dealing with "financial" matters, then submit to the National Emergency Council for clearance those relating to "policy" matters.

In 1937 the President transferred to the Bureau of the Budget the clearance function on all legislative reports on public bills, whether involving appropriations or not, and expanded the procedure to include recommendations made in the course of testimony before congressional committees (Budget Circular No. 344). The clearance procedure was expanded in 1942 to include reports and testimony on private-relief legislation (Budget Circular No. 390). The arrangement was again changed in 1944 to include recommendations made "in an annual or special report" (Budget Circular No. A-19, Revised).

How the Bureau of the Budget Performs Its Clearance Function. The Bureau of the Budget now reviews proposed departmental legislative reports not only from the standpoint of the President's financial program but also from the standpoints of over-all policy, program and administrative planning, and coordination of interdepartmental and other relationships.[5]

In its consideration of proposed legislative recommendations from the departments and agencies, the Bureau of the Budget is confronted with various types of problems. There is usually the basic question as to what effect the enactment of the proposed legislation would have on the economic and social welfare of the nation and groups of its citizens, or what its relation is, from political and other standpoints, to the policy of the President. Even if the objective of the bill is deemed desirable, the bureau must consider whether the contemplated program would be worth the money it would cost. Consideration of this question involves determination as to the probable size of the program, how long it would need to remain in effect, what its benefits would be, and how the contemplated expenditures would relate to the over-all fiscal situation of the government and general economic conditions in the entire country.

Legislative proposals often relate to the operations of more than one department. Occasionally there are conflicts between the recommendations of the departments. In the interest of good

[5] For a statement of the functions and duties of the legislative reference division, which performs most of this work in the bureau, *see Hearings before the House Committee on Civil Service Pursuant to H. Res. 16, 78th Congress,* p. 360.

administration the Bureau of the Budget takes the leadership in trying to get agreement among the departments on controversial issues and, in cases where the differences of opinion cannot be resolved, submits to the President an analysis of the situation and a statement of the specific contentions of the departments involved.

In performing its functions concerning proposed legislation, the legislative reference division makes considerable use of the other divisions of the Bureau of the Budget. It uses particularly the division of estimates, whose examiners are familiar with the financial and other problems in the departments submitting the reports. For coordinating purposes the legislative reference division also frequently requests comments from other interested departments.

In many cases the Bureau of the Budget does not find it necessary to submit a legislative proposal or report directly to the President in order to be able to advise the department as to the relationship of the proposal or report to the President's program. Sometimes the bureau can ascertain this information by examination of previous correspondence on the subject. In other cases the President has already indicated his position on the question to the satisfaction of the bureau through messages to Congress, memorandums to the Bureau of the Budget, statements during personal conversations with the budget director, or other indications of policy which are available to the bureau. In some instances, however, an important question of public policy or a question involving the jurisdiction of two or more departments is referred directly to the President for a decision.

After ascertaining to its satisfaction the nature of the President's policy regarding a proposal, the Bureau of the Budget may advise the submitting department in any one of several ways. In most instances it simply states that there is no objection to the submission of the report to the congressional committee. Occasionally, however, it has not been feasible to obtain information concerning the President's position, or perhaps the President has not yet decided what his position will be. In such cases the bureau may advise the department that there is no objection to submission of the report with the understanding that no commitment will thereby be made regarding relationship of the proposal to the program of the President. Or in such instances it may simply state that there is no objection to submission of such report as the department may deem appropriate. That advice is occasionally followed by a statement which inferentially gives the bureau's attitude toward the matter. In rare instances the bureau states that enactment of the bill would be in accord with the program of the President, thus making it clear that the President is positively supporting the bill. In other occasional instances the bureau states that enactment of the proposed legislation would not be in conflict with the program of the President.

Frequently the Bureau of the Budget advises that enactment of the bill would not be in accord with the program of the President. From time to time such advice is qualified by the statement that such legislation would not be in accord "at this time" or "at least at this time." In some cases this type of advice is given in connection with a bill which the interested department opposes. But difficulty arises when the department has submitted to the Bureau of the Budget, for clearance, a proposed report which recommends passage of a legislative proposal. In such cases the department has several choices. It may discuss the matter further with the Bureau of the Budget. The department head, of course, has the privilege of appealing to the President, but many of these reports discuss questions which the department head might not consider important enough to carry to the President personally. There is nothing to prohibit the department from submitting a favorable report to Congress together with the adverse-clearance advice received from the Bureau of the Budget, but this indicates publicly a difference of opinion between the President and a member of his Cabinet and is, therefore, usually considered in bad taste or undesirable for other reasons. In many, if not most, such cases the department revises its report so as to include all the pertinent information and a statement of the bureau's advice, but to avoid making any recommendation specifically in favor of the bill. In very rare instances the Bureau of the Budget advises not only that the bill would not be in accord with the President's program but also that the report itself would not be in accord. Such advice presents the department with a problem which is even more difficult than when the bureau advises only that the bill is not in accord. In recent years the bureau has sometimes said "The proposed legislation should not be considered as being in accord with the program of the President," or "It is not believed that the proposed legislation should be considered as being in accord with the program of the President." Such phrases seem to imply that the Bureau has not had an opportunity to determine definitely the President's position but that it has reason to believe his policy is thus and so. These cases make the departments' problem even more difficult.

Budget Bureau Clearance Procedure—Good or Bad? There has been relatively little discussion among persons interested in political science and public administration as to whether or not the Budget Bureau clearance procedure is desirable. This is probably because the requirement for submitting all reports on proposed legislation to the bureau is rather new, and relatively few persons are familiar with the procedure and its implications. Both laudatory and critical comments have been made, however.

The procedure sometimes tends to discourage the departments from submitting to Congress complete statements of their views, since the departments naturally hesitate to recommend bills which, according to advice from the Bureau of the Budget, the President opposes. Even though the clearance procedure does not prohibit departments from submitting favorable reports in such instances, so long as the reports include the Budget Bureau's advice, nevertheless in practice, as pointed out earlier, the departments usually revise their reports so that their recommendations will not contradict the President's policy as expressed by the Bureau of the Budget. At a hearing in 1939 Mr. Daniel Bell, then acting director of the Bureau of the Budget, in response to a question as to how that bureau could prevent a departmental legislative proposal from reaching Congress, replied, "We can tell the head of a department who suggests the legislation that it is not in accord with the President's program." But then he went on to say, "I cannot keep bills from being introduced, and I do not think I could keep anyone from informally contacting Members of Congress."[6] Later Mr. F. J. Bailey, an assistant director of the bureau, said, "We never tell a department what to say in a report."[7]

Another point is that the Bureau of the Budget usually does not inform the departments as to why a legislative proposal is not in accord with the program of the President. If the bureau could give the reasons for the President's decisions, not only would the additional information be of value to Congress, but in some cases it might actually change the attitude of the department involved. Such reasons are given by the Bureau of the Budget in some cases.

There have been doubts as to whether the Bureau of the Budget interprets the President's policy correctly in every case. As mentioned earlier, the bureau does not always submit a legislative proposal or report directly to the President for his decision but sometimes relies upon his general statements of policy or some other indication as a basis for determining his views. There is always some danger that the bureau, in order to save the time of the President, will make a decision which he personally would not make if he were fully advised of all the departments concerning legislative proposals, "I must ascer- of the bureau, made this clear when he said that, in advising the departments concerning legislative proposals, "I must ascertain their relationship to the program of the President, either by acting on my own responsibility, or by taking them to the President and discussing them with him."[8]

[6] *House Hearings on 1940 Treasury Department Appropriation Bill,* pp. 946–47.

[7] *Hearings before House Civil Service Committee Pursuant to H. Res. 16, 78th Congress,* p. 366.

[8] *House Hearings on 1940 Treasury Department Appropriation Bill,* p. 497.

Fear has also been expressed that, even when the Bureau of the Budget submits a proposal or report directly to the President for a decision, it may fail to give him a complete understanding of the facts in the same way that the proponents of the bill would. One member of Congress has indicated his feeling that "on one piece of legislation . . . either the conclusion as to its workability or advisability of the legislation was warped, or . . . no adequate consideration was given to the hearings, the committee reports or the debates."[9] On the other hand, Assistant Director Bailey has stated, "We try to be faithful in presenting to the President both sides of the question —all sides of the question."[10]

One Congressman has expressed regret that the committees do not have all the information which the Bureau of the Budget obtains during its clearance process. He stated, "It strikes me that actually, though, if I wanted to have a basis for my opinion I would have to have three things, the two conflicting opinions and your report as to where they ought to flux, and I would have something to work on."[11] It is true that, in some cases where there is an interdepartmental controversy, the congressional committees do not have before them all the contentions of the departments both opposing and favoring a proposal. But it would be difficult in some such instances for this information to be made available to the committees, since much of it arises from informal discussions with the Bureau of the Budget and is not written down so that it can be referred to.

Occasionally the present clearance procedure may discourage the President from utilizing his Cabinet to the fullest extent. Some people claim that legislative recommendations could be coordinated and reviewed from a policy standpoint at the President's Cabinet meetings. Perhaps the Cabinet could perform this function partially. It is doubtful, however, whether Cabinet members would have the time or specific knowledge necessary

[9] *Hearings before House Civil Service Committee Pursuant to H. Res. 16 78th Congress,* pp. 363–64.
[10] *Ibid.,* p. 366.
[11] *Ibid.,* p. 373.

for coordination and review of the multitude of relatively minor administrative questions, many of them highly technical—which frequently is the real reason Congress asks for review of proposals by administrative officials.

There is danger that the Bureau of the Budget, because of the nature of its general responsibilities, may not always give enough weight to the human elements of legislative proposals and may think primarily of administrative and financial phases. It is not certain that the bureau is sufficiently responsive to special-interest groups, whatever may be the evils of such groups, since they do come as near as anything we have, when considered together, to a cross-section of public opinion. The functional departments which report to the bureau, however, are usually very much aware of the sentiment of the interest groups concerned.

Whatever may be the shortcomings of the clearance procedure, by and large it works fairly well and serves useful purposes. It provides for review of proposed legislation and reports by an agency which has an over-all viewpoint rather than the specialized and often one-sided outlook of a functional department with a "burning heart" for pet proposals. Assistant Director Bailey has stated that it "acquires information that puts it in a position to make a fair appraisal of the legislative proposal, not because of arrogating to itself any great amount of wisdom, but simply because of its favorable opportunity to cross-line the views of all the agencies concerned with a proposal. A person of mediocre ability who is acquainted with all angles of a proposal is better qualified to pass upon it than is one of large ability who knows and is concerned with only one angle of it."[12] Frequently the Bureau of the Budget is in a position to correct apparent misunderstandings of one department concerning the relation of a legislative proposal to the problems of other departments.

The review of departmental reports on bills pending in Congress also assists the Bureau of the Budget in doing a good job

[12] *Ibid.*, pp. 367–78.

of reporting to the President after a bill has been passed by Congress. The bureau has stated that "because of the fact that we have to act on enrolled bills sent to us by the President, that previous operation, the clearance procedure on the same legislation, is highly important and valuable to enable us to handle the enrolled bill action."[13] This is particularly true when it is realized that the President has only ten days, exclusive of Sundays, to decide whether to approve or veto a bill.

EXECUTIVE CONSIDERATION OF ENROLLED ENACTMENTS

Obviously the President must rely upon the appropriate executive departments and the Bureau of the Budget for a large portion of the information which he uses in deciding whether to approve or veto "enrolled enactments" or, as they are often called, "enrolled bills" (proposed legislation which has been passed by Congress and is pending for presidential approval or disapproval). The Bureau of the Budget has issued, by direction of the President, Budget Circular A-9 (similar to a previous circular), which sets forth the procedure for obtaining information and recommendations from the departments on such bills. Because of the constitutional limitation on the time available for consideration of enrolled bills by the President, departmental reports on such enactments are given priority over practically all other types of business and are handled with the utmost dispatch by all concerned. Within the departments the examination of such bills is facilitated through the same mechanism as has been discussed earlier in this article in connection with reports to Congress and the Bureau of the Budget on measures pending in Congress.

The departmental reports to the Bureau of the Budget on enrolled enactments ordinarily include statements of the purposes and provisions of the legislation, the effects which it would have upon the programs of the department, its budgetary aspects, and any other background information which may be of value at that stage, ending with a recommendation for ap-

[13] *Ibid.*, p. 363.

proval or disapproval of the measure. If disapproval is recommended, a draft of a proposed veto message, for consideration by the President, must accompany the department's report.

The legislative reference division obtains such reports not only from all the departments and agencies concerned but also from the appropriate officials in the Bureau of the Budget itself. That division then weaves the information so obtained into reports to be forwarded to the President by the director of the bureau. These reports usually include a summary of the bill, the recommendations of the departments concerned, and the recommendations of the Bureau of the Budget. Thus the President can utilize all the resources at his command in the review of enrolled bills, and his decisions are, therefore, much more than one man's opinion.

CONCLUSION

The activities of the executive branch, particularly below the presidential level, in the legislative process are an important and fertile field for further study. There seems to be general agreement with the thought that, because of its administrative experience and technical knowledge, the executive branch can provide real assistance to the legislative branch during the consideration of proposed legislation, and that the departments and the Bureau of the Budget can greatly help the President in deciding whether to approve or veto bills. Many things can probably be done to improve the assistance of the executive branch in the legislative process, from the standpoints of both Congress and the executive agencies. That objective will be attained only if the two branches of government have a respectful, cooperative, and helpful attitude toward each other.

V. The Courts, The Bureaucracy, and Judicial Review

EDITORIAL NOTE. Though it is frequently overlooked, the judicial aspect of bureaucracy is one of the most important. Administrative adjudication has developed because of government regulation, and the entry of government into welfare fields. This requires extensive and flexible adjudication of controversies arising in relation to the law and administrative action. The volume of administrative adjudication far exceeds that handled by the regular judiciary. It is important that some degree of judicial review be maintained if our system of supremacy of law is to have any meaning. The following selections illustrate the dimensions of this problem.

9. THE RIGHT TO JUDICIAL REVIEW

Louis L. Jaffe

THE ROLE OF JUDICIAL REVIEW

The availability of judicial review is the necessary condition, psychologically if not logically, of a system of administrative power which purports to be legitimate, or legally valid. Except for that uncertain ambit of powers directly granted to the Presidency by the Constitution, administrative power is delegated by a representative legislature to the President, to his administration, and to the so-called independent agencies. These delegations may be exceptionally broad and may, indeed should, be taken to grant enormous room for the improvisation and consolidation of policy; but unless we are to abandon the premise that parliamentary grant is an expression of popular consent to the exercise of power, a delegation of power implies some limit. Action beyond that limit is not legitimate. Certain theorists resent any emphasis on the notion of limit. Administration is to them the prime, perhaps only, creative political matrix in a world which badly needs political construction, and they will insist that the administrative hierarchy is itself the most representative of government organs. It is argued that administration properly organized produces within itself the most highly articulated, the most highly representative political creations. Paul Appleby has stated the position eloquently:

> With the growth of knowledge, science, and public expectations, the principal development of government has been in the strictly executive field. . . .
>
> . . . . The administrative search for morality is a search for appropriate ways to serve the popular will in action. . . .
>
> However unclear the distinction between the juridic and the executive functions and processes, it seems at least more illuminating and relevant now to search for it than to go on simply defining administration as the more specific formulation of the more general legislative formulations or to continue to build general administrative thinking around the favorite fictions of legal distinction, "quasi-legislative" and "quasi-judicial."[1]

There is undoubtedly a sharp problem here. We do need political and administrative invention; administration is representative and creative in ways that are true neither of courts nor of legislatures. The day-to-day thrashing out of problems in the cockpit of action brings desire and understanding into a highly charged proximity. And there is a quite remarkably flexible and comprehensive representation of interests in our administrative organs and procedure. It is quite obvious that these desirable creative elements are only spasmodically and faintly present in the isolated lawsuit which may from time to time intervene in the administrative process. And, as has been pointed out by

[1] APPLEBY, MORALITY AND ADMINISTRATION IN DEMOCRATIC GOVERNMENT 81–82 (1952).

very distinguished political and legal philosophers, the lofty intrusion of the judiciary may chill creative responsibility. "Not to make decisions that others should make," says Chester Barnard in a much-quoted passage, "is to preserve morale, to develop competence, to fix responsibility, and to *preserve authority*."[2]

But I nevertheless insist that the availability of judicial review is, in our system and under our tradition, the necessary premise of legal validity. It is no doubt logically possible for the immediate possessor of power to keep within imposed limits. For the most part he does so, and may indeed be very eager to do so; and furthermore, in the vast hierarchy of a modern administration, there is always the possibility of appeal to and rectification by a higher level within the hierarchy. Yet there is in our society a profound, tradition-taught reliance on the courts as the ultimate guardian and assurance of the limits set upon executive power by the constitutions and legislatures. It is true that this feeling, at least in its explicit modern form, is a heritage of the seventeenth-century English revolutions and of the laissez-faire economy which followed. There were a few years—from 1616 to 1643—when the Stuarts and the royal lawyers led by Bacon asserted that the King's officers were not answerable to the common-law courts but only to the King's Council. This was part of what was regarded as an attempt to set up an absolute nonparliamentary executive. When Lord Holt finally established in 1700 the power to review official action by certiorari and mandamus his decision was simply one aspect of the limits set upon monarchy. These events ushered in a long, leisurely century of government by justices of the peace and relative quiescence of central authority. The administrative activities of the justices operated within well-defined areas: laws relating to the poor, to liquor licensing, to apprentices, and to game protection, and to the levy of rates to support these minimum functions. The core of administration itself was thus made judicial; its control by the judges at Westminster was thoroughly acceptable

[2] Barnard, The Functions of the Executive 194 (1938). (Emphasis added.)

and workable. This was the situation and the tradition which we inherited in colonial times and which we carried over more or less intact into the states and the nation. Our Revolution emphasized once more the themes of a limited government and a limited executive.

It will be contended that this tradition is no longer relevant. Our government is committed to objects which demand creative open-ended power. The administration is not the remnant of an alien royalty, but the most intimate and complete mirror of our people. Judicial review is accordingly unfit by temperament, equipment, and resources to the function of control; it is a distortion of effective patterns of responsibility; it is unnecessary for the protection of the governed. In recent years, indeed, the English judiciary has sometimes seemed to accept a theory of its futility and irrelevance. It has fallen into a half-hearted, off-again-on-again performance of judicial review. The English administration has become the dominant committee of an "omnipotent" Parliament, and against this powerful law-making machine the little engines of mandamus and certiorari perhaps have seemed obsolete and pathetic. For a time during the New Deal, our courts, belabored for their hostility to administration (and quite correctly belabored), appeared to yield somewhat to the arguments for executive autonomy and omnipotence. But the conservative interest in this country showed more elasticity, more vigor and self-assurance; the courts, backed by a written Constitution, recovered from their sense of guilty usurpation, and in these latter days even the New Deal liberals have rushed to the defense and reinvigoration of judicial review.

Why then, is judicial review not so obsolete as the eulogists of public administration would have it? What is the flaw in their argument? Basically the flaw is as patent, as obvious, as simply stated as an old saw. We may grant that power is benign and without it we can do nothing. But it is also malign, fearsome, hateful, and dangerous. This multilateral character it shares with all things conceived and acted out by man. Even if we grant, and I do, the magnificent accomplishment of the New Deal, we cannot forget that our age has produced elsewhere, and even on occasion in our own country, the most monstrous expressions of administrative power. The completely representative administration is a professional mirage, whether we look to actual administrations (even the very good ones) or resort to more abstract inquiry. There is presently a shocked discovery of the so-called "industry oriented" agency, the agency thought to be the "captive" of one of the interests which it should balance. There is something slightly absurd about this discovery. From time immemorial, agencies have represented some constituencies more than others. Those who accuse the Interstate Commerce Commission of being "railroad oriented" are often the same persons who accepted labor domination of the National Labor Relations Board as a beneficent fact of nature. But I would insist that this phenomenon is not a perverse rejection of the ideal. It is, I think, a necessary condition of government. The notion of complete representativeness is an illusion, a version of nirvana. It does not exist, because it cannot. Representation means organized purpose, and at one time no more than a fraction of the potential infinity of organized purposes are in being. Policy means choice, decision, direction; and if policy is to have any stability or weight, any creative drive, it will almost inevitably be a choice of one interest over others. Administration, then, as the active principle of choosing, of preferring (be it for the most part wisely, fairly, kindly) has in it the inherent power to hurt, to awaken resentment, to stir the sense of injustice. By its very nature, because it is challenged to hammer out policy against opposition, it is driven almost inevitably to seek allies and to provide cement for its alliances. This is manifested, for example, in *Brannan* v. *Stark*,[3] in which it was claimed that the Department of Agriculture had given advantages in excess of statutory authority to the dominant milk co-operatives.

From the point of view of an agency, the question of the legitimacy of its action is secondary to that of the positive solution of a problem. It is for this reason that we, in common with nearly all of the Western countries, have concluded that the

[3] 342 U.S. 451 (1952).

maintenance of legitimacy requires a judicial body independent of the active administration. In this connection French experience is instructive. In the thinking of 1789 the separation of powers was deemed to require that the administration's actions be completely free of control or question by the regular judiciary. The rectification of administrative excess was the task of higher administrative echelons. But by 1870 there had evolved within the administration an autonomous court, a section of the *Conseil d'Etat* completely judicialized in spiirt and procedure. This court, not hindered as are some courts by a guilty sense of intruding in matters outside of their experience, subjects the administration to an intensive scrutiny which reaches down much deeper into the merits than most of our courts would think proper.

The guarantee of legality by an organ independent of the executive is one of the profoundest, most pervasive premises of our system. Indeed I would venture to say that it is the very condition which makes possible, which makes so acceptable, the wide freedom of our administrative system, and gives it its remarkable vitality and flexibility. It is, of course, true that the agencies make positive contributions to the richness and *ambiance* of our life, which quite clearly the courts could not make. It is also true that the good public servant is devoted to the law. But I feel that in the context these considerations are peripheral. They have to do with the spirit in which judicial review should be exercised but not with the question whether there shall be review. It is clear that the country looks, and looks with good reason, not to the agencies, but to the courts for its ultimate protection against executive abuse. The need for judicial protection has undoubtedly varied and the risks of judicial sabotage under the guise of protection are considerable. But we are dealing with basic institutions and basic attitudes; we must take the bad with the good, the fortuitous with the exigent, the trivial with the necessary. We are dealing here not with what might be, but with what are in fact, the psychological assumptions which sustain cohesion and security.

Furthermore, there is a deep wisdom in this division of function. We have quoted Chester Barnard to the point that not to make decisions that others should make preserves morale, develops competence, and fixes responsibility. Does this argue against judicial intrusion? Yes, if the judiciary forgets its role and tries to run the show. No, if it limits itself to the question of illegality or arbitrariness. Even if we admit that the line between the two cannot be drawn with a ruler, it distinguishes attitudes and tasks. And I think that in the end the administration itself is the gainer. The frightened, timid, unenterprising administrator may hide behind judicial negatives. But the positive and conscientious administrator will be freed from an obsessive preoccupation with the limits of his power. And, since there is a forum in which his alleged excesses may be adjudicated, he has a ready and persuasive answer to claims of usurpation. Anyone familiar with modern delegations knows that there is a large area of legitimate doubt and dispute. Within that area the good administrator's leverage is enhanced and his conscience justifiably eased if he does not have the last word on legality.

But it will be said, finally, that judicial review is not an effective instrument of supervision and control.

> Judicial review is too occasional and cursory, and is exercised from too remote a point, to supply an adequate corrective for arbitrary administration of economic controls. Moreover, unless applied only at the periphery it runs counter to the basic idea of delegation of responsibility to administrative agents.[4]

These words contain a great measure of truth but they are not an argument against judicial review. We must admit that within the area of validity there is great room for corruption, favoritism, inefficiency, and irresponsibility. The courts may occasionally correct even such lapses but they are on the whole incapable of providing a constant check to bad administration or a positive spur to creative administration. This is the area of discretion and of policy making and it is not for the courts. The objectives

[4] REDFORD, ADMINISTRATION OF NATIONAL ECONOMIC CONTROL 346 (1952).

of a good administration must be achieved primarily within the organization itself. But it is in no way inconsistent with the significant role allotted to the courts. This function may be patently exercised only spasmodically but its availability is a constant reminder to the administrator and a constant source of assurance and security to the citizen.

Yet, before leaving the subject with this rather over-precise dichotomy which assigns validity to the judiciary and policy to the administration, I would say a word by way of caveat and qualification. In the hands of imaginative, resourceful, and discreet judges the fashioning of limits is not confined to mere prohibition, to humdrum, journeyman signs, "Smoking prohibited" or "Do not walk on the grass." Questions of power arise in the context of an already developed complex of policy; they demand answers—or at least give room for answers—which may have a propulsive, a co-ordinating effect. I have said in the hands of "discreet" judges. A discreet judge is one who constantly is aware and respectful of the limits of his role. He feels free only in a rarely appropriate occasion to make a positive contribution toward the fulfillment of statutory objectives. He should, even then, make it in such a way that the administration, the senior partner in this area, can eventually write off as much of it as seems impertinent or unworkable. I am adverse to a legal philosophy which insists on completely rigid roles, which stifles and discourages creative expression and interchange between the judges and the executive. By its nature the quest for legality reaches into the area of policy; to attempt or to pretend to draw the distinction with complete logical precision, and without regard to the creative impulses at all levels of authority, leads to a certain cynicism and frustration in which judicial review is seen either as an empty formality or as a usurpation of power masked by lying phrases.

I do not wish to assert the proposition that because important individual interests are at stake judicial review is an invariable requirement. The protection which it effects for some may, in certain situations, reduce the more general protection. This may conceivably be true of judicial review of workmen's-compensation awards. The desiderata in a system of compensation are quick payment and the reduction of administrative expense. It is the rather startling fact that of the total bill for compensation something less than half goes to the worker as cash benefit, the remainder to operating expense. Though the incidence of review is relatively small, it perforce tends to cast compensation in a litigious mold, thus increasing the cost and time factors. Might not workers and employers choose the lesser cost despite the sacrifice of occasional individual interest? Furthermore, it may be that in this system there are certain "built-in" protections due to the equilibrium of the component forces. American administration is, as we are now so much aware, remarkably sensitive to organized pressures. Employees are represented by their unions, employers and insurers by their various associations. Exclusion of review would thus be easier to justify now that the principles of the system have become established and the interested parties know what the system demands of them and are well organized to protect their interests. It is very far from my intention to suggest that there should not be judicial review in compensation cases. I use the example of compensation simply as an analytic model, as an area in which it is not unrealistic to assume certain premises which might support the conclusion that review is inappropriate.

There is a further reason for judicial review which, if not ordinarily present, is implied in the basic role of the courts in our system. The constitutional courts, as I have said elsewhere in defining the scope of judicial review,

> are the acknowledged architects and guarantors of the integrity of the legal system. I use integrity here in its specific sense of unity and coherence and in its more general sense of the effectuation of the values upon which this unity and coherence are built. In a society so complex, so pragmatic as ours, unity is never realized, nor is it necessary that it should be. Indeed there is no possibility of agreement on criteria for absolute unity; what is contradiction to one man is higher synthesis to another. But within a determined context there may be a sense of contradiction sufficient to create social distress; and it is one of the

grand roles of our constitutional courts to detect such contradictions and to affirm the capacity of our society to integrate its purposes. . . . [T]he statute under which an agency operates is not the whole law applicable to its operation. An agency is not an island entire of itself. It is one of the many rooms in the magnificent mansion of the law. The very subordination of the agency to judicial jurisdiction is intended to proclaim the premise that each agency is to be brought into harmony with the totality of the law; the law as it is found in the statute at hand, the statute book at large, the principles and conceptions of the "common law," and the ultimate guarantees associated with the Constitution.[5]

[5] Jaffe, *Judicial Review: Question of Law*, 69 HARV. L. REV. 239, 274–75 (1955).

10. ADMINISTRATIVE JUSTICE: Formal Prescription and Informal Adjudication

Peter Woll

The growth of administrative law has profound implications upon legal theory and judicial practice. It is possible that with the development of administrative law fundamental changes are taking place in the common-law world which have not been taken sufficiently into consideration by judges, practitioners, and scholars in the law. Probably the most significant alteration of common-law practice by administrative agencies is the extensive utilization of informal procedure, indigenous to all areas of administrative adjudication. The purpose of this article is to analyze the importance, merit, and implications of informal administrative adjudication in light of constitutional and common-law theory.

COMMON LAW AND CONSTITUTIONAL FRAMEWORK

The fact of administrative adjudication at once appears to conflict with the common law and the Constitution. Article III requires that "the judicial power of the United States, shall be vested in one Supreme Court, and in such inferior courts as the Congress may from time to time ordain and establish."[1] The courts, however, have constitutionally justified the exercise of judicial power[2] by extra-judicial agencies through distinguish-

[1] Constitution of the United States, Art. III, § 1.

[2] The term "judicial power" is used here in the generic sense. The courts seem reluctant to use this term when referring to administrative adjudication as it is frequently used when referring to the judicial power of the United States under Article III; thus the reader may substitute the term judicial function, judicial act, judicial business, judicial matter, etc., all of which are used with great frequency to avoid using the term "judicial power." Since the author feels that in essence identical power is exercised in many instances both within and outside of the judicial branch the term judicial power will be used in a generic sense and distinguished from "the judicial power of the United States" under Article III.

ing (1) the judicial power of the United States under Article III of the Constitution from (2) judicial power in the generic sense. The courts permit the exercise of judicial power by agencies outside of the judicial branch; however, when the judicial power of the United States under Article III can be identified the courts require its vestment in the Supreme Court and inferior courts established by Congress. Conversely, judicial power which is not encompassed by Article III cannot be vested in the judicial branch.

The utilization of these concepts enables the courts to permit the exercise of judicial power beyond their sphere without an apparent violation of Article III. Judicial power may be vested in administrative agencies at both the national and state level, and if necessary it may be united with legislative functions.

Judicial power, in the generic sense, involves an adversary proceeding[3] in which a final determination is made. In the words of Holmes, "a judicial inquiry investigates, declares and enforces liabilities as they stand on present or past facts and under laws supposed already to exist." Because finality is a necessary attribute of judicial power the courts will not accept jurisdiction which subjects their decisions to further review by an extra-judicial agency; however, this does not prevent final judicial power from legally residing outside of the judicial branch. The Court has stated:

> We do not consider Congress can either withdraw from judicial cognizance any matter which, from its nature, is the subject of a suit at the common law, or in equity, or admiralty; nor, on the other hand, can it bring under the judicial power a matter which, from its nature, is not a subject for judicial determination. At the same time there are matters, involving public rights, which may be presented in such form that the judicial power is capable of

[3] The term "adversary" does not require articulated conflict among parties, but rather an asserted claim on the part of a specific party requiring a determination according to legal standards. The judicial power "is capable of acting only when the subject is submitted to it by a party who asserts his rights in the form prescribed by law. It then becomes a case. . . ." *I.C.C.* v. *Brimson,* 154 U.S. 444, 475 (1894).

> acting on them, and which are susceptible of judicial determination, but which Congress may or may not bring within the cognizance of the courts of the United States, as it may deem proper.[4]

The Court notes further: "It is true, also, that even in a suit between private persons to try a question of private right, the action of the executive power, upon a matter committed to its determination by the Constitution and laws, is conclusive."[5]

Judicial finality may, then, be vested in administrative agencies provided the courts do not find reason for intervention.[6] Such finality results from judicial self-restraint, not *legal* prohibitions upon judicial review. There is little doubt that where the courts want to intervene they can legally find sufficient reason for so doing. Long-standing criteria precluding such review, e.g., judicial refusal to review issues of "fact" *(expertise)* as opposed to those of "law," may be ignored if the courts decide that intervention is necessary. In certain areas where final judicial power is given by Congress solely to an administrative agency the courts have refused to intervene. In others, regardless of apparent congressional intent to limit justifications for judicial review, the courts have intervened to prevent denial of due process of law.

In summary, although Article III of the Constitution vests judicial power in one Supreme Court and inferior courts to be established by Congress, the courts have permitted judicial power to be exercised by administrative agencies. As one notable scholar has concluded,

> . . . though the courts will not perform administrative acts, there is no *constitutional* objection to vesting the performance of acts essentially judicial in character in the hands of the executive or administrative agents, provided the

[4] *Murray* v. *Hoboken Land & Improvement Co.,* 18 How. 272, 284 (1856).

[5] *Ibid.,* at 285, citing *Luther* v. *Borden,* 7 How. 1 (1894); and *Doe* v. *Braden,* 16 How. 635 (1854).

[6] In this sense administrative finality, where it exists, is *de facto,* not *de jure.*

> performance of these functions is properly incidental to the execution by the department in question of functions peculiarly its own. Furthermore . . . there is . . . subject to the same qualification, no objection to rendering the administrative determinations conclusive, that is, without appeal to the courts, provided in general the requirements of due process of law as regards the right of the person affected to a hearing, to produce evidence, etc., have been met.[7]

Provided the criteria of due process of law are followed there is no constitutional inconsistency in the exercise of judicial functions by administrative agencies. Due process generally requires administrative adherence to the judicial model insofar as feasible; however, because of the unique needs of administrative adjudication the courts have permitted administrative practice which would not be acceptable in a court of law.

The common law and administrative adjudication

Although there is apparently no constitutional problem to administrative agencies exercising conclusive jurisdiction over matters of a judicial nature, there is a common-law objection to any exercise of judicial functions outside of the realm of the ordinary court system. A fundamental common-law concept is that of "supremacy of law." One of the best early expressions of this theory is found in Coke's *Institutes*. In speaking of the jurisdiction of the Court of Kings Bench he noted:

> . . . this court hath not only jurisdiction to correct errors in judicial proceeding, but other errors and misdemeanors extrajudicial tending to the breach of the peace, or oppression of the subjects, or raising of faction, controversy, debate, or any other manner of misgovernment; so that no wrong or injury, either public or private, can be done, but that this shall be reformed or punished in one court or other by due course of law.[8]

[7] Westel W. Willoughby, *The Constitutional Law of the United States* (New York: Baker, Voorhis, 1910), II, 1277.
[8] 4 *Institutes* 71.

Perhaps the best known articulation of the doctrine of rule (or supremacy) of law is found in the writings of Dicey. In his terms the essence of supremacy of law is that "no man is punishable or can lawfully be made to suffer in body or goods except for a distinct breach of law established in the ordinary legal manner before the ordinary courts of the land. In this sense the rule of law is contrasted with every system of government based on the exercise by persons in authority of wide, arbitrary, or discretionary powers of constraint."[9] Individuals must have recourse to common-law courts ("ordinary courts"). Dickinson has noted:

> In so far as administrative adjudication is coming in certain fields to take the place of adjudication by law courts, the supremacy of law as formulated in Dicey's first proposition is overridden. But a possible way of escaping this result is left open by his second proposition. An administrative determination is an act of a governmental officer or officers; and if it be true that all the acts of such officers are subject to be questioned in the courts, it is then possible to have the issue of any questionable administrative adjudication raised and decided anew in a law court, with the special advantages and guaranties of the procedure at law. We here see the reason why the question of court review of administrative determinations has come to be of such central importance and has been the focus of so much discussion since the rise of the administrative procedure. For just in so far as administrative determinations are subject to court review, a means exists for maintaining the supremacy of law, though at one remove and as a sort of secondary line of defence.[10]

Dickinson accurately concludes that "administrative justice exists in defiance of the supremacy of law only in so far as administrative adjudications are final or conclusive, and not subject to correction by a law court. To some undefined extent, however, they are final, and there seems to be a tendency at work to

[9] A. V. Dicey, *Introduction to the Study of the Law of the Constitution* (8th ed.; London: Macmillan, 1927), pp. 183–84.

[10] John Dickinson, *Administrative Justice and the Supremacy of Law* (Cambridge, Harvard University Press, 1927), pp. 36–37.

make them increasingly so."[11] Administrative finality, then, conflicts with common-law theory although it is not inconsistent with constitutional doctrine.

Particular note should be taken of the fact that the conflict of legal ideas which developed with reference to administrative adjudication focused upon the conceptual validity of the common law as against that of administrative law. This is particularly interesting in that equity was not discussed even though it was an admittedly valid area of the law within the frame of reference of traditional legal thinking. Equity, which generally relied upon the written deposition and other devices less formal than those of the common law, was more similar in a procedural sense to administrative adjudication. Nevertheless, in writing about administrative law the less formal nature of equity has been forgotten in light of what are considered to be more important safeguards contained in the common law, and the relationship between "law" and "executive justice" is conceptualized in terms of the relationship between the common law and administrative law.[12]

Pound expresses the concern of the legal profession with the rise of administrative adjudication. He notes that common-law doctrine

> assumes that experience will afford the most satisfactory foundation for standards of action and principles of decision. It holds that law is not to be made arbitrarily by a fiat of the sovereign will, but is to be discovered by judicial and juristic experience of the rules and principles which in the past have accomplished or have failed to accomplish justice. Where such doctrine obtains, not merely the interpretation and application of legal rules but in large measure the ascertainment of them must be left to the disciplined reason of the judges. . . .[13]

[11] *Ibid.*, pp. 37–38.

[12] This distinction is well illustrated in three of Pound's best known articles. See Roscoe Pound, "Justice According to Law," 13 *Col. L. Rev.* 696–713 (Pt. 1, 1913); 14 *Col. L. Rev.* 1–26 (Pt. 2, 1914); 14 *Col. L. Rev.* 103–21 (Pt. 3, 1914).

[13] Roscoe Pound, *The Spirit of the Common Law* (Boston: Marshall Jones, 1912), p. 183.

In the common-law courts the citizen is protected by subjecting the determination of the case to one who is trained to administer and determine appropriate legal principles, based upon past experience and the ability to apply legal reasoning in uncharted fields. Professional standards ensure fair adjudication. Within this frame of reference Pound crystallized in 1941 the need for the stricter application of common-law principles to administrative adjudication. Although Pound was effectively refuted, his thinking reflected a concern which ultimately led to the passage of the Administrative Procedure Act of 1946. The judicial model was used in the construction of this statute as it pertains to the control of internal agency procedure. With respect to the broader question of judicial review the APA attempts to increase the scope of review, thereby strengthening the theoretical concept of supremacy of law. The primary failure of this and other proposals for administrative law reform is the inadequate attention given to the informal administrative process.

IMPORTANCE OF INFORMAL ADJUDICATION

From an examination of the common-law and constitutional framework it is evident that judicial review of administrative determinations must be maintained, and that as a minimum administrative agencies must adhere to criteria of due process of law, as defined by the courts, and by the APA, in exercising judicial functions. Due process of law requires that fundamental procedures such as notice, hearing, adequate record, and appeal be maintained; however, the procedures inherent in the concept of due process are *formal* insofar as standards have been developed. As presently defined, in order for due process to be operative in administrative proceedings, private parties must have opportunity for recourse to the formal hearing stage within the agency, for only at that level are procedures sufficiently formalized and opportunity present for further appeal to the judicial branch. Unfortunately it is impossible to generalize concerning standards of due process in administrative proceedings. The Court of Appeals, D.C., noted in *NBC* v. *FCC:*

> Nor has it been made clear by judicial decision what constitutes a minimum compliance with due process in the way of administrative hearing. Presumably this will vary to a considerable extent with the nature of the substantive right, the character and complexity of the issues, the kinds of evidence and factual material, the particular body or official, and the administrative functions involved in the hearing.[14]

Although the APA was designed to remedy this situation, the indefiniteness of standards of due process remains today.

The most significant aspect of administrative law today is that the bulk of administrative determinations are handled informally. Decisions are rendered on the basis of conferences, correspondence, and inspections, rather than on the basis of a formal hearing in which cross-examination takes place, formal rules of procedure are followed with respect to the introduction of evidence, and a decision is made on the basis of a record which may be used later for judicial review. Agencies today reflect in their procedure requirements of *expertise* and expedition, which have developed largely from the volume and technical nature of the cases coming within their jurisdiction. The basic need for informal adjudicative techniques stems from the fact that without their extensive utilization the administrative process would break down, and fail to provide expeditious and expert case disposition.

Generally adjudicative areas within the administrative process can be divided in accordance with the type of case coming within the jurisdiction of the agency. Three areas may be distinguished: (1) application cases; (2) complaint cases; and (3) cases which because of their technical nature offer no opportunity for a hearing (the pure administrative process).[15] These may be determined either at a formal or informal level within any given agency; however, because of recent developments in administrative law there has been a demise of the formal hear-

[14] NBC v. FCC, 132 F.2d 545, 560 (1942).

[15] With the exception of an alteration in the definition of the term "pure administrative process" these categories are taken from Walter Gellhorn and Clark Byse, *Administrative Law* (Brooklyn: Foundation Press, 1960).

ing device, in the common-law sense[16] Traditionally, there has been the belief that if one wants to have a case adjudicated through a formal hearing there will generally be this opportunity; however this is not the case, and the extensive introduction of informal adjudicative techniques into the formal administrative process renders it in many cases basically similar to the informal administrative process.[17] To the extent to which the formal-informal distinction is blurred in reality, administrative law must be conceptualized in informal terms. If this is true, due process, insofar as it requires formal procedure, cannot be applied to administrative adjudication without a fundamental alteration in the practices, jurisdiction, and requirements of administrative agencies.

In the application case area administrative agencies settle most cases coming within their jurisdiction through informal conferences and correspondence with applicants. In an area such as this, for example, the SEC will send a "deficiency letter" to registrants under the Securities Act of 1933 to correct misstatements of fact or supply amendments to registration statements without the necessity of going to the formal process and issuing a stop order.[18] Frequently, conferences in this category take place before particular applications are filed. Thus the complexity of applications under the Holding Company Act of 1935, for example, requires expert administrative advice for proper filing. In this way informal interpretative advice is given to private parties which may in fact constitute the final determition of a case. In some instances agencies will actually *initiate* applications if they feel that the public interest would be served by a particular dispensation. Administrative adjudication of ap-

[16] See the author's "The Development of Shortened Procedure in American Administrative Law," 45 *Cornell Law Quarterly* 56–82 (1959).

[17] These devices consist of prehearing conferences, generally required in each agency's procedural rules, conferences of an informal nature during the course of formal hearings, and specific techniques designed to fit the requirements of particular agencies. See *ibid., passim.*

[18] Needless to say, in a proceeding of this kind any adverse publicity regarding a prospective seller of securities would result automatically in economic deprivation to the private party concerned; thus the efficacy of formal techniques, which usually result in such publicity, as well as in delay and expense, is highly questionable in cases such as this.

plications, then, is accomplished almost entirely on an informal basis.[19]

In the area of administrative complaint cases the informal process is further extended and conferences and correspondence generally effect settlement. Frequently, initial decisions with respect to the merits of a particular case suffice to settle the matter. Stipulation, admissive answer, and consent order procedures are generally accepted techniques in this area. Often, cases are settled "administratively" during the course of a complaint investigation. Adjudicative procedures established by agencies in this area vary in accordance with the type of case handled. No system is haphazard. In some instances, as in the operation of the Internal Revenue Service, elaborate informal settlement systems have been established with a clear definition of substantive and procedural standards to be followed by conferees. In addition the IRS has a highly successful informal appellate division which generally eliminates the necessity of taking a case to the formal process, i.e., to the Tax Court.

The pure administrative process completes the picture of informal administrative adjudication. The area essentially comprises technical adjudication, in which facts are best ascertained through such informal devices as inspections and interviews rather than on the basis of formal hearings. The difference between the informal process generally and the pure administrative process specifically is not one of substance, as all administrative adjudication requires *expertise* to a varying extent; however, the difference is one of *degree*, and it is possible to identify an administrative area in which technical considerations generally are the primary ones in disposing of cases. Adjudication by such benefit agencies as the Veterans' Administration and the Bureau of Old-Age and Survivors Insurance within the Social Security Administration presents an example of the pure administrative process. At numerous other points in the administrative process cases are disposed of purely on a technical basis.[20]

[19] *De facto*, not *de jure*.

[20] This area frequently involves inspection to determine legal violation in accordance with administrative standards. FTC inspection under the Wool, Fur, and Flammable Fabrics Acts illustrates such an area. Field engineering and monitoring by the FCC provides a further example.

Gauging the importance of informal adjudication

The scope of informal adjudication is clearly defined. Well in excess of 95 per cent of administrative adjudication is handled in this manner.[21] This percentage takes into account cases settled informally both at the nonhearing and hearing phases in the administrative process. In order to gauge the importance of this procedural device it is necessary not only to observe the extent to which it is used but also the purposes which it fulfills. Thus the *merits* of informal adjudication relative to more formal procedural techniques must be analyzed.

FORMAL JUSTICE

Common-law procedure developed initially to ensure the accurate establishment of the *facts* of a case under adjudication.[22] Disputes were between individuals acting in their private capacities, and fair adjudication was dependent upon the clear articulation and ascertainment of relevant facts which, when established and applied within the proper legal framework, would result in justice being rendered. Governmental officials committing torts were to be sued in their private capacities.

As the common law developed in the Middle Ages legal procedure came to be thought of not only as a mechanical device for determining fact, but also as a "safeguard" against arbitrary judgments by *public* officials. This distinction was particularly important as public officers came to exercise wide discretionary judicial functions on a broader front and with greater frequency. Insofar as common-law procedure pertained to the protection of the individual against abuse of discretion by public officials it was subsumed under the heading of "due process of law." Due process, first identified in chapter thirty-nine of the Magna Carta and later developed as requiring primarily trial by jury,

[21] This has been determined by the author through independent investigation. See Peter Woll *Administrative Law: The Informal Process* (Berkeley & Los Angeles: University of California Press, 1963).

[22] Initially common-law methods were rather crude, composed of such procedures as ordeal and battle; nevertheless their purpose was, of course, to determine guilt or innocence, i.e., to determine the truth.

required judgments to be made in accordance with a recognized form of legal procedure. Although at first the procedure principally recognized was that of jury trial, time produced the injection of the formula with more subtle procedural devices. Procedures in addition to jury trial were recognized as being of primary importance.

Mott has pointed out:

> Some scholars see in chapter thirty-nine of the Great Charter from the very first the protection of general justice and right. According to such an interpretation, this article was the general norm of all governmental action and should prove valuable at least as a moral precept controlling the government in all its dealings with individuals. . . . The idea of a residual substantive content of "due process of law" was at most exceedingly nebulous. It probably grew out of the general idea that governmental power should be limited; a concept which originated when all powers of government were concentrated in the hands of the sovereign. With the subsequent expansion of governmental activity and governmental forms an extension of the idea of due process was to be expected.[23]

The implementation of the concept of due process controlled arbitrary governmental action in the sense that government was under the law of the land, and could not act in a manner contrary to that law. Common-law devices for establishment of facts, then, insofar as they became associated with due process of law served a corollary function of bringing government under the law of the land and thereby protected citizens against arbitrary exercise of power.

Initially due process was in substance considered to be equivalent to trial by jury; however, as Mott has pointed out, it soon became evident "that there were numerous situations in which a jury trial was not applicable."[24] The courts, after rejecting trial by jury as an absolute criterion of due process turned in other directions. It was particularly emphasized that trial before

[23] R. L. Mott, *Due Process of Law* (Indianapolis: Bobbs-Merrill,1926), pp. 74–75.

[24] Mott, *op. cit.*, pp. 208–09.

some court was necessary; however, the courts finally concluded that there is nothing in the term "that necessarily implies that due process of law must be judicial process."[25] The courts began "to look to the inherent elements of justice in a determination rather than to the form by which that decision might be arrived at. It was then that the courts developed the doctrine of notice and hearing."[26] Although it is true that the criteria of notice and hearing have not been applied consistently by the courts when reviewing administrative action, the desire is present to enforce such standards where it is at all feasible. Administrative exigencies sometimes require elimination of notice and hearing requirements, but the courts are never happy with this solution.

The Court expressed the traditional view regarding the necessity for administrative hearings in *Interstate Commerce Commission* v. *Louisville & Nashville R.R. Co.*[27]

> A finding without evidence is arbitrary and baseless. And if the Government's contention is correct, it would mean that the Commission had a power possessed by no other officer, administrative body, or tribunal under our Government. It would mean that where rights depended upon facts, the Commission could disregard all rules of evidence, and capriciously make findings by administrative fiat. Such authority, however, beneficently exercised in one case, could be injuriously exerted in another; is inconsistent with rational justice, and comes under the Constitution's condemnation of all arbitrary exercise of power.
>
> In the comparatively few cases in which such questions have arisen it has been distinctly recognized that administrative orders, quasi-judicial in character, are void if a hearing was denied; if that granted was inadequate or manifestly unfair; if the finding was contrary to the "indisputable character of the evidence."[28]

[25] *Weimer* v. *Bunbury,* 30 Mich. 201, 211 (1874).

[26] Mott, *op. cit.,* p. 216.

[27] 227 U.S. 88 (1913).

[28] 227 U.S. 88, 91. In the instant case a statutory provision was involved requiring a hearing; however, the language of the Court generalizes the proposition that judgments determining rights require hearing in order to conform to standards of due process.

In *Southern Ry. Co.* v. *Va.*,[29] the Court stated emphatically that a state statute authorizing an administrative officer to require railroads to substitute overhead crossings for existing grade crossings whenever he felt it necessary for the public safety and convenience violated the Fourteenth Amendment because of its failure to provide for notice and hearing. The Court noted that "before its property can be taken under the edict of an administrative officer the appellant is entitled to a fair hearing upon the fundamental facts."[30]

Ideally, then, notice and hearing are considered necessary components to due process. The ideal has been limited at numerous points by practice, but the opportunity for hearing at some stage in most administrative proceedings of a judicial nature is considered a minimum requirement. The principal *raison d'être* of administrative hearings is prevention of arbitrary administrative action through accurate determination of facts.

FORMAL AND INFORMAL JUSTICE CONTRASTED

It is possible, in analyzing the requirements of administrative law, to construct a model which will delineate the criteria of administrative justice. Such a model, of course, will have its limitations; nevertheless it is impossible to contrast formal and informal procedure unless a definite frame of reference is developed. As a basis for such a model the British concept of "natural justice" may be used, for it essentially coincides with broad criteria of due process of law. In the Report of the Committee on Ministers' Powers this concept is developed and applied to administrative law in Great Britain.[31] The committee notes with respect to the definition of tenets of natural justice that "it is beyond doubt that there are certain canons of judicial conduct to which all tribunals and persons who have to give judicial or quasi-judicial decisions ought to conform. The principles on which they rest are . . . implicit in the rule of law."[32]

[29] 290 U.S. 190 (1933).
[30] *Ibid.*, p. 199.
[31] Report of the Committee on Ministers' Powers, Cmd. 4060, April 1932.
[32] *Ibid.*, p. 76.

The first principle of natural justice is that a man cannot be judge in his own cause. Disqualifying bias is a difficult thing to define; however as a minimum requirement an official should not have a direct *personal* interest in the outcome of a case which he is to judge. The Committee on Ministers' Powers felt that bias as to public policy should constitute disqualification; however American administrative law makes a distinction between a personal and policy bias, tending to support disqualification in the former situation but not in the latter. A reasonable policy bias does not result in disqualification, but no official should be permitted to adjudicate a case in which he *might* have a personal interest. Presumably a policy bias can be changed if the evidence presented during a hearing is convincing enough; however, a personal bias is irrational with regard to the factual context, and can result normally in only one judgment which favors the interests of the biased adjudicator. A policy bias is based upon rational consideration of the facts, whereas a personal bias stems from self-interest.

The second principle of natural justice has two phases. In the words of the Committee on Ministers' Powers:

> No party ought to be condemned unheard; and if his right to be heard is to be a reality, he must know in good time the case which he has to meet. But on neither branch of this principle can any particular procedure (i) by which the party is informed of the case which he has to meet, or (ii) by which his evidence and argument are "heard" be regarded as fundamental. That a Minister or a Ministerial Tribunal does not conform to the procedure of the Courts in either respect imports no disregard of natural justice. There is, for instance, no natural right to an oral hearing.[33]

The Committee advanced two further corollary principles of natural justice: (1) parties must know the reason for the decision made in their case; (2) parties must know the nature of any material or recommendations made at an initial administrative level, e.g., an inspector's report, which is taken into account by officials authorized to render a final decision.

[33] Report of the Committee on Ministers' Powers, *op. cit.*, pp. 79–80.

It is evident that administrative justice is not dependent upon strict adherence to particular procedures, but upon maintenance of a sense of fairness in the procedures determining the rights and obligations of private parties. What is "fair" will vary to some extent procedurally from one proceeding to the next. The concept of natural justice delineates procedural necessities in administrative adjudication; however, it is necessary to consider other requirements of administrative justice before the model is complete.

Aside from the concept of natural justice, three additional components of a model for administrative justice should be noted: (1) the need for review of administrative decisions; (2) the need for accurate fact-finding; (3) the need for *policy* considerations to be taken into account properly in the process of exercising quasi-judicial functions. Ideally, under the terms of the rule of law concept *judicial* review must be maintained over administrative determinations of a judicial nature. The possibility of review should be open even if rarely used for a system to be in accordance with common-law doctrine; however, it may be questioned whether review must always be by courts. A sense of fairness may be maintained if review exists within the administrative agency concerned, or within the administrative branch. Nevertheless, there is little doubt that ideally the possibility of review by courts of law is a desirable characteristic of administrative justice, although not always a necessity.

A second important need for administrative justice to be realized is accurate fact-finding. Machinery must exist for proper determination of facts in any given case. This is the principal function of common-law procedural rules, and a vital need in any type of adjudication; however, the types of cases and characteristics of personnel differ markedly in the administrative process relative to the common-law realm. Insofar as juries are used in common-law cases adjudication depends upon personnel with less continuity of service and less *expertise* than found in the administrative process. The judge may counterbalance this lack on the part of juries to some extent; however, the basic distinction remains. With regard to the type of case handled by administrative agencies it is doubtful that the formal testimonial process of proof, designed to keep irrelevancies and prejudicial matter away from juries and gain the advantage of demeanor evidence, is as efficacious to administrative justice as it is in a normal case tried in a common-law court. Administrative fact-finding must depend to a large extent upon independent investigation accomplished through an institutional decision-making process in which experts participate. Demeanor evidence is of little importance in administrative proceedings, and such techniques as cross-examination are cumbersome in attempting to arrive at expert determinations. Efficient fact-finding requires flexibility and the utilization of modern research techniques which cannot be used within the framework of traditional common-law doctrine. Due process may require, in accordance with the right to a hearing, limited cross-examination under certain circumstances; however from the standpoint of efficient fact-finding the effectiveness of certain common-law devices may be questioned with regard to the administrative process.

A final component to a model for administrative justice is the existence of a proper relationship between policy and adjudication. Administrative determinations must be made not only in accordance with facts presented during the course of a hearing, but also in terms of policy considerations. The agency involved in adjudication must roam beyond the boundaries which would normally be set by strict adherence to common-law procedure and take official notice of circumstances bearing upon policy interests defined by statute or administrative rules and directives.[34] In line with its policy function the administrative agency must be able and willing to seize the initiative and take necessary corrective action when required. The umpire theory of law cannot operate effectively in the modern regulatory realm.

Having outlined a model for administrative justice it is now possible to contrast the effectiveness of formal and informal

[34] Such statutory definitions are usually vague, couched in such terms as "public interest," "just and reasonable," etc. The agency fills in the details of statutory prescriptions through rule-making.

adjudicative techniques. First, there is little doubt that formal adjudication, with requirements for adequate notice and apprisal, hearing with cross-examination, right to counsel, a decision on the record, and opportunity for review, meets the standards of natural justice. In the formal area (i.e., where formal adjudication is required by statute or, in rare instances, by constitutional due process) the Administrative Procedure Act applies and aids directly in implementing the standards of natural justice. Further, except in rare instances, appeal may be taken from a decision made in the formal administrative process to a court of law, provided the necessary legal requirements have been fulfilled and the court accepts review. Standards of natural justice may not be as adequately fulfilled in the formal administrative process as in a court of law; however, relative to the informal adjudicative realm, criteria of natural justice are followed more consistently and with more predictability in the formal realm. This is particularly true because of the clear definition of standards in this area and the existence of greater outside control by the courts.

In the informal area, on the other hand, it is largely within the discretion of the agency and the administrator involved whether or not strict standards of due process and natural justice will be followed. It is important to point out that due process does not require formal procedure; however, due process is more likely to be followed where such procedure is operative. It is quite possible that a sense of fairness will be present in the informal adjudicative area which would fulfill the requirements of natural justice and due process of law. This *possibility*, and in many instances probability, is of considerable importance because informal procedure, which does not fulfill criteria of natural justice as adequately as formal procedure, nor provide for review as adequately as that done by courts of law, does provide more appropriate machinery for fact-finding and greater flexibility for taking into account policy considerations than the approach of formal adjudication.

The *raison d'être* of the administrative process is the increasing need for more flexibility than is provided by either Congress or the courts. Modern regulation requires specialization, *expertise,* continuity of policy, and flexibility for utilization of a variety of skills which would not be possible operating within a strict common-law framework. Even the formal administrative process was to be more flexible than a court of law, and the courts have permitted this utilization of more flexible procedure; however, it is actually the informal administrative process which epitomizes those characteristics for which there was a felt need at the time of the creation of the administrative agency as a regulatory device. Informal procedure offers the best possibility of effective use of a combination of techniques in the regulatory realm; thus informal investigation through an institutional process is the most effective way in which to ascertain relevant facts pertaining to any given situation, and policy considerations may shape the final decision insofar as necessary for the protection of the public interest, convenience, or necessity.

In contrasting the fact-finding possibilities of the administrative as opposed to the judicial process Landis has noted:

> The test of the judicial process, traditionally, is not the fair disposition of the controversy; it is the fair disposition of the controversy *upon the record as made by the parties.* True, there are collateral sources of information which often affect judicial determinations. There is the more or less limited discretion under the doctrine of judicial notice; and there is the inarticulated but nonetheless substantial power to choose between competing premises based upon off-the-record considerations. But, in strictness, the judge must not know of the events of the controversy except as these may have been presented to him, in due form, by the parties. . . . Nor is he permitted to conduct an investigation to determine what policy is best adapted to the demands of time and place, even though he is aware that sooner or later he will be confronted with the necessity, through the processes of judicial decision, of shaping policy in that particular field.[35]

On the other hand, in order for the administrative process to be successful, "it is imperative that controversies be decided as 'rightly' as possible, independently of the formal record the

[35] James M. Landis, *The Administrative Process* (New Haven: Yale University Press, 1938), p. 38.

parties themselves produce. The ultimate test of the administrative is the policy that it formulates; not the fairness as between the parties of the disposition of a controversy on a record of their own making."[36] The underlying assumption of formal adjudication in accordance with common-law criteria is that all the relevant facts of a particular case will be produced through an adversary process; however, this is not the case in administrative law where relevant "facts" are gained from a broad and complex area, and where in addition a case cannot by statutory law be disposed of purely on the basis of such facts. Policy, in terms of the "public interest," must be taken into account.

Administrative adjudication meets the conditions of administrative justice most consistently through utilization of flexible, informal procedure. Administrative procedure must, then, differ markedly from that used in the judicial branch because of different requirements in the two areas. The exigencies of administrative law have been essentially recognized by the courts and by Congress, although strong interests still are attempting to "formalize" the administrative process to a greater extent than presently exists. This is not to say that within the administrative process itself the so-called formal adjudicative area is not as appropriate to the realization of administrative justice as the informal area, for in fact the two are less distinguishable than commonly believed. Formal administrative adjudication is itself highly informal when contrasted with the judicial process, although even in the latter informal devices are being utilized which shorten proceedings. Administrative law, like equity, developed to meet a deficiency in the common law and like equity it relies upon procedures which could not be developed within the common-law framework. The efficacy of administrative procedure must be recognized, and the administrative process must not be forced into a judicial mold.

CONCLUSION

The modern administrative process has developed virtually total reliance upon informal procedure in the adjudication of

[36] *Ibid.*, p. 39.

cases. Although extensive utilization of such procedure presents some drawbacks in terms of common-law doctrine, requirements of administrative adjudication make utilization of such procedure more consonant with administrative justice than would result from strict adherence to formal procedure in fact-finding and adjudication. Perhaps the most significant limitation placed upon common-law theory by informal adjudication is with respect to the doctrine of supremacy of law, which requires review of administrative decisions by courts of law. Private parties always have a theoretical right of appeal within the administrative process to the formal realm and subsequently to the courts in most instances; however, although this recourse exists in law it does not exist in fact in many instances, for appeal to the formal administrative realm automatically results in publicity and delay which defeat the very purposes of fair adjudication.[37] Apart from this limitation, which is an important one, it is more likely that other important elements in administrative justice will be realized more consistently through utilization of flexible, informal procedure. The sense of fairness required by natural justice may be present at the same time effective fact-finding techniques are being employed within a proper policy framework.

The essential informal nature of administrative law today raises questions of vital concern to every lawyer and his client. When the common law is operative an automatic check is provided with respect to the decisions of administrative officials, particularly through judicial review; however, common-law procedures are not followed, resulting in an automatic increase in administrative discretion. The problem of control is vital; however, the complexity of the administrative process coupled with the large volume of cases handled makes control by any outside group difficult. The problem of responsibility in administrative law is one of the most crucial in the modern administrative state.

[37] Thus administrative sanctions are frequently automatically invoked, e.g., when it is publicized that a registration statement under the Securities Act of 1933 is under formal investigation for the issuance of a stop order, a procedure which would result in severe financial deprivation for the registrant.

VI. The Problem of Administrative Responsibility

EDITORIAL NOTE. All of the selections in this book have dealt in one way or another with the problem of administrative responsibility. Empirical evidence has been given regarding the way in which agencies function. In reading the following selections that outline proposals to achieve "administrative responsibility" students should bear in mind the relevance of the theories that are given to the facts that have preceded in the case studies and selections of this book.

11. PUBLIC POLICY AND THE NATURE OF ADMINISTRATIVE RESPONSIBILITY

Carl Joachim Friedrich

As the scope and functions of modern administration have widened, the difficulty of securing responsibility has greatly increased. Pious myth-makers have continued to take it for granted that in England, at least, the formal dependence of the Cabinet upon the confidence of the House of Commons—what used to be known as parliamentary responsibility—effectively insures responsible conduct of public affairs by officials, high and low. One of these mentors has gone so far as to suggest that the United States will never have a healthy political system until it adopts the British scheme by clear and direct constitutional amendment. To be sure, he advanced this "bold" advice prior to the events leading up to the Munich pact, but he had before him the British elections of 1931 and 1935, which admittedly provided the only check for holding the government responsible.

A realistic analysis of responsibility must take account of these developments, so markedly out of tune with formerly accepted views regarding the nature of parliamentary influence.[1]

RESPONSIBILITY AND POLICY FORMATION

The starting point of any study of responsibility must be that even under the best arrangements a considerable margin of irresponsible conduct of administrative activities is inevitable. For if a responsible person is one who is answerable for his act to some other person or body, who has to give an account of his doings (Oxford English Dictionary), it should be clear without further argument that there must be some agreement between such a responsible agent and his principal concerning the action in hand or at least the end to be achieved. When one considers the complexity of modern governmental activities, it is at once evident that such agreement can only be partial and incomplete, no matter who is involved. Once the electorate and legislative assemblies are seen, not through the smoke screen of traditional prejudice, but as they are, it is evident that such principals cannot effectively bring about the responsible conduct of public affairs, unless elaborate techniques make explicit what purposes and activities are involved in all the many different phases of public policy. It is at this point that the decisive importance of policy determination becomes apparent. Too often it is taken for granted that as long as we can keep the government from doing wrong we have made it responsible. What is more important is to insure effective action of any sort. To stimulate initiative, even at the risk of mistakes, must nowadays never be lost sight of as a task in making the government's services responsible. An official should be as responsible for inaction as for wrong action; certainly the average voter will criticize the government as severely for one as for the other.

[1] See Clarence A. Dykstra, "The Quest for Responsibility," *American Political Science Review,* vol. XXXIII, no. 1 (February 1939), p. 1; also Charles Aiken, "The British Bureaucracy and the Origins of Parliamentary Policy," *ibid.,* vol. XXXIII, no. 1 (February 1939), p. 26, and vol. XXXIII, No. 2 (April 1939), p. 219.

Without a well-defined and well-worked-out policy, responsibility becomes very difficult to bring about. Yet such policies are the exception rather than the rule. Many of the most severe breakdowns in contemporary administration, accompanied by violent public reactions against irresponsible bureaucracy, will be found to trace back to contradictory and ill-defined policy, as embodied in faulty legislation. There are numerous familiar illustrations. Nor should it be imagined that legislation in this sense is merely embodied in the formal statutes passed by Congress or Parliament. An even more common source of contradictory policy is administrative rules and regulations adopted by the several departments in the process of executing the statutory provisions. In England the Report on Ministers' Powers (1932) dealt extensively with the field of delegated legislation and found that many of these regulations suffer from poor draftsmanship. There appeared to prevail a fairly irresponsible tendency to adopt such rules and regulations without much regard for public and parliamentary opinion. In the United States the situation has become equally bad. The courts have shown little aptitude for dealing with the situation. The general inclination has been to reject the idea of such delegated legislation, with highly objectionable results, such as the Supreme Court decision holding the AAA unconstitutional because of its wide delegation of legislative power.[2] Many of those who hailed the decision would be surprised to recall that Elihu Root, who certainly was no radical, declared in his presidential address to the American Bar Association:

> Before these agencies (namely administrative commissions), the old doctrine prohibiting the delegation of legislative powers has virtually retired from the field and given up the fight. There will be no withdrawal from these experiments. We shall go on; we shall expand them, whether we approve theoretically or not, because such agencies furnish protection to right, and obstacles to wrong-doing, which under our new social and industrial conditions can-

[2] *U. S.* v. *Butler et al., Receivers of Hoosac Mills Corporation,* 297 U.S. 1 (1936). See also *Schechter Poultry Corp.* v. *U. S.,* 295 U.S. 495 (1935).

> not be practically accomplished by the old and simple procedure of legislature and courts as in the last generation.[3]

With this view, any informed analysis of contemporary legislation must concur. In the light of the large amount of legislative work performed by administrative agencies, the task of clear and consistent policy formation has passed likewise into the hands of administrators, and is bound to continue to do so. Hence, administrative responsibility can no longer be looked upon as merely a responsibility for executing policies already formulated. We have to face the fact that this responsibility is much more comprehensive in scope.

POLICY-MAKING AND POLICY EXECUTION

It has long been customary to distinguish between policy-making and policy execution. Frank J. Goodnow, in his well-known work, *Politics and Administration*, undertook to build an almost absolute distinction upon this functional difference.

> There are, then, in all governmental systems two primary or ultimate functions of government, viz. the expression of the will of the state and the execution of that will. There are also in all states separate organs, each of which is mainly busied with the discharge of one of these functions. These functions are, respectively, Politics and Administration.[4]

But while the distinction has a great deal of value as a relative matter of emphasis, it cannot any longer be accepted in this absolute form. Admittedly, this misleading distinction has become a fetish, a stereotype in the minds of theorists and practitioners alike. The result has been a great deal of confusion and

[3] Elihu Root, "Public Service by the Bar," address as president of the American Bar Association at the annual meeting in Chicago, August 30, 1916. Reprinted in *Addresses on Government and Citizenship*, Robert Bacon and James Brown Scott, eds. (Cambridge: Harvard University Press, 1916), p. 535.

[4] Frank J. Goodnow, *Politics and Administration* (New York: Macmillan, 1900), p. 22.

argument. The reason for making this distinction an absolute antithesis is probably to be found in building it upon the metaphysical, if not abstruse, idea of a will of the state. This neo-Hegelian (and Fascist) notion is purely speculative. Even if the concept "state" is retained—and I personally see no good ground for it—the idea that this state has a will immediately entangles one in all the difficulties of assuming a group personality or something akin to it.[5] In other words, a problem which is already complicated enough by itself—that is, how a public policy is adopted and carried out—is bogged down by a vast ideological superstructure which contributes little or nothing to its solution. Take a case like the AAA. In simple terms, AAA was a policy adopted with a view to helping the farmer to weather the storm of the depression. This admittedly was AAA's broad purpose. To accomplish this purpose, crop reduction, price-fixing, and a number of lesser devices were adopted. Crop reduction in turn led to processing taxes. Processing taxes required reports by the processors, inspection of their plants. Crop reduction itself necessitated reports by the farmers, so-called work sheets, and agreements between them and the government as to what was to be done, and so forth and so on. What here is politics, and what administration? Will anyone understand better the complex processes involved in the articulation of this important public policy if we talk about the expression and the execution of the state will? The concrete patterns of public policy formation and execution reveal that politics and administration are not two mutually exclusive boxes, or absolute distinctions, but that they are two closely linked aspects of the same process. Public policy, to put it flatly, is a continuous process, the formation of which is inseparable from its execution. Public policy is being formed as it is being executed, and it is likewise being executed as it is being formed. Politics and administration play a continuous role in both formation and execution, though there is probably more politics in the formation of policy, more administration in the execution of it. In so far as

[5] See Carl J. Friedrich, *Constitutional Government and Politics* (New York: Harpers, 1936), pp. 29 ff. and elsewhere.

particular individuals or groups are gaining or losing power or control in a given area, there is politics; in so far as officials act or propose action in the name of public interest, there is administration.

The same problem may be considered from another angle. Policies in the common meaning of the term are decisions about what to do or not to do in given situations. It is characteristic of our age that most legislation is looked upon as policy-deciding. Hence policy-making in the broad sense is not supposed to be part of administration. While these propositions are true in a general way, they tend to obscure two important facts, namely, (1) that many policies are not ordained with a stroke of the legislative or dictatorial pen but evolve slowly over long periods of time, and (2) that administrative officials participate continuously and significantly in this process of evolving policy. To commence with the latter fact, it is evident that in the process of doing something the administrator may discover another and better way of accomplishing the same result, or he discovers that the thing cannot be done at all, or that something else has to be done first, before the desired step can be taken. In our recent agricultural policy, examples of all these "administrative" policy determinations can be cited, as likewise in our social security policy. The discussions now taking place in both fields amply illustrate these points. What is more, such administrative participation alone renders policy-making a continuous process, so much in a state of flux that it is difficult, if not impossible, to state with precision what the policy in any given field is at any particular time. But, if this is true, it follows as a corollary that public policy will often be contradictory and conflicting in its effects upon society. Our myth-makers, of course, remain adamant in proclaiming that this should not be so, and let it go at that. It is hard to disagree with them, but we still have to face the question of responsibility, seeing that policies are in fact contradictory and conflicting. Who is responsible for what, and to whom? To what extent does such responsibility affect the actual conduct of affairs? A complex pattern appears when we attempt to answer such questions.

Some time ago I pointed out that administrative responsibility had not kept pace with our administrative tasks. In relying upon the political responsibility of policy-making persons and bodies, we had lost sight of the deeper issues involved. At that time I wrote:

> . . . autocratic and arbitrary abuse of power has characterized the officialdom of a government service bound only by the dictates of conscience. Nor has the political responsibility based upon the election of legislatures and chief executives succeeded in permeating a highly technical, differentiated government service any more than the religious responsibility of well-intentioned kings. Even a good and pious king would be discredited by arbitrary "bureaucrats"; even a high-minded legislature or an aspiring chief executive pursuing the public interest would be thwarted by a restive officialdom.

An offended commentator from the British Isles exclaimed loudly that if I imagined that to be true of England I was "simply wrong." But I think it would be easy to show that the officials of a seventeenth-century prince were more responsible, i.e., answerable, to him, this sovereign, than the officials of any modern democracy are as yet to the people, their supposed sovereign. In the comparison there was no judgment as to the positive amount of responsibility found in either. Admittedly, many commentators have dwelt at length upon the frequently irresponsible conduct of public affairs in Great Britain and elsewhere.

THE NEW IMPERATIVE: FUNCTIONAL RESPONSIBILITY

It is interesting that the administrators themselves attach so little weight to the influence of parliamentary or legislative bodies. Leading Swiss officials—and Switzerland has as responsible a government service as any country in the world—told the author that "responsibility of the public service in Switzerland results from a sense of duty, a desire to be approved by his fellow officials, and a tendency to subordinate one's own judgment as a matter of course. Still, in a case like the arrival of

Social Democrats into the Federal Council, it might happen that official conduct would be slow to respond to the new situation." They also felt that officials are not unwilling to allow a measure to lapse, although actually provided for in legislation, if considerable opposition is felt which the public might be expected to share. Thus a wine tax was quietly allowed to drop out of sight, just as the potato control act remained a dead letter in the United States.[6] There are, of course, ways by which the legislature secures a measure of control that enables it to enforce responsibility, usually of the negative kind which prevents abuses. Legislative committees act as watchdogs over all expenditure.[7]

What is true of Switzerland and the United States without "parliamentary responsibility" seems to be equally true of England and France. In both countries complaints against the increasing independence of officials are constantly being voiced. In a very important discourse, Sir Josiah Stamp called attention to the creative role the civil servant is called upon to play in Great Britain. "I am quite clear that the official must be the mainspring of the new society, suggesting, promoting, advising at every stage." Sir Josiah insisted that this trend was inevitable, irresistible, and therefore called for a new type of administrator. An editorial writer of *The Times,* though critical of this development, agreed "that the practice, as opposed to the theory, of administration has long been moving in this direction." He added, "In practice, they (the officials) possess that influence which cannot be denied to exhaustive knowledge; and this influence, owing to the congestion of parliamentary business and other causes, manifests itself more and more effectively as an initiative in public affairs." Testimony of this sort could be indefinitely multiplied; and as we are interested in practice, not in ideology, we must consider the question of responsibility in terms of the actualities. Such cases throw a disquieting light upon the

[6] See Schuyler C. Wallace, "Nullification: A Process of Government," *Political Science Quarterly,* vol. XLV, no. 3 (September 1930), p. 347.

[7] See George C. S. Benson, *Financial Control and Integration* (New York: Harpers, 1934).

idea that the mere dependence of a cabinet upon the "confidence" of an elected assembly insures responsible conduct on the part of the officials in charge of the initiation and execution of public policy, when those officials hold permanent positions. It is no accident that the Goodnow school should fully share such illusions. After pointing out that the British Cabinet unites in its hands power of legislation and administration, and thus both formulates and executes policies, Goodnow remarks:

> So long as their action meets with the approval of Parliament . . . there is none to gainsay them. If, however, they fail to gain such approval . . . they must resign their powers to others whose policy is approved by Parliament. . . . In this way the entire English government is made responsible to Parliament, which in turn is responsible to the people.[8]

This is no longer very true. It is objectionable to consider administrative responsibility secure by this simple device, not merely because of interstitial violations but because there is a fundamental flaw in the view of politics and policy here assumed. The range of public policy is nowadays so far-flung that the largely inoperative "right" of the parliamentary majority to oust a Cabinet from power belongs in that rather numerous group of rights for which there is no remedy. The majority supporting the Cabinet may violently disagree with this, that, and the other policy advocated and adopted by the Cabinet, but considerations of party politics, in the broadest sense, will throttle their objections because the particular issue is "not worth a general election" and the chance of the M.P.'s losing his seat.[9] As contrasted with the detailed and continuous criticism and control of administrative activity afforded by Congressional committees, this parliamentary responsibility is largely inoperative and certainly ineffectual. When one considers the extent of public disapproval directed against Franklin D. Roosevelt's Congressional supporters who were commonly dubbed "rubber

[8] Goodnow, *op. cit.*, p. 154.

[9] See Ramsay Muir, *How Britain is Governed* (New York: Richard R. Smith, Inc., 1930), pp. 81–91, 120–132.

stamps," it is astonishing that anyone extolling the virtues of British parliamentarism should get a hearing at all. For what has the parliamentary majority in Britain been in the last few years but a rubber stamp of an automatic docility undreamt of in the United States?

THE MODERN PHASE: ADMINISTRATIVE DISCRETION

British observers are not unaware of this development. Indeed, the Committee on Ministers' Powers, whose able report has already been cited, was created in response to widespread criticism of the irresponsible bueraucracy which was supposed to be developing. While Lord Hewart's *The New Despotism* undoubtedly exaggerated, his critical attack upon the growth of discretion allowed administrative agencies corresponded to a widespread sentiment. Unfortunately, his views were expressive of an unrealistic nostalgia for legal traditions which the forward march of social development has irrevocably assigned to limbo. Like Beck's *Our Wonderland of Bureaucracy,* Lord Hewart's denunciation of policy-determining officials failed to take into account that this "bureaucracy" had arisen in response to undeniable needs, and that therefore the real problem is how to render these functionaries responsible, not how to take all power away from them. The Committee on Ministers' Powers addressed itself to the real task. They set out to reduce the extent of the rule-making power of administrative agencies and to subject the making of such rules and regulations to a measure of parliamentary control. A standing committee of each house was to scrutinize bills with a view to whether they contained any such delegated legislative power, and, if so, to report upon the provisions in the light of given standards. Without going into the details of these recommendations—for they have not been put into effect—it must be said that they fail to cope with the decisive issue, the responsibility of officials for the policy adopted. No doubt technical improvements would result here and there, errors would be corrected, and mistakes avoided. But wherever the acquisition of discretionary rule-making power would be considered desirable by the government in power, or its exercise in a particular instance justifiable in terms of its policies, it is scarcely probable that under the British parliamentary system a committee composed of a majority of the government's party would cause any real difficulties. Either in getting such discretionary power on the statute books, or in exercising it as the permanent officials see fit, the government's view is more than likely to prevail.

The Report itself is illuminating on this score, though it softpedals the real trouble. The Report states that tactical considerations of party politics will play a role, and that, as realists, the committee members recognize it. An interesting illustration is afforded by their discussion of the so-called "Henry VIII Clause." This clause bears its nickname reminiscent of Tudor absolutism because it empowers the appropriate minister to modify the provisions of an act he is called upon to administer so far as may appear to him necessary for the purpose of bringing the act into operation. A number of important statutes in the last few decades contain such a clause. By way of illustrating the inevitability of such a clause, the Report remarks that the Committee had been assured that the National Insurance Act, 1911, could never have been brought into operation without the powers conferred by the Henry VIII Clause. Furthermore, it says:

> We have been told, rightly or wrongly, that if that Bill had not passed into law in 1911, the chance of it passing the Parliamentary ordeal with success in 1912 or 1913 would have been small; with the result that a social measure . . . of far-reaching importance would never have passed at all. In other words, the practical politician has to seize the tide when it serves or may lose his venture. We admit this truth: and because we admit it, we consider that the Henry VIII clause is a political instrument which must (*sic*) occasionally be used.[10]

The Committee recommended, of course, its sparing use and all that, but the only sanction they could think of was a parliamen-

[10] Committee on Ministers' Powers, *Report* (London, 1936; Cmd. 4060), p. 61.

tary standing committee dominated by the government's majority. Evidently, a monarch could count on his officials' acting more nearly responsibly and in accordance with his will than the people can under such arrangements.

A DUAL STANDARD OF ADMINISTRATIVE RESPONSIBILITY

But are there any possible arrangements under which the exercise of such discretionary power can be made more responsible? The difficulties are evidently very great. Before we go any further in suggesting institutional safeguards, it becomes necessary to elucidate a bit more the actual psychic conditions which might predispose any agent toward responsible conduct. Palpably, a modern administrator is in many cases dealing with problems so novel and complex that they call for the highest creative ability. This need for creative solutions effectively focuses attention upon the need for action. The pious formulas about the will of the people are all very well, but when it comes to these issues of social maladjustment the popular will has little content, except the desire to see such maladjustments removed. A solution which fails in this regard, or which causes new and perhaps greater maladjustments, is bad; we have a right to call such a policy irresponsible if it can be shown that it was adopted without proper regard to the existing sum of human knowledge concerning the technical issues involved; we also have a right to call it irresponsible if it can be shown that it was adopted without proper regard for existing preferences in the community, and more particularly its prevailing majority. Consequently, the responsible administrator is one who is responsive to these two dominant factors: technical knowledge and popular sentiment. Any policy which violates either standard, or which fails to crystallize in spite of their urgent imperatives, renders the official responsible for it liable to the charge of irresponsible conduct.

In writing of the first of these factors, technical knowledge, I said some years ago:

> Administrative officials seeking to apply scientific "stand-

ards" have to account for their action in terms of a somewhat rationalized and previously established set of hypotheses. Any deviation from these hypotheses will be subjected to thorough scrutiny by their colleagues in what is known as the "fellowship of science." . . . If a specific designation were desirable, it might be well to call this type of responsibility "functional" and "objective," as contrasted with the general and "subjective" types, such as religious, moral and political responsibility. For in the former case, action is tested in terms of relatively objective problems which, if their presence is not evident, can be demonstrated to exist, since they refer to specific functions. Subjective elements appear wherever the possibility of relatively voluntary choice enters in, and here political responsibility is the only method which will insure action in accordance with popular preference.[11]

Similarly, John M. Gaus writes:

> The responsibility of the civil servant to the standards of his profession, in so far as those standards make for the public interest, may be given official recognition. . . . Certainly, in the system of government which is now emerging, one important kind of responsibility will be that which the individual civil servant recognizes as due to the standards and ideals of his profession. This is "his inner check.[12]

Yet this view has been objected to as inconceivable by one who claimed that he could not see how the term "responsibility" could be applied except where the governed have the power to dismiss or at least seriously damage the officeholder.[13] Thus, with one stroke of the pen, all the permanent officials of the British government, as well as our own and other supposedly popular governments, are once and for all rendered irresponsible. According to this commentator, political responsibility alone is

[11] Carl J. Friedrich, "Responsible Government Service under the American Constitution," *Problems of the American Public Service* (New York: McGraw-Hill, 1935), p. 38.

[12] John M. Gaus, "The Responsibility of Public Administration," *The Frontiers of Public Administration* (University of Chicago Press, 1936), pp. 39–40.

[13] Herman Finer, "Better Government Personnel," *Political Science Quarterly*, vol. LI, no. 4 (December 1936), pp. 569 ff., esp. pp. 580 ff.

"objective," because it involves a control by a body external to the one who is responsible. He also claims that its standards may be stated with finality and exactitude and its rewards and punishments made peremptory. For all of which British foreign policy leading up to Munich no doubt provides a particularly illuminating illustration.

It seems like an argument over words. The words, as a matter of fact, do not matter particularly. If you happen to feel that the word "objective" spells praise, and the word "subjective" blame, it may be better to speak of "technical" as contrasted with "political" responsibility, or perhaps "functional' and "political" will appeal. Whether we call it "objective" or "functional" or "technical," the fact remains that throughout the length and breadth of our technical civilization there is arising a type of responsibility on the part of the permanent administrator, the man who is called upon to seek and find the creative solutions for our crying technical needs, which cannot be effectively enforced except by fellow-technicians who are capable of judging his policy in terms of the scientific knowledge bearing upon it. "Nature's laws are always enforced," and a public policy which negelcts them is bound to come to grief, no matter how eloquently it may be advocated by popular orators, eager partisans, or smart careerists.

POLITICAL RESPONSIBILITY

The foregoing reflections must not deceive us, however, into believing that a public policy may be pursued just because the technicians are agreed on its desirability. Responsible public policy has to follow a double standard, as we stated before. We are entirely agreed that technical responsibility is not sufficient to keep a civil service wholesome and zealous, and that political responsibility is needed to produce truly responsible policy in a popular government. Discarding the wishful thinking of those who would tell us that Great Britain has solved this difficult problem, it is first necessary to repeat that such truly responsible policy is a noble goal rather than an actual achievement at the present time, and may forever remain so.

All institutional safeguards designed to make public policy thus truly responsible represent approximations, and not very near approximations at that. One reason is the intrusion of party politics, already discussed; another is the tremendous difficulty which the public encounters in trying to grasp the broader implications of policy issues, such as foreign affairs, agriculture, and labor today. Concerning unemployment, all the general public really is sure about is that it should disappear. Many people, in defending Hitler, declare that, after all, he did away with unemployment. If you try to object by explaining what tremendous cost in national welfare this "accomplishment" has entailed, the average citizen is apt to be bewildered. "After all . . . ," he reiterates.

THE ROLE OF CITIZEN-PARTICIPATION

There are, of course, those who would altogether deny the impact of the people or its representatives, whether Congress or Parliament, upon the emerging policies. Such observers assert that even the most far-reaching of public policies are often formed by executive agencies under the pressure of circumstances and are merely legalized by subsequent legislation. It was thus recently put by an able student of our labor policy:

> It is a problem for the bureaucracy to foresee a situation and evolve a solution which will break gradually upon the political consciousness and be sufficiently entrenched so that its formal adoption in the legislative chamber is not an embarcation upon an uncharted sea.

Lest our British friends rush in to tell us that this is another American heresy, let me hasten to add that a similar view is even more common among British students of these matters, and quite naturally, since the role of the permanent administrative group in the drafting of legislation is so much more openly acknowledged under the cabinet system of government. Indeed, apropos the previously quoted address of Sir Josiah Stamp the commentator in *The Times* felt it necessary to remark upon the neglect of Parliament which Sir Josiah's views seemed to spell. Nor is this trend so very novel. Long before the war Sir Eyre Crowe, a leading permanent official of the Foreign Office, once wrote a confidential memorandum on parliamentary and public influence upon the course of British foreign policy. He stated that there was very little or none; he could recall only one instance, the Venezuela imbroglio, when the Foreign Office had been obliged to change its policy in response to public opinion. But it is our opinion that Sir Eyre Crowe, as well as all others who maintain the virtual aloofness of the permanent administrator from politics, are deceiving themselves. It is our view that such officials are more or less responsible to the people and its representatives, the press and Parliament, right along. Sir Eyre Crowe forgot that policy-making officials deliberated almost daily upon what would be the reaction of the public to this, the reaction of Parliament to that move. By correctly anticipating these reactions, the Foreign Office avoided getting embroiled and having to reverse its course. Who can say, then, that it was free from influence by Parliament and the public?

The same thing would, I believe, be found to be true here. The mere knowledge that the representative assemblies can stop a policy from going forward, that a row in the public press may destroy all chances of initiating an activity which the administrator holds to be desirable, will make him keenly interested in and desirous of anticipating the reactions of public and Parliament or Congress alike. Too little attention has been directed to the fact that political influence works most effectively through such anticipation, rather than through the reversal of policies after they have been adopted. But while the press and Parliament still provide very potent sources of influence, and hence their reactions are keenly watched by policy-formulating officials, newer and equally potent instruments have been developed in recent years. Through its informational services, administrative officials have begun to tap independent sources of insight into the views and reactions of the general public which are increasingly important in guiding them towards the making of public policy in a responsible fashion.

It is quite common to look upon the informational services which are being developed in this country at the present time as largely devoted to the handing-out of routine news items to the daily press. A more comprehensive discussion of these activities is not intended here. Their many-sided function is being increasingly recognized. In fields with novel policies to administer, such as Social Security or AAA, educational and promotional functions are being recognized. But along with all this outward flow of information on emerging policies, there is an ever-increasing quantity of intake. This intake of all sorts of communicable views, opinions, facts, and criticisms is becoming a potent factor in the shaping of public policy, particularly in areas where the government is entering new or experimental ground. But even in established realms of governmental activity new lines of approach are being pushed as a result of the activity of informational services. It is the function of the administrator to make every conceivable effort toward the enforcement of the law which he is called upon to administer. The authoritarian tradition of the past was inclined to take the attitude that it was up to the citizen to find out what the law was; if he did not, it was just too bad. Ignorance was no excuse. This conception of the government as mere police is quite outmoded, though undoubtedly many government offices are still administered according to such outworn notions. The modern conception of government as the largest "public service" with vast and diversified activities to administer cannot be made to work in such terms. The continuously changing pattern of our society requires that the administrator be responsive to whatever trends may be affecting his activities. Laws do not embody static and universal truths; they represent expedient policies which are subject to continuous change and must be so considered. Instead of administering according to precedent, the responsible administrator today works according to anticipation. Within the limits of existing laws, it is the function of the administrator to do everything possible which will make the legislation work. The idea of enforcing commands yields to the idea of effectuating policy. For most of the policies of a modern government, at any rate under democratic conditions, require collaboration rather than force for their accomplishment.

It is very natural that policies which are novel in their creative impact upon society should elicit a great many diverse public reactions. These will flow into the administrative offices in the form of inquiries, criticisms, and suggestions. Under democratic conditions, the average citizen feels entirely free to communicate with the government, because he considers it his own. According to the traditional conception of representative government, such communications would be sent to the citizen's representative in Congress or Parliament, who in turn would make them the basis of suitable action, official or unofficial inquiries, remarks in the debates of the House, and so on. A great deal of public reaction still takes this form, and, while elected representatives at times are inclined to feel that their mail is getting to be too much of a good thing, they would surely be agreed that the more important communications of this kind constitute an intrinsically valuable source of information and guidance. In Great Britain, the question hour still serves this purpose fairly well. In the United States much would depend upon the representative's being a member of the strategically important committees. However, the great pressure of legislative work has made it increasingly difficult for parliamentarians to attend to such matters. Moreover, a citizen, no matter how competent or well-informed, would be handicapped if his views were patently different from those of the representatives, whether for political or technical reasons. It is evident that in these and similar situations the citizen has become more and more accustomed to turn directly to the administrator. Some far-sighted administrators, like M. L. Wilson, Undersecretary of Agriculture, have made persistent efforts to secure such citizen-participation. Actually, referenda have been held to ascertain what would be the reaction of large groups of affected citizens to a proposed policy. On December 10, 1938, the United States Department of Agriculture held a regular referendum to determine AAA crop control.[14] Other such consultations have been held on a more limited scale on potatoes, milk, and the like. The Social Security Board, from its very inception, has realized

[14] See *New York Times*, December 11, 1938, p. 1.

the extent to which citizen-interest must be aroused and citizen-coöperation maintained in order to realize the far-flung policies which the Act had embodied into law. Hence the Board's information service has been called upon to advise the Board and its various bureaus and the regional and field offices not only on public relations matters but on all policy matters which affect public relations of the Board and its agents. Markedly similar conceptions prevail in the Department of Agriculture, more particularly the AAA, and many other agencies. Indeed, there has lately developed an interesting tendency for administrative authorities to avail themselves of the large mail Congressmen receive on all sorts of questions. A Senator may just pass on to the administrator the letters he is receiving, or he may add his own comments from time to time. A representative is apt to be rather alert concerning the attitudes prevailing among his constituency; he is bound to become a specialist in public relations after a bit of experience! Hence legislators can often gauge much more accurately than an administrator what the significance of a particular communication might be. This tendency represents an interesting modern adaptation of the question hour in the House of Commons.

It seems that the United States federal government has gone farther than any government abroad in developing such direct citizen participation in policy formation at the administrative level. This much may be asserted, even though in the field of agriculture the Scandinavian countries and Switzerland have progressed rapidly in the same direction. The whole movement suggests a significant shift of emphasis, when contrasted with the legislative referendum so characteristically molded by Switzerland and developed throughout the United States. Perhaps federal leadership in this sphere is not wholly unrelated to the fact that we have refused to extend the earlier referendum procedure to that sector of our government. But, quite apart from that, it is a rather natural development, compensating democratically for the gradual disappearance of effective legislation by individual members of legislative assemblies. As a result, the basic pattern of securing responsibility has been altered. Put quite broadly, it may be said that the public relations work of the administrative agencies has the task of anticipating clashes between the administrative efforts at effectuating a policy and the set habits of thought and behavior of the public which constitutes its "environment." There is, we might say, a laudable tendency here to adopt the department store slogan: "The customer is always right." For if such friction develops, the presumption exists that there is a flaw in the policy or in the methods by which the policy is being administered. Many questions asked of the information services of important federal agencies have no answer. The questions raise issues of policy which either have not been anticipated, or at least have not been settled by the administrative officer involved, or reported back to Congress for settlement.

SHALL WE ENFORCE OR ELICIT RESPONSIBLE CONDUCT?

Those old-timers who are enamored of strict subserviency undoubtedly will be inclined to argue that the foregoing is all very well, but that it depends entirely for its effectiveness upon the good will of the administrator, and that as soon as he is indifferent or hostile to such public reactions he can and will discard them. There is unquestionably some truth in this objection. Responsible conduct of administrative functions is not so much enforced as it is elicited. But it has been the contention all along that responsible conduct is never strictly enforceable, that even under the most tyrannical despot administrative officials will escape effective control—in short, that the problem of how to bring about responsible conduct of the administrative staff of a large organization is, particularly in a democratic society, very largely a question of sound work rules and effective morale. As an able student of great practical experience has put it:

> This matter of administrative power commensurate with administrative responsibility, or the administrator's freedom from control, is not, under our system of government, anything absolute or complete: it is a question of degree. . . . Nothing which has been said should be construed to mean that preservation of administrative freedom, initiative and

> resourcefulness is not an important factor to be considered in organization: quite the contrary, it is one of the major factors.[15]

The whole range of activities involving constant direct contact of the administrator with the public and its problems shows that our conception of administrative responsibility is undergoing profound change. The emphasis is shifting; instead of subserviency to arbitrary will we require responsiveness to commonly felt needs and wants. The trend of the creative evolution of American democracy from a negative conception to a positive ideal of social service posits such a transformation. As the range of government services expands, we are all becoming each other's servants in the common endeavor of operating our complex industrial society.

It seems desirable to consider one further problem of especial significance in this area, and that is the role and the importance of satisfactory relations of the government to its employees of all ranks and classes. Private employers are becoming increasingly aware of the decisive role which all their empolyees must play in the public relations of business concerns. Competition through service is becoming an ever more important factor, and the contact of the general public with particular businesses is through their employees. It is evident that the government through its expanding services is placed in a similar position.[16] The Postal Service has long recognized this and has evolved careful regulations concerning the dealings of its employees with the public. As a result, the letter carrier has become a symbol of cheerful service. By contrast, the arbitrary official of authoritarian regimes abroad has always been acknowledged as the

[15] Lewis Meriam, *Public Personnel Problems* (Washington: Brookings Institution, 1938), p. 340.

[16] These trends were discussed at a conference on personnel problems held at the Brookings Institution, under the auspices of the Harvard Graduate School of Public Administration, in 1938. See manuscript, "Report of a Conference on the Relations of Personnel Problems and Public Relations, February 3, 1938," now at the Littauer Center of Public Administration, Harvard.

antithesis of democracy. Atlhough such conduct was often condoned as part of administrative efficiency, we know today that this view is mistaken. Just as morale within the service is of decisive importance in bringing about responsible administration, so likewise morale should extend beyond the confines of the service itself.

The most serious issue revolves around the problem of the employees' right to organize, to bargain collectively, and to strike if their demands are rejected. It is difficult to see how popular government can recognize a right to strike, though it seems equally questionable to deny it. Whatever the abstract arguments the right to strike is not recognized by most democratic governments. At any rate, most public employees recognize that such strikes really are not in their true interest. But it is obvious that in lieu of the possibility of bringing their complaints and grievances forcibly to the attention of their employer, the government, government employees must be provided with exceptionally well-ordered institutional safeguards for mediation and arbitration. Such mechanisms have a fairly long tradition in some countries; they are rapidly developing in this country. The American Federation of Government Employees has always staunchly defended this right of government employees to organize and present their views collectively. Recently, a C.I.O. union, the United Federal Workers of America, has taken an even more militant attitude, including a demand for the recognition of the right to strike. Here again, it is evident, a democracy has to face the issues which are being raised by the ever-expanding size of its administrative activities. It cannot possibly hope to develop and maintain responsible conduct unless it accords its employees a status at least equal in dignity and self-respect to the status its labor laws impose upon and demand from private employers. In short, even though the government did not feel justified in conceding the right to strike, it should not discriminate against employees who join an organization which advances this claim. For merely to demand this right is not a crime, since reasonable men may differ as to the right answer. Employees who are denied the rights of ordinary citizens cannot possibly be expected to remain loyal and responsible public servants.

The right policy is to be sure that all necessary disciplinary rules are loyally accepted by the entire staff, irrespective of what organization they belong to. This formula works well as long as those responsible for the rules respect the rights of the persons working under them. It must be kept in mind, however, that there are quite a few difficult border-line cases, where the infraction of a given rule has been due to faulty behavior or hostile attitudes on the part of the higher-ups. Some time ago two or three members of the staff of a certain agency in Washington stayed away from the office to attend a hearing at the Civil Service Commission which bore upon an important point at issue between themselves and their agency. When their superiors learned of it, they wanted to fire them, because these employees had stayed away from the office without permission, which the disciplinary rules forbade them to do. But the men pointed out that their superiors were so hostile to their C.I.O. union that permission to attend the hearing would have been refused. It is evident that in such a case the rule is at fault, since members of the staff duly appointed to represent it should be free to leave the office to attend a hearing at the arbitral authority, such as the Civil Service Commission, without asking permission to go. The possible frictions of this type are endless; it is evident that adequate representative organization of the employees is the only possible way of coping with the situations as they arise.

Another important problem which is closely related to the foregoing, and equally controversial, is the right of officials to talk and write about issues of general public policy, more particularly those on which they themselves possess exceptional information and understanding because of their official position. There was a time when officials were supposed never to speak their mind in public. But the American and other democratic governments have gradually relaxed these restrictions. It must seriously be doubted whether technical responsibility, which, as we have shown, is coming to play an ever more important role in our time, can be effectively secured without granting responsible officials considerable leeway and making it possible for them to submit their views to outside criticism. The issue is a very complex one. Opinions vary widely. People try to escape facing these difficulties by drawing facile distinctions, such as that officials might discuss facts but not policy. It might cogently be objected that facts and policies cannot be separated. Any presentation of facts requires a selection, and this selection is affected by views, opinions, and hence bears upon policy. What is worse, in many of the most important matters intelligent and well-informed students disagree frequently on what are the facts.

The simplest solution, and one to which the authority-loving politician has recourse without much hesitancy, is to forbid such public utterances altogether. It is undeniable that great inconveniences might and often do result from technical authorities' bringing out "facts" which make the official policy appear in a questionable light. Hence instances of "gag rules" are quite frequent. At one time a federal department head ruled that no official in his organization was to give any more interviews, because one of them had annoyed him. Thereupon six reporters proceeded to that department and got six different stories, all of which were printed and sent to the administrative head to show him that his rule had been foolish and could not really be enforced. In this case the power of the press forced the abandonment of an unsound policy which would seriously interfere with making the administration responsible in the formulation and execution of policy. While many cautious administrators will aver that an official should not discuss policy, it seems wiser, in a democracy, to avoid such a gag rule. Many officials will hesitate to express themselves, anyway, for obvious reasons. A great deal depends upon the nature of the case. In matters of vital importance the general public is entitled to the views of its permanent servants. Such views may often provide a salutary check on partisan extravagances. Such views should be available not only to the executive but to the legislature and the public as well. Gag rules seek to insulate the specialist so that he is no longer heard. A large benefit is thus lost. Irrespective of what one thinks of the particular policies involved, a presidential order not to talk against administration bills to Congress is particularly doubtful, for Congress certainly is entitled to the advice and expert opinion of permanent officials of the government, who may be presumed to have a less partisan viewpoint on particular policy proposals. In fact, the rule can easily be circumvented by an official determined to make his views known: he can prime Congressional questioners to ask the right questions, and, as the officials must answer, their views become available to whole committees. This is true, but while it is alleged that no president would dare punish a man for what he says in answer to a Congressional query, it may often seem to the official undesirable to incur the presidential wrath. Hence no such rule should be allowed at all.

What applies to enlightening Congress really applies likewise to a wider field. It seems inexcusable that highly trained professional economists, for example, should be handicapped in addressing themselves to their colleagues in a frank and scientifically candid manner. Even when they are permitted to do so, they will be only too prone to be overcautious. The only sound standard in a vast and technically complex government such as ours is to insist that the public statements of officials be in keeping with the highest requirements of scientific work. If a man's superiors disagree with him, let them mount the same rostrum and prove that he is wrong; before the goddess of science all men are equal. Without this conviction the present volume could not have been conceived. In its pages men of science inside and outside the government service match their views and findings in a common effort to reach the right conclusions.

CONCLUSION

The ways, then, by which a measure of genuine responsibility can be secured under modern conditions appear to be manifold, and they must all be utilized for achieving the best effect. No mere reliance upon some one traditional device, like the dependence of the Cabinet upon majority support in Parliament, or popular election of the chief executive (neither of which exists in Switzerland), can be accepted as satisfactory evidence. At best, responsibility in a democracy will remain fragmentary because of the indistinct voice of the principal whose agents the officials are supposed to be—the vast heterogeneous masses composing the people. Even the greatest faith in the common man (and I am prepared to carry this very far) cannot any longer justify a simple acceptance of the mythology of "the will of the people." Still, if all the different devices are kept operative and new ones developed as opportunity offers, democratic government by pooling many different interests and points of view continues to provide the nearest approximation to a policy-making process which will give the "right" results. Right policies are policies which seem right to the community at large and at the same time do not violate "objective" scientific standards. Only thus can public policy contribute to what the people consider their happiness.

EDITORIAL NOTE: The following article is a direct response to Friedrich's thesis in the preceding essay.

12. ADMINISTRATIVE RESPONSIBILITY IN DEMOCRATIC GOVERNMENT

Herman Finer

Administrative responsibility is not less important to democratic government than administrative efficiency; it is even a contributor to efficiency in the long run. Indeed, it is tempting to argue that the first requisite is responsibility, and if that is properly instituted efficiency will follow. Elaboration of this point should be unnecessary in the era and under the stress of the events which now make up our days.

To the subject of administrative responsibility, Professor Carl J. Friedrich has made several interesting and sagacious contributions,[1] and he deserves our gratitude for having reintroduced its discussion among primary problems. Yet these contributions have by no means said the last word on the subject. Indeed, he has put forward a number of propositions which must arouse earnest dissent. In answer to an earlier contribution of his I said,

> It is most important clearly to distinguish a "sense of duty" or a "sense of responsibility" from the fact of responsibility, that is, effective answerability. I am anxious to emphasize once again that the notion of *subjective* responsibility (in my definition of it), whether as intellectual integrity or general loyalty to the spirit and purpose of one's function, is of very great importance in maintaining the level of efficiency. It is stimulating and sustaining, like the will to believe. But we must first of all be perfectly clear about its nature in order that we may not burke the question of whether or not such responsibility is sufficient to keep a civil service wholesome and zealous, and how far, in its own nature, it is likely to break down so that political responsibility must be introduced as the adamant

[1] "Responsible Government Service under the American Constitution," in Friedrich and others, *Problems of the American Public Service* (McGraw-Hill, 1935).

> monitor of the public services. For the first commandment is, Subservience.[2]

My chief difference with Professor Friedrich was and is my insistence upon distinguishing responsibility as an arrangement of correction and punishment even up to dismissal both of politicians and officials, while he believed and believes in reliance upon responsibility as a sense of responsibility, largely unsanctioned, except by deference or loyalty to professional standards. I still maintain my belief while in a more recent article[3] Professor Friedrich still maintains his, so far as I am able to follow his argument. I propose therefore to treat the subject in two divisions, first, a more extended version of my own beliefs and, second, a critical examination of his article.

I

Most of the things I have to say are extremely elementary, but since it has been possible for a writer of eminence to discount their significance I may be forgiven for reaffirming them. The modern state is concerned with a vast sphere of services of a mixed nature. They are repressive, controlling, remedial, and go as far as the actual conduct of industrial, commercial, and agricultural operations. The state, which used to be negative —that is to say which was concerned to abolish its own earlier interventions and reduce such controls as ancient and medieval polity had caused it to undertake—has for some decades now abandoned laissez faire and can be called ministrant. Its work ranges over practically every sector of modern individual and social interest, from sheer police work, in the sense of apprehending and punishing assaults on person, peace, and property, to the actual ownership and management of utilities. I need not dwell on this point further, nor upon the range and detailed intensity of the state's operation, nor the large percentage of

[2] 51 *Political Scince Quarterly* 582 (1936).

[3] "Public Policy and the Nature of Administrative Responsibility," in *Public Policy, 1940* (Harvard, 1940), pp. 3–24.

men and women among the gainfully occupied population it employs in the strategic positions in society. The weight and immensity and domination of this behemoth, for our good as well as for our control, are well known to all of us. But academic persons are less subject to the power of the colossus than the worker, the economic entrepreneur, the sick and the needy of all kinds. The academic person is therefore likely to regard the weight of the administrator's hand as not needing to be stayed or directed by the public custodian.

Are the servants of the public to decide their own course, or is their course of action to be decided by a body outside themselves? My answer is that the servants of the public are not to decide their own course; they are to be responsible to the elected representatives of the public, and these are to determine the course of action of the public servants to the most minute degree that is technically feasible. Both of these propositions are important: the main proposition of responsibility, as well as the limitation and auxiliary institutions implied in the phrase, "that is technically feasible." This kind of responsibility is what democracy means; and though there may be other devices which provide "good" government, I cannot yield on the cardinal issue of democratic government. In the ensuing discussion I have in mind that there is the dual problem of securing the responsibility of officials, (a) through the courts and disciplinary controls within the hierarchy of the administrative departments, and also (b) through the authority exercised over officials by responsible ministers based on sanctions exercised by the representative assembly. In one way or another this dual control obtains in all the democratic countries, though naturally its purposes and procedures vary from country to country.

What are we to mean by responsibility? There are two definitions. First, responsibility may mean that X is accountable for Y *to* Z. Second, responsibility may mean an inward personal sense of moral obligation. In the first definition the essence is the externality of the agency or persons to whom an account is to be rendered, and it can mean very little without that agency having authority over X, determining the lines of X's obligation and the terms of its continuance or revocation. The second definition puts the emphasis on the conscience of the agent, and it follows from the definition that if he commits an error it is an error only when recognized by his own conscience, and that the punishment of the agent will be merely the twinges thereof. The one implies public execution; the other hara-kiri. While reliance on an official's conscience may be reliance on an official's accomplice, in democratic administration all parties, official, public, and Parliament, will breathe more freely if a censor is in the offing. To convince himself of this the student needs to scrutinize once again the rather uncomfortable relationship between Sir John Reith of the B.B.C. and the public and Parliament[4] (Sir John was a man of moral hauteur), the deep shelter policy of Sir John Anderson's technical experts and parliamentary opinion thereof, and Sir John's Defence Regulations in draft and Parliament's attitude thereto.[5]

Democratic systems are chiefly embodiments of the first mentioned notion of responsibility, and dictatorial systems chiefly of the second. The leading textbooks by Germans on the Nazi system of government explain the essence of the Nazi system by a slavish dressing up of Hitler's dictum that all authority proceeds from above downward, and all responsibility from below upward. But when responsibility gets to Hitler, where does it go then? Mussolini's essay on fascism is nothing but an exercise revolving around the central thesis that since One Man can at times represent the people more validly than any other arrangement, that One Man owes no responsibility outside himself. The Stalinite doctrine is "democratic centralism," which simply means that after a period of discussion the central authority, that is to say Stalin and a few self-chosen friends, decides the course of policy and bears no responsibility to an agency outside himself.

In the democratic system, however, there is either a direct

[4] Cf. Finer, "Personnel of Public Corporations," in *The British Civil Servant* (Allen and Unwin, 1937).

[5] Cf. Finer, "British Cabinet and Commons in War Time," 56 *Political Science Quarterly*, (September, 1941).

declaration in the constitution of the primacy of the people over officeholders, whether politicians or employees, or else in authoritative documents or popular proverbs the constitutional omission is made good. Thus, in the Weimar Constitution, Article I declared the issuance of sovereignty from the people. Thus, the Committee on Indian Reforms of 1934 said, "so there arise two familiar British conceptions; that good government is not an acceptable substitute for self government and that the only form of self government worthy of the name is government through ministers responsible to an elective legislature." And thus, we are all familiar with the essential meaning of the American dictum, "where annual election ends tyranny begins."

Democratic governments, in attempting to secure the responsibility of politicians and officeholders to the people, have founded themselves broadly upon the recognition of three doctrines. First, the mastership of the public, in the sense that politicians and employees are working not for the good of the public in the sense of what the public *needs,* but of the *wants* of the public as expressed by the public. Second, recognition that this mastership needs institutions, and particularly the centrality of an elected organ, for its expression and the exertion of its authority. More important than these two is the third notion, namely, that the function of the public and of its elected institutions is not merely the exhibition of its mastership by informing governments and officials of what it wants, but the authority and power to exercise an effect upon the course which the latter are to pursue, the power to exact obedience to orders. The Soviet government claimed (in the years when the claim seemed profitable to it internationally) that it was a democratic government; but its claim was supported by two arguments only, that the government worked for the good of the people, their economic well-being, and that the people were allowed to inform the government of their will through a multitude of institutions. The Soviet government never sought to employ with any cogency the third and really vital argument that it could be made to conform to the pepole's will by the people and against its own will. This last alone is responsibility in democratic government.

Democratic government proceeded upon the lines mentioned because the political and administrative history of all ages, the benevolent as well as the tyrannical, the theological as well as the secular, has demonstrated without the shadow of a doubt that sooner or later there is an abuse of power when external punitive controls are lacking. This abuse of power has shown itself roughly in three ways. Governments and officials have been guilty of nonfeasance,[6] that is to say, they have not done what law or custom required them to do owing to laziness, ignorance, or want of care for their charges, or corrupt influence. Again there may be malfeasance, where a duty is carried out, but is carried out with waste and damage because of ignorance, negligence, and technical incompetence. Third, there is what may be called *over*feasance, where a duty is undertaken beyond what law and custom oblige or empower; overfeasance may result from dictatorial temper, the vanity and ambition of the jack in office, or genuine, sincere, public-spirited zeal. As a matter of fact, the doctrine of the separation of powers as developed by Montesquieu was as much concerned with the aberrations of public-spirited zeal on the part of the executive as with the other classes of the abuse of power. Indeed, his phrase deserves to be put into the center of every modern discussion of administrative responsibility, *virtue itself hath need of limits.* We in public administration must beware of the too good man as well as the too bad; each in his own way may give the public what it doesn't want. If we wish the public to want things that are better in our estimation, there is a stronger case for teaching the public than for the imposition of our zealotry. A system which gives the "good" man freedom of action, in the expectation of benefiting from all the "good" he has in him, must sooner or later (since no man is without faults) cause his faults to be loaded on to the public also.

[6] I use the terms nonfeasance and malfeasance in a common sense, not a legal sense—they are convenient.

As a consequence of bitter experience and sad reflection, democratic governments have gradually devised the responsible executive and an elected assembly which enacts the responsibility. Within the system, there has been a particular concentration on the subservience of the officials to the legislature, ultimately through ministers and cabinet in a cabinet system, and through the chief executive where the separation of powers is the essential form of the organization of authority. Where officials have been or are spoilsmen, the need for holding them to subservience is particularly acute, since the spoilsman has not even a professional preparation to act as a support and guide and guarantee of capacity. With career men, the capacity may be present. What is needed, however, is not technical capacity per se, but technical capacity in the service of the public welfare as defined by the public and its authorized representatives.

Legislatures and public have realized that officials are monopolist no less than the grand men of business who have arrogated to themselves the exclusive control of the manufacture or sale of a commodity and therewith the domination, without appeal by the victim, of an entire sector of national life. The philosophy and experience of the Sherman Anti-Trust Act have significant applications to administrative procedures in public administration. The official participates in the monopoly of a service to society so outstanding that it has been taken over from a potential private monopolist by the government. This monopoly is exercisable through a sovereign agency armed with all the force of society and subject to no appeal outside the institutions which the government itself creates. This is to be subject to a potentially grievous servitude.

How grievous can be surmised in one or both of two ways. One can reflect on the merits of competitive industry which satisfies the consumers best as to price and quality and variety while it remains competitive, so that the consumer can cast a more than daily vote most effectively for the producer he prefers by buying his goods or services, and expel the others from office by *not* buying from them. One can notice, too, how producers, on the plea of "service before self" and the like, attempt to escape consumer's control; and memories are stirred of Adam Smith's dig at traders who affect to trade "for the public good." Or, second, one can have experience at first hand, not merely of the coercive side of public monopolies, say that the contract powers of a municipal electricity undertaking, but of its administration of charitable undertakings, say in the feeding of school children or hospital management. The conceit of Caesar making concessions *ex gratia* to "subjects" can be noticed too palpably.

To overcome the potential evils flowing from public monopoly, democratic governments have set up various controls. It is these controls, and especially their modern deficiencies, which seem to have worried Professor Friedrich into a position where he practically throws the baby out with the bath. He feels that there is need of some elasticity in the power of the official, some discretion, some space for the "inner check," and he sees also that existent controls (either intentionally or by the accident of their own institutional deficiencies) do actually leave some latitude to the official. He argues therefore that heavy and, indeed, primary reliance in the making of public policy and its execution should be placed on *moral* responsibility, and he pooh-poohs the efficacy of and need for political responsibility. He gives the impression of stepping over the dead body of political responsibiilty to grasp the promissory incandescence of the moral variety.

Let us review the chief controls exercised over politicians and officials in democratic government, and their deficiencies and the remedy of these deficiencies. In traversing their inadequacies I am dealing with those loopholes for administrative discretion or the policy-making power of officials which have given Professor Friedrich so much concern. First, the legislative definition of the duties and powers of officials may not be precise because the legislators were not very clear about what they wanted. It is doubtful, for example, whether the planning clauses in the T.V.A. statute represented any clarity of purpose in the legislative mind. Legislative draftsmanship may be slipshod. Or the statute may be simply misunderstood, thus offering latitude to officials. If all the items of administrative determination arising out of the elbowroom allowed by these causes were gathered together they would no doubt be considerable. Since this latitude exists, it calls for one or both of the available remedies: the continuing control of the representative and judicial agencies over the official and an omnipresent sense of duty *to the public* on the part of the official. But the remedy is not, as Professor Friedrich suggests, the institution of specific legislative policies which may please the heart of the technical expert or the technocrat. I again insist upon subservience, for I still am of the belief with Rousseau that the people can be unwise but cannot be wrong. The devices for securing the continuing responsiveness of the official are, of course, the law courts, the procedure of criticism, question, debate, and fact-finding, and parliamentary control of the purse within the assembly, and, in the U.S.A., the election of executive or administrative officials and their recall.

It has been suggested by Professor Laski that to overcome judicial bias in the interpretation of social legislation a preamble might be set at the head of every statute so that the intention of it should be rendered less mistakable.[7] Such a device might serve the purpose of making the official amenable to the legislature, except that I have grave doubts whether the legislature can express its intention any better in a preamble than it does in the particulars of the whole statute.

Next, the enormous congestion of modern legislative assemblies and the heritage of antiquated procedure mean that a sufficiently frequent review of legislation and its administrative outcrops cannot be secured to remedy, or to punish, or to act by power of anticipation on the official mind. But these are not insuperable problems and there is no need for us, seeing contemporary deficiencies, to jettison political responsibility prematurely.

Third, there may be a want of understanding by members of Parliament and congressmen of technical issues involved in the law and the administration, and this shortcoming has meant a

[7] Committee on Ministers' Powers, *Report, 1932, Addendum.*

leaning upon the supply of these things available in public employees. But the growth of advisory bodies, formal and informal, in the major governments of our own time has tremendously limited the need to rely wholly upon official initiative. Attention to the further development of advisory bodies is the line of progress here, not surely the handing over of our fate to officials who, by the way, are themselves only too grateful for instruction by such bodies.[8]

It is true, further, that the exercise of the power of control by the legislature, such for example as Congress' detailed attention to and itemization of financial appropriations, may destroy movement, flexibility, and the like, on the part of the administration. This point is stressed by Professor Friedrich; queerly enough, he does not deduce from this criticism that a more rational parliamentary procedure is required, but that there is need of more administrative discretion. He even goes to the inexplicable extreme of proposing that some action is better than none, whatever the action is!

In short, these various drawbacks of political control can be remedied. They can be highly improved, and it is therefore unnecessary to proceed along the line definitely approved by Professor Friedrich of more administrative policy making. As a democrat, I should incline to the belief that the remedying of these drawbacks is precisely our task for the future. The legitimate conclusion from the analysis of the relationship between Parliament and administration is not that the administration should be given its head, but on the contrary that legislative bodies should be improved. Conceding the growing power of officials we may discover the remedy in the improvement of the quality of political parties and elections, if our minds are ready to explore.

Even then I am willing to admit an external agency could not attend to every administrative particular without introducing an element of coercion and fear into administration which

[8] Cf. R. V. Vernon and N. Mansergh, *Advisory Bodies* (Allen and Unwin, 1941).

might damage originality, joy in work, the capacity for creative suggestion, and day-by-day flexibility. No external agency could do this; and none that we know would want to. But because some latitude must be given—both owing to the technical impossibility of complete political coverage, and the wise recognition that the permitted latitude can be used for technically good policy which though not immediately acclaimed or wanted may become so in a short while upon demonstration to the public—there is no need to overstress the auxiliaries to political control. Such auxiliaries as approved by Professor Friedrich are: referenda by government departments, public relations offices, consultation of academic colleagues in order to temper "partisan extravagance," "education and promotional functions," the administrative scrutiny of a congressman's mail. These are harmless enough.

But when Professor Friedrich advocates the official's responsibility to "the fellowship of science," the discard of official anonymity, the entry of the official into the political arena as an advocate of policy and teacher of fact versus "partisan extravagance," the result to be feared is the enhancement of official conceit and what has come to be known as "the new despotism." It seems to me that in the article in *Public Policy* a theoretical aberration regarding the value of devices for eliciting public opinion, auxiliary to the medium of the legislative assembly, has led to pushing these auxiliaries into the principal place. Where the external, propelling, remedial, and punitive power of legislative bodies and administrative superiors acting after the administrative event, and upon the imagination of the official before it (and therefore relying upon fear), is weak, other techniques can be and have been added.

For example, statesmen have invited the expression of public opinion through letters, and the departments are deluged with complaints and, let us hope, occasional praise. The rise of the public relations officer has led to the education of public opinion and the evocation of that public opinion other than through Parliament. (But beware lest he become a tout!) The British Broadcasting Corporation, for instance, has set up various councils of listeners, and it seeks their advice—and no doubt at the same time explains to them why it is not really so bad as the public thinks it is. There is the inspectorial contact of the central government with the local authorities. A few months ago the Ministry of Information began to avail itself of the services of a number of people formerly employed in the Market Research Bureau to take samples of public opinion, and they came to be known as "Duff Cooper's Snoopers." Members of Parliament challenged the need for these, seeing that they themselves are channels of public opinion.

All these devices have their value, but let it be remembered that they do not and cannot commit and compel the official to change his course. Officials may, in spite of them, still think that what they are doing is for the good of the public, although the public is too ignorant to recognize what is for its good. However, the more the official knows of public reactions the better. My qualm is that the official is very likely to give himself the benefit of the doubt where the information he elicits admits of doubt, whereas when the legislative assembly asserts an opinion it also asserts a command. This is the very essence of the *Report of the Committee on Ministers' Powers*—upon this, you may say, hang all the laws and the prophets. It said:

> It is unfair to impose on a practical administrator the duty of adjudicating in any matter in which it could fairly be argued that his impartiality would be in inverse ratio to his strength and ability as a Minister. An easy going and cynical Minister, rather bored with his office and sceptical of the value of his Department, would find it far easier to apply a judicial mind to purely judicial problems connected with the Department's administration than a Minister whose head and heart were in his work. *It is for these reasons and not because we entertain the slightest suspicion of the good faith or the intellectual honesty of Ministers and their advisers* that we are of opinion that Parliament should be chary of imposing on Ministers the ungrateful task of giving judicial decisions in matters in which *their very zeal for the public service can scarcely fail to bias them unconsciously.*[9]

[9] Pp. 78, 79. The italics are mine.

Besides these arrangements the official may be kept responsive to the will of the legislative assembly by all the devices of legal responsibility. This point need not be adumbrated in any detail as it has been the subject of so many recent analyses and proposals for reform in the standard works of administrative law. I need only refer to works like Port's *Administrative Law* and John Dickinson's *Administrative Justice and the Supremacy of the Law*. In addition, there is the regular intradepartmental discipline resting upon the professional prospects and career, the salary, the retirement pay, and the chances of promotion, transfer, distinction, and honors, or vice versa, of the civil servant, going right up the hierarchy to those who are in direct contact with the secretaries of departments and the chief executive in the United States and the permanent secretaries and the ministers in Great Britain.

Even when the best has been accomplished with all this mechanism and the rewards, punishments, and incentives by which it functions, there may be still a gap between the controls and those official actions which would give the greatest public satisfaction. We should do all we can to reduce this gap to its minimum. Where our powers reach an impasse we will be obliged to rely upon two ways out: the education of the official and the influence of his professional organizations.

As for education—which should be part of the official's training before entry and then should be continued in various ways after entry[10]—besides the purpose of technical excellence, it should be shaped to make the official aware of the basic importance of his responsibility to the parliamentary assembly, and the errors into which he will be liable to fall unless he makes this his criterion. He should realize the dangers in the belief that he has a mission to act for the good of the public outside the declared or clearly deducible intention of the representative assembly. No one in his right mind would deny the importance of suggestions persuasively presented by the expert; but there is a world of difference between acknowledging the

[10] Cf. Finer, *The British Civil Service* (The Fabian Society, and Allen and Unwin, 1937), pp. 243 *et seq.*

value of such suggestions and following the path of increasing administrative independence simply because there is *faute de mieux* already some independence.

Again, my own studies in the field of the professional organizations of local and central government officials in Great Britain have taught me what a great power for the good can be exercised by them.[11] Besides keeping members up to the mark and up-to-date in the exercise of their profession, they do embody a sense of responsibility in the second sense in which we use that term, as devotion to the highest standards of a craft or to a special body of people in the community—such as the consumers of electricity or passengers on petrol or trolley buses, or the frequenters of public baths, or the payers of income tax. They engender and develop this sense of responsibility, and it is a valuable product. But even with this we must require principally and austerely the subservience of the public official. Without this requirement, we shall gradually slip into a new version of taxation without representation. There will result the development of a profession or corporate spirit, and bodies which at first are beneficial in their freshness become what Rousseau and Hobbes have called "worms in the entrails of the body politic." We shall become subject to what has, in a short time, almost always been to the detriment of the public welfare—producer's control of the products, the services, the commodities which the producer thinks are good for the consumer and therefore ought to be produced at the consumer's expense, though the consumer does not want the service or commodities in question and strongly prefers something else.

II

In the article in *Public Policy* to which reference has been made, Professor Friedrich takes a position radically different from my own as hitherto stated, though most of the facts to which both of us refer are common ground. Before turning to a detailed criticism of his thesis, it is useful to state his position

[11] Cf. *Municipal Trading* (Allen and Unwin, 1941), especially the last two chapters, for a development of this point.

in general. He argues (a) that the responsibility of the official that is of any moment to us today is not political responsibility but moral responsibility; (b) that the quality of administration and policy making depends almost entirely (and justifiably so) upon the official's sense of responsibility to the standards of his profession, a sense of duty to the public that is entirely inward, and an adherence to the technological basis of his particular job or the branch of the service in which he works; (c) that the public and the political assemblies do not understand the issues of policy well enough to give him socially beneficial commands in terms of a policy; (d) that, in fact, legislatures and the public have been obliged to allow or positively to organize more and more latitude for official policy making; (e) that there are satisfactory substitutes for the direction of officials and information as to the state of public opinion through the electorate and the legislature in the form of administratively conducted referenda, public relations contacts, etc.; and, therefore, (f) that political responsibility, i.e., the responsibility of the administrative officials to the legislature and the public, is and should only be considered as a minor term in the mechanism of democratic government, so much so, indeed, that officials may rightly state and urge policies in public to counteract those advocated by the members of the elected legislatures.

Let us commence the critical discussion with a passage of Professor Friedrich's on Goodnow's *Politics and Administration*. In 1900 Professor F. J. Goodnow's work, one of the pioneer incursions into a fairly untilled field, made the following distinction between politics and administration. "There are then, in all governmental systems, two primary or ultimate functions of government, viz. the expression of the will of the state and the execution of that will. There are also in all states separate organs, each of which is mainly busied with the discharge of one of these functions." Professor Friedrich imputes to Goodnow "an almost absolute distinction" in this functional difference. As a matter of fact, Goodnow uses the term "*mainly* busied with the discharge of one of these functions," and deserves credit for the broad distinction.

The distinction in the present writer's mind is this. By the "political" phase of government we mean all that part which is concerned with eliciting the will and winning the authority of the people. The process is carried on differently in democratic and dictatorial states. The elements of coercion and persuasion differ in magnitude and kind, and the place of the electorate, parties, parliaments, and ministers differs. This process ends with a law; with the approval (by positive ratification or by lapse of time for rejection) of administrative rules based on the original statute; and with control of the application of the law. The distinctive mark of this political part of the governmental process is that its agencies are practically unfettered in their authority over the making of policy and its execution. Where a written constitution and judicial review are absent, these political agencies are bounded only by the hopes and fears arising out of the electoral process. What of the administrative side? Administration begins where the legislature says it shall begin. It begins where the administrator begins, and the legislature decides that. Administration may include the making of rules and policy, which *looks* like legislation or politics. But its essence is that the administrator, elected or appointed (and most usually in modern states the latter), cannot himself determine the range or object of that policy. He has authority, but it is a conditioned, derived authority.

Thus, in the governmental process in general, there are agencies which are concerned with making and executing policy, and there is a descending narrowing latitude of discretion in the making of policy. The latitude is greatest where electorate meets legislature; it then tapers down through a descending line of the administrative hierarchy until the discretion left to the messenger and the charwoman and the minor manipulative grades is almost nil. There have been polities where there was an almost complete fusion of these functions, e.g., at some stages of Athenian democracy. But modern states are obliged at some point convenient to each in a different degree to distinguish them, with the first as authority and master over the second.

Professor Friedrich calls this distinction of Goodnow's (shared by all other authorities I can recall) "misleading," a "fetish," a "stereotype," in the minds of theorists and practitioners alike. Are we then to be permitted to offer worship only to fallacies? He produces the queerest explanation for this alleged "absolute antithesis" of Goodnow's. It is this:

> That it is built upon the metaphysical, if not abstruse, idea of a will of the state. This neo-hegelian (and Fascist) notion is purely speculative. Even if the concept "state" is retained—and I personally see no good ground for it—the idea that this state has a will immediately entangles one in all the difficulties of assuming a group personality or something akin to it (p. 6).[12]

This explanation is surely very fanciful. Later on, Professor Friedrich is constrained to admit: "Politics and administration play a continuous role in both formation and execution [of policy], though there is probably more politics in the formation of policy, more administration in the execution of it." "More" is a delicious understatement. But the understatement is not intended; it is part of a thesis that the amount of policy made by modern officials is of very great magnitude, in terms of proposing and later executing with latitude of interpretation. But this is only a play on the words "making" and "policy." What important "policy" does any federal official "make"? Has any federal official more authority than to propose? Certainly we expect those who are paid by the public to think and propound solutions to do their job well. But this is nothing new. By misusing the word "make" to suggest instituting and carrying into the law of the land, and only by this torsion of meaning, can Professor Friedrich's thesis at all come into court—that administrative responsibility to the legislature, the real policy-forming body of the nation, is in modern conditions impossible or unnecessary.

Professor Friedrich then reiterates an earlier statement of his: "Nor has the political responsibility based upon the election of legislatures and chief executives succeeded in permeating a highly technical, differentiated government service any more

[12] Page references are to *Public Policy, 1940.*

than the religious responsibility of well-intentioned kings." He then says, "An offended commentator from the British Isles [who appears to be the present writer] exclaimed that if I imagined that to be true of England I was 'simply wrong.'" Yes! that the power of the House of Commons in permeating the British civil service, right down to its local offices, and making it responsive to the House as the master delegate of the electorate, is most effective, is true, is demonstrably true, and ought not be denied. Nor can it be compared in delicateness or constancy with the "religious responsibility of well-intentioned kings," which appears to be an enthusiasm of Professor Friedrich's, for he undertakes to defend it by history, though he does not do so. Does it hold good of the Tudors, Stuarts, and Hanoverians? If so, why has British history been one long resolute struggle for the supremacy of Parliament and the reduction of the monarch to a dignified cipher?

Professor Friedrich begins his article in *Public Policy* with some remarks on the Munich Pact, with the intention presumably of showing that administrative responsibility to Parliament is ineffective. He offers it as evidence that "pious mythmakers" have no right to accept the claim that the formal dependence of the Cabinet upon the confidence of the House of Commons effectively insures responsible conduct of public affairs by officials, high and low. (He reverts to this example later also.) As a matter of fact, this example proves the exact converse of Professor Friedrich's intention. The Munich Pact only too well carried out the will of Parliament. Mr. Harold Nicolson, M.P., now Under Secretary to the Ministry of Information, even jeopardized his career by denouncing the hysteria with which the invitation to Munich and peace was received by Parliament. It is true that thereafter, as the consequences came to light, Parliament and people felt that the Government had been wrong—but they too were completely implicated. The revulsion of feeling caused the Government, under paliamentary pressure, to give up its appeasement policy and push on with civil defense preparations and rearmament.

Professor Friedrich argues that "even under the best arrangements a considerable margin of irresponsible conduct of administrative activities is inevitable." He is sanguine enough to continue (p. 4): "Too often it is taken for granted that as long as we can keep the government from doing wrong we have made it responsible. What is more important is to ensure effective action of any sort." Of any sort! This surely is exactly the doctrine to stimulate a swelling of the official head. Though I am not inclined to argue by *reductio ad absurdum*, such a phrase, if taken seriously, must encourage public employees to undertake actions which would very soon arouse the cry of Bureaucracy! and New Despotism! Friedrich himself tones down his own objurgation shortly afterward, but does not discard it.

Professor Friedrich has somehow come to believe that "parliamentary responsibility is largely inoperative and certainly ineffectual" (p. 10). Is he referring to the policy-making powers of administrators, or the acts of the Cabinet? His criticism seems to apply to the Cabinet, and not to the subject of his essay, viz., the responsibility of *officials*, for, citing the case of Munich and "the last few years," he seems to be concerned mainly with a foreign policy of which he did not approve but of which a large majority of his "ineffectual" Parliament emphatically did. And then he claims the benefit of this demonstration, I suppose, for the thesis that in England the civil service is out of hand?

On this point there are two records which might be summed up as follows. On questions of foreign policy, the Government, misguided as it may have been (in my view as well as Professor Friedrich's), was steadily supported by a large majority in Parliament, and I should guess a large one in the country. As for control over the administration, has Professor Friedrich heard of Parliament's actions on the Unemployment Regulations of 1934, the reform of the Post Office, the reform of the constitution of the B.B.C., the special areas, the preparation of the scheme of civil defense, the partial success in getting a Minister for the Coordination of Defense, the overthrow of Sir Samuel Hoare, the speeding up of arms production? And, during the war, the successful pressure of Parliament for the removal of certain ministers, e.g., from the Ministry of Information, for more reasonable use of the powers of interning refugees, its control over government contract methods, over appointments in the civil service, over the Defence Regulations proposed by the Home Secretary, over economic and fiscal policies and administration, and, finally, over the very existence of the Chamberlain Government itself? I have listed only a few of the outstanding successes of Parliament in controlling (a) the government in general, and (b) the proposals of administrators and their parliamentary chiefs before they were "made" into policy by Parliament.

The conclusion of this section of the essay (p. 7) reads: "Admittedly, many commentators have dwelt at length upon the frequently irresponsible conduct of public affairs in Great Britain and elsewhere." This is of course true; they have; and they have been right. But that does not mean that the examples are many, important, or long continuing. Nor would any person claim perfection for any system. You do not prove the value of your enthusiasm by showing that there are some flaws in existing political arrangements. Rather is political science a comparative weighing of the imperfections of alternative consequences. Even so, this should hardly lead the author to the conclusion that runs like a scarlet thread throughout the entire treatment, that if political responsibility is imperfect it is to be cast out in favor of a sense of responsibility in the bosom of the official: "a sense of duty, a desire to be approved by his fellow officials, and a tendency to subordinate one's own judgment as a matter of course" (p. 8), a point that Friedrich cites with evident approval from shaky evidence given to him orally by a Swiss official. Without the existence of the Federal Assembly, for how long does Professor Friedrich think the Swiss civil service would remain in tune with the humor of the people and responsive to its wants?

Professor Friedrich then turns to that agitation against the civil service which was summed up in Lord Hewart's book, *The New Despotism.* Alas, for the thesis of the author! *The Report of the Committee on Ministers' Powers,* while showing that, certainly, our civil service was very useful, showed that only in a few respects, and those not very important or deep-seated, were its members escaping control. He seems to harbor an objection to the power which the parliamentary majority would have over the rule-making authority of the administrator though submitted to a committee of the House for sanction (p. 12). What is wrong with this? Even if a special scrutinizing committee is organized, why should not the majority views of the whole House prevail? What is wrong with the majority? As for "the Henry VIII clause" (i.e., the power given by statute to the Minister heading a department to "remove difficulties" which are obstacles to the putting of the act into effect), this sounds very gruesome; but a glance at Mr. Willis' book on the *Legislative Powers of Government Departments* will show how trivial were the uses of it.[13] And Sir Cecil Carr has more recently shown that the hullabaloo was about very little indeed.[14] In the light of these authors and the distinguished membership of the committee, is not the suggestion that the Committee on Ministers' Powers "soft-pedals the real trouble" somewhat daring?

In the effort not to let reconsideration correct his first misconception of "responsibility," Professor Friedrich finds himself compelled to adopt an undemocratic view of government, and to throw scorn upon the popular will. I do not think for a moment that he really is antidemocratic, but his line of argument presses him to enunciate views which might lead to this suspicion. The error in his conception leads to an error in the consequence; and the error in the consequence is precisely what officials (not constrained by principle and institutions to the dictates of political responsibility) would begin to use as an

[13] Cf. also Finer, *British Civil Service,* pp. 217–230.

[14] *Concerning English Administrative Law* (Columbia University Press, 1941).

argument to justify their irresponsibility: conceit of themselves and scorn of the popular will. Thus (p. 12)

> The pious formulas about the will of the people are all very well, but when it comes to these issues of social maladjustment the popular will has little content, except the desire to see such maladjustments removed. A solution which fails in this regard, or which causes new and perhaps great maladjustments, is bad; we have a right to call such a policy irresponsible if it can be shown that it was adopted without proper regard to the existing sum of human knowledge concerning the technical issues involved; we also have a right to call it irresponsible if it can be shown that it was adopted without proper regard for existing preferences in the community, and more particularly its prevailing majority.

The answer to this argument is this. It is demonstrable that the will of the people *has* content, not only about what it desires, but how maladjustments can be remedied, and some of its ideas are quite wise. The popular will may not be learned, but nevertheless the public's own experience teaches it something, the press of all kinds teaches it more, and political parties and the more instructed members of the community play quite a part. "The people" consists of many kinds of minds and degrees of talent, not of undifferentiated ignorance and empty-mindedness. Legislative assemblies created by election, in which political parties play a vital part, also exist; and they are not so dumb. Their sagacity is not to be ignored or derided. Second, a policy which is based upon an incomplete or faulty grasp of technical knowledge is *not* an irresponsible policy, for to use the word "irresponsible" here is to pervert it by substituting it for the words "incomplete" or "faulty" or "unwise." It is surely wisest to say that the full grasp of knowledge is to be used by the official within the terms of the obligation and policy established for him by the legislature or his departmental superior; otherwise it looks as though an independent position were being claimed for the official. Nor is it wise to make responsibility to "the community" an addendum to a "proper regard to the existing sum of human knowledge, etc., etc." And, by the way, the state seems to have cropped up again in the word community!

"Consequently," continues Professor Friedrich, "the responsible administrator is one who is responsible to these two dominant factors: technical knowledge and popular sentiment. Any policy which violates either standard, or which fails to crystallize in spite of their urgent imperatives, renders the official responsible for it liable to the charge of irresponsible conduct." But just as surely there is no responsibility unless there is an obligation to someone else; no one is interested in a question of responsibility as a relationship between a man and a science, but as it involves a problem of duty—and the problem of duty is an interpersonal, not a personal, matter. Responsibility in the sense of an interpersonal, externally sanctioned duty is, then, the dominant consideration for public administration; and it includes and does not merely stand by the side of responsibility to the standards of one's craft in the dubious position of a Cinderella. If the community does not command, there is no call for the technical knowledge whatever; and, however magnificent the grasp of technical knowledge and the desire to use it, it must be declared irresponsible whenever it becomes operative except under a direct or implied obligation. Many a burglar has been positively hated for his technical skill.

There is another consequence of his thesis which Professor Friedrich would not like, I feel certain, if he had developed its implications. He declares: "Administrative officials seeking to apply scientific 'standards' have to account for their action in terms of a somewhat rationalized and previously established set of hypotheses. Any deviation from these hypotheses will be subjected to thorough scrutiny by their colleagues in what is known as the 'fellowship of science.'" What is the force of the phrase "have to account for their action?" Exactly to whom? By what compulsion? Does this phrase mean only that there is left to the official the vague, tenuous reaching out of his qualms in view of the known or possible public opinions of the men with whom he studied or those who are the present leaders of the profession? Suppose he despises their grasp of knowledge and scorns their judgment—is he therefore irresponsible? Suppose that they are conservative, while he is one of a minority of progressive practitioners? When is he responsible and when irresponsible? When he follows the ancients or marches with, perhaps even leads, the pioneers?

This question takes us directly into the history of these professional organizations of colleagues, "the fellowship of science," the associations, the guilds, of medical men, engineers, accountants, lawyers, and others. Even if such fellowship were fully organized to implement Professor Friedrich's wish, whom could the ordinary man trust for a better deal, the great osteopath, Mr. (later Sir as a mark of popular gratitude) Herbert Barker, or the elders of the British Medical Association, the organization which banned him; Whistler, Charles Ricketts, or the Royal Academy; an Epstein or the stone chippers favored by the Society of Sculptors? I do not err, I believe, in thinking that there are analogous instances in American experience, which Professor Friedrich could supply better than I can. But there is before us the judgment of the District Court of the District of Columbia regarding the American Medical Association's action against medical practitioners—their expulsion because they participated in a group medicine clinic. Which criterion: groupist or anti-groupist?

I do not deny all value to such guild organization; I affirm and applaud some of these organizations. Yet, appraised from the very angle of the theory which I am here opposing, they must be seen as broken reeds in a long-run view of governmental devices to keep men in the van of social progress, technically defined, and still less to satisfy progress as the populace, the consumer, asks for it. Professor J. M. Gaus, who is quoted in support of the claim that responsibility is professional, is by no means so zealous in the service of the notion as Professor Friedrich who quotes him, for he says: "The responsibility of the civil servant to the standards of his profession, *in so far as those standards make for the public interest,* may be given official recognition." I have italicized the proviso, and it is essential, I am sure, to Professor Gaus's view. Who would define the public interest—who could define it? Only the public, I believe, or its deputies.

Professor Friedrich seems to be so obsessed by modern technology, and the important part which the knowledge of it must play in the establishment of policy, that he seems to forget how old this problem is, and what the answer of the ages has been to the very problem he poses. Does he think there was no question of "technical needs" three hundred years or three thousand years ago, or of the relationship of those who provided the knowledge and service to those members of the public who were its consumers? Governments owned warships, weapons, sewers, baths, roads, and irrigation works, and even had mines and forests to administer, and domestic and foreign trade to regulate. The relationship of the public to the mysteries of religion and ecclesiastical procedures—a very important technique in the context of good living—was for centuries one of the most critical problems in the history of political responsibility. "The creative solutions for our crying technical needs," as Professor Friedrich calls them, have for centuries been offered by the experts of various kinds, and the verdict of mankind has been that they need the expert on tap and not on top. All important questions are begged by throwing in the word "creative." It is no news to tell us, as we are told here, that nature will have her revenge if her laws are not understood and followed in any particular piece of administration. Of course that is so. But there is a wider concept of nature than that which relates to interest in the "technical"; there is also the nature of man as a political animal. We are entitled to believe, from the reading of his millennial administrative history, that *his* nature, as well as physical nature, is thwarted where the primacy of public responsibility is challenged by blurred interpretations, theoretical and practical, of the term responsibility.

Nor is there any novelty in the fact that political responsibility (the importance of which Professor Friedrich admits in a scanty oasis of one paragraph in twenty-four pages) acts by its power on the official mind in anticipation of action by the sanctioning organs of popular control. In pursuance of his denigration of the British system of political responsibility he rather misinterprets the function of questions in the House of Commons. Their principal function is not to inform ministers of public reaction to policy, but to discipline administration. Ministers know already through other procedures. Questions are a *force*. Only ask the officials who prepare the information for the ministers whether they are not in an anxious sweat until the House is appeased!

Why, this is almost the ideal instrument for exercising that power of anticipation over the officials' mind, and therefore upon his sense of obligation to the community, which indirectly implies an obligation to the expertness he commands. I say this with diffidence, since the article seems a little severe on British experience. Nor am I an idolator of every item of parliamentary technique as it now operates. It should certainly be improved; but it ought not to be scouted.

There are occasions when Professor Friedrich seems to admit the fundamentality of political responsibility, but the relapse certainly and fatally follows. Thus he says (pp. 19, 20): "The whole range of activities involving constant direct contact of the administrator with the public and its problems shows that our conception of administrative responsibility is undergoing profound change. The emphasis is shifting; instead of subserviency to arbitrary will we require responsiveness to commonly felt needs and wants." Whose is the arbitrary will? The parliamentary assembly's emanating from popular election? Let us beware in this age lest we destroy our treasure altogether because it is not the purest of pure gold.

I come now to the last matter in which I care to take issue with Professor Friedrich, the relationship between administrative responsibility and the doctrine of official anonymity.

Professor Friedrich believes:

> It must seriously be doubted whether technical responsibility, which, as we have shown, is coming to play an ever more important role in our time, can be effectively secured without granting responsible officials considerable leeway and making it possible for them to submit their views to outside criticism. The issue is a very complex one. Opinions vary widely. People try to escape facing these difficulties by drawing facile distinctions, such as that officials might discuss facts but not policy. It might cogently be objected that facts and policies cannot be separated (p. 22).

The rejoinder to this statement in the first place is that it is possible in some cases at any rate to distinguish facts and policy quite clearly. For example, the government or the representative assembly in seeking a policy to deal with rural water supplies might properly expect to receive from an official a description of the existing situation, in terms of the total water resources of the country, the supplies and the sources of supply in various rural vicinities, what those supplies cost per thousand gallons, whether the nearest supplies beyond the jurisdiction of each unit need pumping stations or whether the water will come down by being piped, what are the costs of pumping and distribution in various other areas, and so on. What the assembly shall do about it, once these facts are before it, it is a matter of policy. A wise civil servant, careful to preserve his own usefulness and that of his colleagues, and not reckless in the face of the always imminent cry of bureaucracy and despotism, would not urge a policy upon it. Still less would he use public advocacy to spur on his political chief or connive with reformist groups having a purposeful policy. He would rather confine himself to frank private demonstration of the alternatives and their advantages, to his political chief, or where the political system requires, to the committee of the assembly at their request.

That, however, is not all. If Professor Friedrich really believes that the severance of fact and policy is impossible, then a fortiori the civil servant should preserve his anonymity, on pain of bringing himself and his colleagues into partisan contempt. And

Professor Friedrich does really seem to contemplate a war of all against all. He seems to approve of the fact that six reporters proceeded to a federal department whose head had ruled that his subordinates were not to give interviews and violated the chief's rule by getting six different stories. Is this the way to promote official responsibility to the chief? To the technical standards? To the "fellowship of science"? Does Professor Friedrich approve of this piece of press impudence? Has he ever investigated what such impudence cost the T.V.A. in prestige, morale, and administrative efficiency in the old days? Nor can I view with equanimity the grave consequences of such proposals as this: "In matters of vital importance the general public is entitled to the views of its permanent servants. Such views may often provide a salutary check on partisan extravagances. Such views should be available not only to the executive but to the legislature and the public as well" (p. 23).

This doctrine surely is to set up the official against the political parties, to make the official the instrument of conflict between the "general public" (which I thought had already been thrown out of court earlier in Friedrich's article) and the legislature. He would set the official, I suppose, against the chief executive also, for he has been elected by the general public, and may utter as many "partisan extravagances" as he pleases in the course of a four-year term. It is not clear whether Professor Friedrich thinks that the civil servant shall pursue moral responsibility as far as a crown of thorns, whether once he has embroiled parties and public and legislature he must resign. As matters are, he would certainly be kicked out by the legislature or chief executive, and it would serve him right. For democracy is ill served by and justifiably abhors those who, appointed to be its servants, assume the status and demeanor of masters.

III

The foregoing critical analysis of Professor Friedrich's view on administrative responsibility as stated in *Public Policy* shows,

I think, its untenability both in its main drift and in most of its particular secondary though related aspects. The analysis reveals the following propositions as cogent and justifiable, in contradiction to Professor Friedrich's contentions.

Never was the political responsibility of officials so momentous a necessity as in our own era. Moral responsibility is likely to operate in direct proportion to the strictness and efficiency of political responsibility, and to fall away into all sorts of perversions when the latter is weakly enforced. While professional standards, duty to the public, and pursuit of technological efficiency are factors in sound administrative operation, they are but ingredients, and not continuously motivating factors, of sound policy, and they require public and political control and direction.

The public and the political assemblies are adequately sagacious to direct policy— they know not only where the shoe pinches, but have a shrewd idea as to the last and leather of their footwear: and where they lack technical knowledge their officials are appointed to offer it to them for their guidance, and not to secure official domination; and within these limits the practice of giving administrative latitude to officials is sound.

Contemporary devices to secure closer cooperation of officials with public and legislatures are properly auxiliaries to and not substitutes for political control of public officials through exertion of the sovereign authority of the public. Thus, political responsibility is the major concern of those who work for healthy relationships between the officials and the public, and moral responsibility, although a valuable conception and institutional form, is minor and subsidiary.

Contributors and Sources

Woodrow Wilson, "The Study of Administration." Reprinted with permission from the *Political Science Quarterly*, Vol. 56, No. 2 (June, 1887), pp. 481-506. Before entering politics and becoming President, Woodrow Wilson was both a historian and political scientist. He wrote a number of important scholarly works, including: *Congressional Government* and *Constitutional Government in the United States.*

Norton Long, "Power and Administration." Reprinted from the *Public Administration Review,* The Journal of the American Society for Public Administration, Vol. 9, No. 9 (1949), pp. 257-264, by permission of the publisher. Professor of Politics at Brandeis University, Norton Long has had extensive experience as a consultant to all levels of government. His collected essays in *The Polity* and other studies provide fresh insights into many facets of political science.

Samuel P. Huntington, "The Marasmus of the ICC." Reprint by permission of the author and of the copyright holder from the *Yale Law Journal,* Vol. 61, No. 4 (1952), pp. 467-509. Single issues, as well as back issues available at $2.50 from Fred B. Rothman Co., 57 Leuning St., South Hackensack, New Jersey. Subscriptions, $10.00 per volume available from Business Office, Yale Law Journal, 401-A Yale Station, New Haven, Conn. 16520. Copyright 1952 by the Yale Law Journal Company. Samuel P. Huntington is Professor of Government at Harvard. His study of the Interstate Commerce Commission is a classic in political science. His other works include: *The Soldier and the State: The Theory and Politics of Civil-Military Relations.*

Joseph P. Harris, "The Senatorial Rejection of Leland Olds." Reprinted with permission of the author and publisher from

The American Political Science Review, Vol. 45 (1951), pp. 674-692. Professor of Political Science at the University of California, Berkeley, Joseph P. Harris has had extensive governmental experience in public administration. His scholarly works include: *Advice and Consent of the Senate: A Study of Confirmation of Appointments;* and *Congressional Control of Administration.*

Herman M. Somers, "The President as Administrator." *The Annals of the American Academy of Political and Social Science,* Vol. 283 (1952), pp. 104-114. Reprinted with permission of the author and publisher. Herman M. Somers is Professor of Politics and Public Affairs at Princeton University. He has been a consultant to numerous government agencies, congressional committees, and private groups. His scholarly works include: *Presidential Agency: Office of War Mobilization and Reconversion;* and *Doctors, Patients, and Health Insurance* (with Anne Somers).

Arthur Maass, "In Accord with the Program of the President." *Public Policy,* Vol. 4 (1953), pp. 77-93. Reprinted by permission of the publishers from Carl J. Friedrich, Editor, *Public Policy,* Cambridge, Mass.: Harvard University Press, copyright, 1953, by the President and Fellows of Harvard College. Arthur Maass is Professor of Government at Harvard. A frequent contributor to scholarly journals in public administration and political science, he is the author of a classic study: *Muddy Waters: The Army Engineers and the Nation's Rivers.*

Edwin E. Witte, "Administrative Agencies and Statute Lawmaking." Reprinted from the *Public Administration Review,* the journal of the American Society for Public Administration, Vol. 2, No. 2 (1942), pp. 116-125, by permission of the publisher. Edwin E. Witte had long experience in both government and academic life, serving at all levels of government and as Professor of Economics at the University of Wisconsin. He was instrumental in helping to draft the Social Security Act of 1935, as Director of the Committee on Economic Security appointed by President Roosevelt in 1934 charged with the responsibility of devising an acceptable social security scheme. His numerous scholarly works include: *The Development of the Social Security Act.*

Carl Sapp, "Executive Assistance in the Legislative Process." Reprinted from the *Public Administration Review,* the Journal of the American Society for Public Administration, Vol. 6, No. 1 (1946), pp. 10-19, by permission of the publisher. When this article was written, Carl Sapp was Chief, Legislative Reports and Service Section in the United States Department of Agriculture.

Louis L. Jaffe, "The Right to Judicial Review." *Harvard Law Review,* Vol. 71 (1958), pp. 401-437. Copyright 1958 by The Harvard Law Review Association. Reprinted with permission of the author and publisher. Professor Louis L. Jaffe of the Harvard Law School is a leading scholar of administrative law, adviser to many governmental groups, and author of numerous articles. His writings on the problems of judicial review are classics in the field.

Peter Woll, "Administrative Justice: Formal Prescription and Informal Adjudication." *The Western Political Quarterly,* Vol. 14, No. 3 (September, 1961), pp. 647-662. Reprinted with permission. Peter Woll is Associate Professor of Politics at Brandeis University. He is the author of many scholarly articles and books, including: *Administrative Law: The Informal Process* and *American Bureaucracy.*

Carl J. Friedrich, "The Nature of Administrative Responsibility." *Public Policy,* (1940), pp. 3-24. Reprinted by permission of the publishers from Carl J. Friedrich, Editor, *Public Policy,* Cambridge, Mass.: Harvard University Press, Copyright 1940, by the President and Fellows of Harvard College. Carl J. Friedrich is Professor of Government at Harvard, a consultant to many governments here and abroad, and the author of numerous distinguished articles and books. His works include: *Constitutional Government and Democracy* and *Totalitarian Dictatorship and Autocracy* (with Z. K. Brzezinski).

Herman Finer, "Administrative Responsibility in Democratic Government." Reprinted from the *Public Administration Review*, the journal of the American Society for Public Administration, Vol. 1, No. 4, (1941), pp. 335-350, by permission of the publisher. Herman Finer is Professor of Political Science at the University of Chicago and an authority in comparative government, public administration, and many other areas of political science. He has combined extensive governmental experience in the United States and abroad with scholarly research. His works include: *Theory and Practice of Modern Government; Major Governments of Modern Europe;* and *The Presidency, Crisis and Regeneration.*